THE KOREAN CONUNDRUM

*America's Troubled Relations
with North and South Korea*

ALSO BY TED GALEN CARPENTER

Peace and Freedom: Foreign Policy for a Constitutional Republic

The Captive Press: Foreign Policy Crises and the First Amendment

Beyond NATO: Staying out of Europe's Wars

A Search for Enemies: America's Alliances after the Cold War

Bad Neighbor Policy: Washington's Futile War on Drugs in Latin America

ALSO BY DOUG BANDOW

Tripwire: Korea and U.S. Foreign Policy in a Changed World

The Politics of Envy: Statism as Theology

Human Resources and Defense Manpower

Beyond Good Intentions: A Biblical View of Politics

Edited by Doug Bandow and Ted Galen Carpenter

The U.S.-South Korean Alliance: Time for a Change

THE KOREAN CONUNDRUM

*America's Troubled Relations
with North and South Korea*

Ted Galen Carpenter and Doug Bandow

palgrave
macmillan

THE KOREAN CONUNDRUM
Copyright © Ted Galen Carpenter and Doug Bandow, 2004.
All rights reserved. No part of this book may be used or reproduced in any manner
whatsoever without written permission except in the case of brief quotations embodied in
critical articles or reviews.

First published 2004 by
PALGRAVE MACMILLAN™
175 Fifth Avenue, New York, N.Y. 10010 and
Houndmills, Basingstoke, Hampshire, England RG21 6XS.
Companies and representatives throughout the world.

PALGRAVE MACMILLAN is the global academic imprint of the Palgrave Macmillan
division of St. Martin's Press, LLC and of Palgrave Macmillan Ltd. Macmillan® is a
registered trademark in the United States, United Kingdom and other countries. Palgrave
is a registered trademark in the European Union and other countries.

ISBN 1-4039-6545-5 hardback

Library of Congress Cataloging-in-Publication Data
Carpenter, Ted Galen.
The Korean conundrum : America's troubled relations with North and South Korea /
Ted Galen Carpenter and Doug Bandow.
     p.   cm.
   Includes bibliographical references and index.
   ISBN 1-4039-6545-5
   1. Nuclear weapons—Korea (North)   2. Korea—Military relations—United States.
3. United States—Military relations—Korea.   4. United States—Military policy.
I. Bandow, Doug.   II. Title.

UA853.K5C37   2004
355'.031'097309519—dc22

2004043460

A catalogue record for this book is available from the British Library.

Design by Letra Libre, Inc.

First edition: December 2004.
10 9 8 7 6 5 4 3 2 1

Printed in the United States of America

CONTENTS

ACKNOWLEDGMENTS

We owe a debt of gratitude to numerous people for helping to make this book possible. Edward H. Crane, president of the Cato Institute, has provided sustained and enthusiastic backing for this project and so many other aspects of the Institute's foreign policy program for more than two decades. The same can be said of William Niskanen and David Boaz, respectively the chairman and executive vice president of the Institute.

Our appreciation goes out as well to Michael Flamini and Anthony Wahl, our project editors at Palgrave Macmillan. Alan Bradshaw and Amanda Johnson at Palgrave provided significant help keeping the production process on track. Key members of the Cato Institute staff, most notably Justin Logan, Feliz Ventura, and Joshua Dunn, were invaluable in helping to prepare the manuscript for publication. Martha Sencindiver did her usual fine job with the index.

Most of all, we want to thank our families for the emotional support they gave us throughout this project.

INTRODUCTION

Perhaps unique among America's security commitments, the guarantee for the Republic of Korea (ROK) arose from inadvertence. As the victor in a bitter struggle with Japan during World War II, Washington was left to dispose of the detritus of the Japanese empire. Korea, a once-independent kingdom formally seized as a colony by Tokyo in 1910, was divided between the United States and Soviet Union. The Cold War quickly froze the temporary administrative division into a permanent border between two hostile states.

Although there was much to criticize in U.S. policy before North Korea's 1950 invasion of South Korea, the most likely alternative to division of the peninsula would have been a unified communist state. If that had happened, nearly 70 million Koreans today would be living in an impoverished tyranny. And the ability of what we now call the "North" to commit mischief and even mayhem would be magnified dramatically.

Unfortunately, the price of preventing reunification on Kim Il-sung's terms was the three-year Korean War. The conflict changed little on the peninsula other than wreaking horrendous death and destruction, but it put America and China at war with one another and deepened the dependence of both Koreas on their respective allies—China and the Soviet Union, in the case of the North, and the United States for the Republic of Korea. A half century later the Democratic People's Republic of Korea (DPRK) remains frozen in time, a Stalinist monument to totalitarianism and collectivism, enshrouded in probably the most pervasive, and certainly the most persistent, personality cult in modern history.

Unfortunately, the U.S.–ROK alliance also seems to be frozen in time. America continues to guarantee the security of the South, as if the latter remained an impoverished dwarf facing an imposing regional communist alliance and the Cold War continued to rage, with a geopolitical "loss" anywhere on the globe weakening the United States in its life-and-death struggle against the Soviet Union. American officials plan military force modernization programs; analysts worry about "who" will defend Seoul; every member of the American security establishment proclaims the need to preserve Washington's military presence.

Yet anyone whose academic, military, or political career is not tied to the U.S.–South Korean status quo must wonder at the world in which these discussions are occurring. Beyond Pyongyang one sees economic globalization, advancing democracy, and American dominance. North Korea's fulminations continue unabated, but the DPRK has lost its allies and has been surpassed by the ROK in every measure of power other than military force. South Korea, with the world's twelfth largest economy, is an increasing global presence, while the impoverished North matters not.

Except. Except for the fact that North Korea has embarked on the development of nuclear weapons.

Although it is possible that the North is engaged in one of the grandest bluffs of all time, it would be foolish to assume that Pyongyang is not deadly serious in its intention to acquire atomic weapons and in its development efforts. Whether the DPRK possesses as few as two or as many as six weapons (common estimates when in the spring of 2003 it began reprocessing nuclear fuel that had been stored as part of the 1994 Agreed Framework), the ongoing reprocessing effort could yield several more. And operation of its nuclear reactor could generate enough plutonium for North Korea to develop a small but significant arsenal over time—and, even more ominously, to open a fully stocked Nukes 'R Us on the side.

The North's nuclear ambitions have stirred tension and fear throughout the region. Ironically, if Washington did not deploy troops in the South and had not effectively smothered allied defense efforts in the past, America's involvement would be only tangential. Obviously, nuclear weapons in the hands of North Korea would primarily threaten its neighbors, not distant America. And the potential terrorist threat wasn't even a gleam in most policymakers' eyes more than a decade ago, when the "crisis" first erupted.

But everyone now looks to the United States for answers—while criticizing Washington for its policies. Dealing with the North would never have been easy, but the process is made more difficult by two factors. First, Pyongyang offers an opaque foreign window through which American policymakers must peer. The North may be brandishing its nuclear option as a means to gain respect and attention, and, in turn, bribes in the form of aid, trade, security guarantees, and diplomatic recognition. It may be talking about negotiation to disguise its determination to build a nuclear arsenal. Or it may be holding its options open, undecided about its ultimate course. There is no way to be certain about Pyongyang's motives or intentions.

Second, the United States and its allies have created the worst possible negotiating dynamic. The North learned long ago that no positive steps would be forthcoming voluntarily from America, Japan, or South Korea; even after China and the Soviet Union recognized the ROK, the United States, in particular, evinced little interest in forming any relationship with the North. But when Pyongyang started discussing its nuclear plans, near panic ensued in Seoul, Tokyo, and Washington. The DPRK was recognized and accommodated. Little changed in the decade after Washington inked the Agreed Framework. North Korea may have decided to cheat from day 1, but even if so, America's failure to follow through with its commitments under the 1994 agreement gave the DPRK ample excuse to cheat. And Pyongyang could be forgiven for believing that future improvements in its relations with the United States and Japan, if not with the ROK, required returning to the politics of confrontation.

Responding to the North's challenge has grown more complex with the divergence in views between Seoul and Washington. The South Korean shift from the hard-line policy of Kim Young-sam to the "sunshine policy" of Kim Dae-jung caused little angst in the Clinton administration, but clashed sharply with President George W. Bush's characterization of the DPRK as a member of the "axis of evil." The split obviously impeded coordination between the two capitals; it also helped feed growing antagonism toward the United States. Indeed, anti-American feeling helped propel Roh Moo-hyun into Korea's Blue House in December 2002. Although he subsequently backpedaled feverishly, proclaiming his fealty to the U.S.–ROK alliance, even many hawkish American policymakers were appalled at the rhetorical and sometimes physical attacks on American soldiers and suggested that if the South Koreans did not want us, maybe it was time to go.

The two countries worked hard to patch up their relationship, but proposed solutions, such as moving Yongsan base out of downtown Seoul, were mere Band-Aids. The two nations have grown apart: they perceive the threat from the North differently, advance very different responses to the DPRK's nuclear threats, and foresee a significantly different future relationship. Indeed, the latter conflict of visions almost ensures a not-too-distant alliance crack-up.

Today many South Koreans see little threat from the North. And while some ROK policymakers hope American forces will remain even after reunification as a deterrent to China or Japan, they evince no interest in aiding the

United States should it come to blows with China over, say, Taiwan. Indeed, Washington's request that the South provide 5,000 combat troops for garrison duty in Iraq was summarily rejected; Seoul nervously cut the number and talked of noncombatant support, and even then hesitated. South Koreans who bravely talked of the need for alliance "equality" in terms of formulating policy toward the North ignored the corresponding need for "mutuality" in helping to meet America's as well as South Korea's security needs.

The current U.S.–ROK relationship is unsustainable. America's security interest in the Korean peninsula was rooted in the Cold War: any advance of communism appeared to be a loss for Washington in the struggle between rival global hegemons. Today the Koreas are a peripheral interest at best. South Korea is but a modest U.S. trading partner. There are strong personal and cultural ties between Americans and Koreans; however, the ROK has little security relevance. War on the Korean peninsula would be tragic, but essentially irrelevant to America were it not for the U.S. troop presence.

In any case, the South is well positioned to defend itself. It possesses nearly 40 times the economic strength and twice the population of the DPRK. It has a vast technological lead and has stolen away the North's allies, as well as the friendship of most other states. North Korea can count on the support of another impoverished dictatorship, Cuba, and is trying to rebuild its relationship with a third, Burma—long antagonistic because of Pyongyang's 1987 bombing attack on South Korean president Chun Doo-hwan and his entourage in Rangoon. Beyond them, the DPRK's dance card is empty.

The ROK's military lags in quantity of soldiers and materiel, but only because Seoul has chosen to rely on the U.S. military tripwire (the troop presence that guarantees U.S. involvement in any war on the peninsula) rather than build up its own forces. South Korean military deficiencies could be made up virtually at will, should Seoul decide to invest the necessary resources.

But it will do so only if it must do so. And that will be the case only if Washington drops its unnecessary and unnatural defense subsidy of the South.

Thus, Washington should prepare a phased withdrawal of its forces from the ROK. The United States should sell South Korea whatever weapons it needs and aid its ally in reconfiguring its forces to adjust to America's absence. But Washington must end the South's military free-ride. Defending South Korea is not necessary for America's defense; to the contrary, garrisoning the South ensnares the United States in a volatile region where a future conflict conceivably could go nuclear. And the troops will remain a flashpoint in U.S.–ROK relations, preventing the two countries from developing a far more healthy, and equal, cooperative relationship.

Indeed, a withdrawal is as important for the future as it is for the present. Many American analysts apparently hope to preserve U.S. bases and troop deployments even in a reunified Korea. Despite general talk about regional stability, a few thousand American soldiers would do nothing to halt a region bent on war. Indeed, the most likely contingencies for conflict—a break-up of Indonesia, border clashes between Burma and Thailand—would not warrant U.S. military involvement.

What some Washington policymakers really hope to do is encircle and contain China. As noted earlier, some South Koreans desire a continued U.S. presence to deter Japanese aggression (which is about as likely as an invasion from Mars) or Chinese pressure (economic influence is inevitable, while military invasion is hardly imaginable), but America has little cause to station a permanent garrison in East Asia to protect a small client state from such unlikely threats—which are of little concern to Washington in any case. Instead, the United States is interested in permanent bases for use in other, more likely contingencies, such as a Sino-American conflict over Taiwan. However, officials in Seoul respond with horror when questioned about their potential involvement in such a conflict: they have no interest in turning their nation into a permanent enemy of China over an issue about which they have no concern. Yet they cannot expect Washington to promise to make war only on their terms.

As the conventional arguments against an American withdrawal have dissipated, some advocates of a continued U.S. presence say "not yet" because of the nuclear issue. But Korean and American policymakers have been saying "not yet" for decades. They will never believe the time has come, even after Korean reunification, China's transformation into a democratic, capitalist republic, the Second Coming, and the lion lying down with the lamb. There will always be a reason to delay placing responsibility for the ROK's defense on the ROK.

In fact, America's garrison is an impediment to resolving the nuclear issue. The U.S. presence places Washington in the center of the controversy, causing all of the DPRK's neighbors to look to America for an answer. Were the United States not guaranteeing the South's security, the problem would naturally be viewed as one requiring a regional, not a U.S., solution.

Moreover, Washington has essentially created 37,000 nuclear hostages through its troop presence. It is likely to be years before North Korea can develop a missile capable of hitting America with any degree of accuracy, but stationing soldiers nearby offers a much easier, alternative target. That threat inevitably will constrain U.S. policy.

Nevertheless, the unfortunate reality is that Washington today is stuck in the region, so it cannot easily walk away from the nuclear issue. America's options are limited: military strikes might not destroy all of the North's nuclear facilities and likely would engulf the peninsula in war. The DPRK's willingness to bargain might be equally limited: Pyongyang may have irrevocably decided on a nuclear course.

Given these uncertainties, Washington should proceed on the negotiating track, offering diplomatic recognition, the end of trade sanctions, official security guarantees, and the withdrawal of U.S. forces in return for the end of the North's nuclear program, backed by a rigorous inspection program. Multilateral negotiations are best, but bilateral talks might prove to be a useful supplement. In any case, Washington should point out that if the DPRK desires economic aid and subsidies, it needs to look elsewhere, principally to Japan and South Korea. Basically, the United States will address security concerns; its allies are in charge of de facto bribes.

Washington also needs to encourage China to use its leverage to move the North toward a negotiated settlement. Exactly how much influence Beijing possesses and exactly how much Beijing is willing to use its influence remain highly controversial issues. But the United States should point out that proliferation once started is unlikely to stop, and nuclear weapons could easily spread to South Korea, Japan, and even Taiwan. The People's Republic of China (PRC) might not worry about a North Korean nuclear arsenal; it would not likely feel so comfortable should Japan—and especially what Beijing considers to be the "breakaway province" of Taiwan—brandish one.

America also must prepare for the possibility that the North might reject any proffered deal and choose to formally join the nuclear club. This prospect is yet another reason for continued construction of a limited missile defense system to protect the American homeland. It also suggests the value in refusing to pressure the ROK and Japan not to develop countervailing nuclear weapons. Such proliferation would be unsettling, of course, but even greater and far more dangerous regional entanglement for the United States through nuclear guarantees for any nation threatened by the North would be much worse.

The possibility of DPRK sales of nuclear materials to terrorists would remain a worrisome prospect. Washington should make clear that even the hint of such sales would be viewed as a casus belli, and the result would be the destruction not only of Pyongyang's nuclear facilities, but of the entire regime. Targets would start with Kim Jong-il's palace, but would include the entire economic, political, and military infrastructure of the Korean Worker's Party.

The Kim regime is evil, not stupid, and would be unlikely to undertake such risks, especially if alternative means existed to raise money; in fact, DPRK officials so far have indicated that they are building a deterrent weapon but have no interest in sharing it with anyone. The North apparently understands that vital American interests are at stake in preventing any nuclear transfers.

Obviously, reducing U.S. responsibilities and devolving security obligations on allies are inconsistent with the Bush administration's policy of unilateral dominance and preventive war. Yet these policies look increasingly myopic and unsustainable as the world turns progressively uglier—an interminable guerrilla conflict in Iraq; enduring hostility in Arab and Muslim nations; increasing cooperation among countries (i.e., China, India, and Russia) that fear U.S. hegemony; speedier attempts to acquire the deterrent power of nuclear weapons by such "rogue" states as Iran and North Korea; growing criticism of America even in allied nations, including the European countries; and persistent refusal of most nations, including South Korea and Japan, to offer meaningful help in garrisoning and rebuilding Iraq.

Washington must be prepared to use unilateral military action if necessary to protect what it believes to be vital security interests. It should not dissipate its strength around the globe in frivolous deployments that primarily serve the interests of populous and prosperous allies, especially when they show no interest in aiding the United States in return. American officials should be particularly chary of making promiscuous commitments when they involve nuclear guarantees, which would dramatically raise the costs of any mistakes or failures of deterrence.

South Korea is a valued friend. It will continue to be one even if the United States insists that the ROK do what every serious nation has done throughout human history: take responsibility for its own security. North Korea is a totalitarian hellhole. Everyone, and most particularly its own citizens, will benefit when the existing regime falls, or is tossed, into history's dustbin. No policy can guarantee the peaceful disappearance of today's tyrannical regime, but peaceful engagement offers more hope of speeding the process. Should that process fail, the North's neighbors, and not America, should deal with consequences.

The U.S. security commitment to South Korea began inadvertently. Washington should now end it intentionally. American policy has succeeded brilliantly in allowing the ROK to develop and join the first rank of nations. Now the United States can fade into the region's background, putting the interests of its own citizens first. Which is, especially in a world full of uncertainty, violence, and threats, its most important duty.

Chapter One

GROWING TENSIONS WITH BOTH NORTH AND SOUTH KOREA

The United States and the Republic of Korea (ROK) have been allied for more than a half century. Like any relationship between great power and protectorate, the parties frequently have been irritated and angry with one another. Nevertheless, the tie, however strained, has survived. But tensions are growing and will almost certainly worsen in coming years.

Put simply, the alliance is suffering from the consequences of its own success. The end of the Cold War has isolated North Korea and diminished the threat to both the United States and the ROK. South Korea has grown economically, politically, and internationally, far outstripping its longtime communist rival. And virtually every other allied state in East Asia has similarly advanced. Military necessity no longer can bridge the deep differences between Seoul and Washington.

Both nations are beginning to look away. The Bush administration is preparing to eliminate America's celebrated troop "tripwire" along the demilitarized zone (DMZ) between North and South Korea. Although Washington has promised to maintain deterrence, it plans on reducing U.S. force levels and moving most soldiers southward, well away from the DMZ. South Korean officials, even some who once called for a U.S. withdrawal, have protested, to no avail.

Washington also continues to threaten to strike North Korea's nuclear facilities. There may be no more effective way to generate fear throughout South

Korea than to suggest a course that might trigger a general war, but both the Clinton and Bush administrations have seemed airily unconcerned about winning Seoul's agreement before acting.

Perhaps no surprise, even more doubtful is South Korean support for the alliance. Despite Seoul's recent protestations of fidelity, real commitment seems to be lacking. For instance, before leaving office in early 2003, President Kim Dae-jung, chastened by Washington's dismissal of his "sunshine policy" toward the North and belligerent threats of military action, explicitly attempted to chart an independent course between the United States and Pyongyang. After his election Kim's successor, Roh Moo-hyun, suggested that the ROK "mediate" in any war between America and the North and called for "concessions from both sides."[1] Indeed, he even stated that "we should proudly say we will not side with North Korea or the United States."[2] The head of Roh's transition team, Lim Chae-jung, developed a proposal that sought "a concession" from both America and North Korea.[3] For a time it did not sound as if there were much of an alliance, at least one of any value.

Although a degree of civility eventually returned to the relationship, the two nations' differences were merely set aside, not resolved. And tensions again will grow. The so-called Mutual Defense Treaty, ratified in 1954, was forged in a different era to deal with different threats. Circumstances have passed it by, and no amount of friendly rhetoric can rehabilitate it.

DIFFICULT HISTORY

To some degree, relations between the two countries never have been smooth. Early contacts between the isolated monarchy known as the Hermit Kingdom and the United States included loot-minded American sailors losing their vessel and lives, followed by Washington's demands, simply ignored by Seoul, for redress. Friendly relations eventually were opened, but then were abandoned after Japan swallowed the peninsula. Contact was reestablished after World War II when the United States and the Soviet Union jointly occupied what had been a Japanese colony. (Although some South Korean leftists have blamed Washington for Korea's division, the alternative would have been full control by communist leader Kim Il-sung. If that was the case, those leftists, along with any other defenders of democracy and human rights, would be dead or imprisoned, and their fellow citizens would be impoverished and oppressed. Division was bad, but it was not the worst alternative.)

Forging a new country, and especially one with a sufficiently compliant government, proved difficult for Washington. Indeed, perhaps never have the tensions been greater than after the United States settled on the cantankerous Rhee Syngman as its strongman for the southern sector of the Korean peninsula. Washington ended up backing Rhee because, according to historian Callum MacDonald, it considered his regime to be "an instrument of containment" and "the only reliable barrier against communism."[4] Yet Rhee was constantly at odds with Washington: threatening war even before the North invaded in 1950, pressing for coercive unification even after the United States decided to limit its war aims, obstructing the peace negotiations, and refusing to sign the armistice. The Eisenhower administration considered forcibly removing him.[5]

Even after Rhee's fall from power in 1960 in the face of popular demonstrations (with a push from Washington, tired of his authoritarian rule), relations were uneasy. The United States ultimately accepted military rule. Although initially displeased with Park Chung-hee's coup, the Kennedy administration came to back Park, who visited Washington shortly after taking power and was narrowly elected president in what appeared to be relatively free elections in 1963.[6] Tensions increased when Nixon withdrew some U.S. troops and when the Carter administration emphasized human rights, a commodity often absent in the South. (North Korea was obviously worse, but Washington was subsidizing and defending Seoul, not Pyongyang.[7]) Even the Reagan administration was forced to draw lines, demanding that President Chun Doo-hwan, who eventually succeeded Park, not murder Kim Dae-jung—longtime dissident, human rights activist, and opposition presidential candidate—after the regime kidnapped him from Japan.

Cooperative relations between the U.S. and the ROK governments stoked unhappiness among the Korean population. Although most Americans were blissfully ignorant of U.S. support for successive ROK dictatorships, Koreans were quite aware of that policy. And they were increasingly angered by it.

For instance, between 1985 and 1988 a number of radical student organizations targeted American citizens and institutions for protests, taking over offices of the Chamber of Commerce and the U.S. Information Service.[8] As street demonstrations escalated during the summer of 1987, many protestors blamed America not only for the political intransigence of the Chun government, but for its very existence. At the same time, the Reagan administration became more interested in human rights and pressed the regime to forge a peaceful, democratic solution.[9] Then the 1988 Olympics in South Korea showcased obnoxious behavior by some U.S. athletes—two swimmers stealing a hotel statue, for instance—and generated public disapproval. So did acrimonious trade disputes over automobiles, food, and other products. After the fall of the Berlin Wall led to Germany's reunification, polls found that many younger Koreans blamed the United States for impeding reunification of the peninsula. "It's not that we don't like Americans," explained one demonstrator in July 1987, "but for 37 years you've been supporting the wrong guy here."[10]

One of the wrong guys was Rhee, of course. Barely a year after his fall the military seized power. As noted earlier, the United States accepted Park Chung-hee with few public qualms until the Carter administration. Although Park's assassination in 1979 eliminated this blight on America's record, another soon followed: Chun Doo-hwan. Alas, many Koreans suspected America of having been involved in Chun's 1980 coup. Although General John Wickham, then U.S. commander in the ROK, said that he had no opportunity to block the Korean troop movements, and it is doubtful that South Korean field officers would have refused to obey orders from their own commanders, he fanned suspicions by saying that Koreans were "lemming-like" and needed "a strong leader."[11]

Perhaps an even worse blow to America's reputation was inflicted later the same year by the Chun regime's brutal suppression of the student demonstrations in the city of Kwangju. The official death toll is 191, but private observers estimated the actual number killed to be as high as 2,000.[12] Many residents blamed Washington. Linda Lewis, an American anthropologist in Kwangju at the time, wrote of "the oft-repeated expectation that the American government would (and should) actively intervene."[13]

It was almost certainly unfair for Koreans to accuse the United States of complicity in the Kwangju fight. Wickham did not have operational control of the special forces used to crush the demonstrations, and, again, it is unlikely that U.S. disapproval would have stopped Chun from employing the Korean military to bolster his control. But the fact that Wickham raised no objection to Chun's use of the troops and later publicly stated that the Koreans were not ready for democracy made it appear that Washington would blindly support any pro-American government regardless of its cruelty.[14]

The Chun dictatorship ended in the midst of massive demonstrations in 1987, and the Reagan administration ultimately encouraged Chun to implement democratic reforms. Yet Koreans may be forgiven for their irritation with America's ambivalence. After all, observed Edward A. Olsen of the Naval Postgraduate School, "South Korea is joining the ranks of democratic nations," but more despite than because of the United States.[15]

Important policy differences continued even with democratic rule; the Kim Young-sam administration worried about being ignored by President Bill Clinton when he approached the DPRK.[16] But with the election of Kim Dae-jung, the third civilian president (after former General Roh Tae-woo, who won in 1987), fears of American interference in the ROK's internal political affairs diminished. Still, although the end of military rule eliminated the most serious sources of tension, anger persisted over support for past military regimes.[17] Even a decade ago, wrote historian James Matray during a period of seeming quiet, "Burning the American flag, carrying banners denouncing the United States, and chanting anti-American slogans have become standard features at student demonstrations regardless of the issue."[18]

Moreover, democracy magnified another problem inherent to Washington's military role: cultural conflicts. To place 37,000 military personnel—largely young and male—in a foreign nation guarantees social friction. It is impossible for Koreans to ignore the American presence. Many conservative businessmen as well as radical students long have been irritated by the presence of a U.S. base, Yongsan, near the center of the capital city of Seoul. (The base now is set to be moved.)

And many Koreans were angered by the special treatment accorded American soldiers accused of a crime. Issues of custody, trial, and punishment were easily handled by a military dictatorship, but became explosive for a democratic government. A 1992 case involving a serviceman who murdered a prostitute led to huge anti-American demonstrations. In the summer of 1995 the Kim Young-sam and Clinton administrations faced a bitter controversy arising out of a subway melee. South Koreans protested the Status of Forces Agreement (SOFA), which outlines special treatment for U.S. soldiers by the Korean judicial system.[19] (The United States negotiates similar agreements with other nations that host American bases, but the exact terms vary.) Washington blamed the ROK media and pointed to the fact that four Americans but no Koreans were indicted for the brawl as evidence that some protection for U.S. soldiers was required.[20]

Defense Secretary William Perry later promised to consider changes in the SOFA, but that did not end the controversy. Whatever the merits of any particular case, the SOFA issue created serious discontent. Explained a student leader at Yonsei University: "The problem is not in the crime itself, but in the criminal process. This process reflects the imperialist characteristics of the U.S. government."[21] His opinion might have been extreme, but he was not alone in his unhappiness about the U.S.–ROK relationship: a decade ago one activist collected 40,000 signatures demanding revision of the SOFA. Moreover, with the local media citing a supposed wave of 800 crimes in 1994 through 1995 (most being traffic violations), public opinion polls showed a 20-point plunge in public support for maintenance of American forces.[22] Even U.S. ambassador James Laney acknowledged that "the Korean public is led to believe that these things are getting out of hand, and it's affecting our welcome here. It's cause for great concern."[23]

In fact, the ROK's very success made its dependence on Washington more insufferable. Opined South Korean scholar Manwoo Lee, "anti-Americanism in Korea symbolizes a renaissance of Korean nationalism."[24] His argument was supported by poll data. The United States long ranked at or near the top in terms of nations admired by Koreans. However, during the 1980s America slipped dramatically, falling to number nine in 1988, rebounding a little, and then sliding again to number eight in 1992.[25] Ominously, the favorable rating for America fell among urban dwellers, professionals, and the young. Thus, while the North Korean threat forced South Koreans to accept an unnatural security dependency on the United States, an older, independent heritage was reasserting itself.

SURGING TENSIONS

The tensions are worse today. Nationalism, cultural conflicts, and policy differences have come together in a very powerful combination. Explained Kim Jin-wung of Kyungpook National University in 2003: with the U.S. presence seemingly less important in protecting the ROK's security, the American troops "have been increasingly perceived as a social irritant and a remnant of the almost forgotten Cold War."[26]

Hostility toward America burst forth particularly strongly as the ROK began to improve its relationship with Pyongyang. President Kim Dae-jung had barely set foot back in Seoul after the 2000 summit with North Korean leader Kim Jong-il before thousands of students took to the streets demanding that the Americans go home. Protestors also used June 25 of that year, the fiftieth anniversary of the onset of the Korean War, as an opportunity to demand Washington's withdrawal. The U.S. military established a "civil disturbance hot line" and, in the aftermath of the murder of an army officer at a shopping mall, warned of anti-American "strike squads."[27] Amid the summit euphoria a U.S. soldier was sentenced by a U.S. military court to eight years in prison for murdering a South Korean bar waitress who refused to have sex with him. The case rekindled public anger over the SOFA's limits on Seoul's jurisdiction over U.S. soldiers accused of crimes. Although the most hostile sentiments seemed to reflect only fringe opinions, they were a harbinger of future events.

Little more than two years later, these issues returned with even greater force. In late 2002, after an accident in which an American military vehicle killed two teenage girls, demonstrations swept the country. Anger spilled out of universities into the middle class and seemed to grow along with the nuclear crisis.[28] Explained Kim Sung-han of the Institute for Foreign Affairs and National Security, "Anti-Americanism is getting intense. It used to be widespread and not so deep. Now it's getting widespread and deep."[29]

Although polls showed that a majority of South Koreans still supported the U.S. troop presence, a majority also pronounced its dislike of America. Aidan Foster-Carter of Leeds University complained of the South's "swollen yet strangely selective spleen": "In this mood, the U.S. is resented as a bully, just as Japan is forever a war criminal. Conversely, China—despite repressing North Korean refugees—is seen as a benign protector, and North Korea indulged as a wayward sibling—let the family sort him out."[30]

Although passions cooled in 2003, the ROK will never go back to the Korea of 1953. The world is too different. South Korea is too different. South Koreans no longer perceive their independence to be based solely on American support in the face of the threat of communist aggression from the North.

One significant trend is the change in the public's perceptions of North Korea. In Kim Jin-wung's view, this is "the most important factor to influence South Korean views of the United States."[31] With the end of military rule, both the educational establishment and media, driven perhaps by a mixture of leftist ideology and fear of upsetting the status quo, have begun promoting more positive views of the North.[32] One sign of the shift is the increasing willingness of ROK textbooks to acknowledge Kim Il-sung's role (much overstated in the North, of course) as an anti-Japanese guerrilla leader.[33] Another is a string of movies romanticizing the DPRK and demonizing the United States.[34]

More disturbing is the development of naively favorable views of the North. For instance, between 1992 and 2002 the percentage of South Koreans believing there to be a risk of North Korean aggression dropped from 69 percent to 33 percent.[35] A majority of ROK citizens believe that the DPRK is most likely to use any nuclear weapons against other nations.[36] Some South Koreans confidently state that the North would never use nuclear weapons against them.[37] One person told the Washington Post: "I want North Koreans to develop nuclear weapons. After all, we are one nation."[38] More South Korean children identify the DPRK than America as "the friendliest nation toward South Korea."[39] Most bizarrely, for a time the ROK government stopped publishing a defense "white paper" because it did not want to designate the DPRK as its "main enemy."[40] Yet this seems less surprising after President Roh said that the ROK should treat North Koreans not "as criminals but as counterparts for dialogue."[41]

Demographics, too, are playing a role. The generation grateful for American aid in the Korean War is passing from the scene; 82 percent of the population was born after the war. Explained one diplomat: "It may be difficult for us to sustain the same mood we grew up with. We know the U.S. helped us. But those under 40 . . . aren't swayed by what we think."[42] The percentage of people who profess to like America falls off dramatically among younger South Koreans.[43] In an April 2003 poll, more people in their twenties and thirties expressed their dislike for the United States than for North Korea.[44] A similarly sharp divide reflects support for an American troop withdrawal: those in their twenties favor a pull-out while those in their fifties strongly oppose such a step.[45]

The same factors that are softening attitudes toward the North are hardening feelings toward the United States. A politicized educational system, including biased textbooks, has helped spawn anti-Americanism.[46] Antagonism toward America also reflects Korea's move to the left politically.[47] And the same younger people who look more to the DPRK than to the United States point to Washington's support for various military regimes and the indignities (and tragedies) of a foreign troop presence.[48]

There is more than the problem of past behavior. While anti-Americanism in the 1980s was directed at U.S. backing for military dictators, it now stems "from enhanced confidence and pride in the nation," observes Gi-wook Shin of the Asia/Pacific Research Center at Stanford University.[49] Similarly, argues Kim Jin-wung, "The new generation, having grown up in a more prosperous and proud country than their parents, is assertive, nationalistic, and critical of what it views as South Korea's subservient position vis-à-vis the United States."[50] Thus, as the ROK continues to develop, the sentiments will not only spread but inevitably will grow stronger.

Perceived American arrogance adds fuel to the fire. Bong Youngshik, at Wellesley College, writes that South Korean anti-Americanism "is basically a collective resentment against the political and economic domination of the United States and the fear of becoming a potential victim of U.S. military strategy, following global patterns."[51] One student complained that "the U.S. acts as boss of the world."[52] More ominously, those sentiments were shared by a war veteran, who said: "At the time of the war, I was very thankful for the

Americans. But now I have a negative image of them because they are acting like oppressors—they are too unilateral."[53]

Widespread are feelings that the United States does not respect the ROK.[54] A large majority of South Koreans believe that Americans look down on them.[55] One young South Korean declared that Americans "are actually ruling South Korea with the excuse that they are protecting us."[56] Some ROK residents view Washington's intentions in an even more negative light. A number of students blame Washington for the peninsula's continuing as well as past division. "The U.S. government is in Korea to divide us. The U.S. wants us weak and divided. They are not here for our security," charged one.[57] Said 28-year-old consultant Choi Mee-jin, "It's the U.S. that's a threat to us, not North Korea."[58]

Even stranger was a 1999 poll, which found that 12.2 percent of South Koreans believed that America would be their nation's chief *military* rival after reunification; nearly one in five believed the United States to represent the greatest military danger to the ROK.[59] In July 2003 a poll found that one-third of all South Koreans considered America to be "the most threatening country" for ROK security. Half of the college students held that view.[60] Not surprisingly, Pyongyang exploits these sentiments: for instance, it has attempted to ignore the United States and United Nations Command in working with Seoul, making the former appear to be obstructionists.[61]

It comes as no surprise, then, that to many South Koreans, the burdens of the U.S. presence increasingly seem to outweigh the benefits.[62] More than just radical students perceive the decreasing utility of the American presence. Even conservative policymakers believe that Pyongyang has neither the will nor the ability to stage a successful invasion; those who desire the continued presence of American soldiers usually point to other potential threats, most notably Japan. Yet the belief that Tokyo is likely to attempt to relive its colonial past in the peninsula is but a paranoid fantasy. Nor is it clear how Japan would do so, given the fact that South and North separately possess larger armies and Japan lacks the kind of airlift and sea-lift capabilities necessary for an invasion.

Moreover, as noted earlier, hosting a foreign military is not cheap. In the ROK, U.S. forces are ubiquitous. (They even have their own television channel.) American soldiers are high-profile travelers at Seoul's international airport, and many are based at the 630-acre Yongsan Army Garrison in downtown Seoul.[63] Thus constant contact occurs, leading to purposeless violent altercations and tragic traffic deaths.

In late 2002, after the acquittal in military court of two soldiers charged in the accidental deaths of two children, demonstrations erupted.[64] Americans were barred from restaurants, jeered, and in a few cases physically attacked.[65] One soldier even was kidnapped by a mob after another serviceman refused to accept a leaflet attacking the United States over the deaths of the girls.[66] Some Koreans boycotted U.S. goods.[67]

These anti-American sentiments, perhaps more widespread then ever before, drove the 2002 presidential election. Despite substantial differences, all of the presidential candidates, including conservative Lee Hoi-chang, demanded a change in the SOFA. (The United States, despite initial reluctance, agreed to renegotiate the treatment of American servicemen.[68]) President-elect Roh went a step further, calling for a more "equal" relationship and promising not to "kowtow" to Washington.[69]

THE QUEST FOR AN EQUAL RELATIONSHIP

The demand for "equality" has become common among South Korean policymakers and academics. Candidate Roh called for an "equal partnership" characterized by "horizontal relations."[70] The "alliance should be gradually transformed into a more equal mechanism," writes Kim Tae-hyo, of the Institute of Foreign Affairs and National Security.[71] Another IFANS scholar, Kim Sung-han, argues that the alliance can become more "equal and reciprocal" by developing a more "comprehensive ROK–U.S. alliance that includes human security and economic cooperation."[72] Kim Jin-wung advocates "'decision sharing' through close consultation and cooperation."[73] The majority of South Koreans also say that they want equality.[74]

Some Americans have sought to satisfy this desire. A panel formed by the Center for Strategic and International Studies in Washington and the Seoul Forum for International Affairs in Seoul recommended that the two nations "strive for a more equal partnership, buttressed by effective consultation and alliance management."[75] Seongho Sheen, a research fellow at the Asia-Pacific Center for Security Studies, says: "To develop a more mature alliance, the two governments need to make a conscious effort to promote an equal partnership based on mutual respect."[76] Yet, despite such sentiment, genuine equality is impossible for three reasons.

First, the interests of America and South Korea are diverging. The ROK is an emerging regional power, concerned about maintaining good relations with its immediate neighbors, particularly North Korea and China. It is relatively unconcerned about larger global issues, such as terrorism, democracy in the Mideast, and the like. In contrast, write security analysts Gregory F. Treverton, Eric V. Larson, and Spencer H. Kim, "It would be difficult to overstate the importance of 11 September 2001 on the U.S. psyche and on public support for a wide range of actions—including military action—to eliminate terrorist organizations."[77] As the perceived threat from the North recedes, the cement of the U.S.–ROK relationship is crumbling. While Washington has favored confrontation with North Korea over its nuclear program, neoconservative luminaries David Frum and Richard Perle observe that "the South Koreans, to speak plainly, favor a policy of appeasement of the North."[78] Although there are other issues about which the countries can cooperate, on none are they likely to do so equally.

Second, the alliance as constituted lacks mutuality, the necessary foundation for equality. While the United States is to defend the ROK, Seoul need do nothing for America. This lack of mutuality was evident in the lengthy debate over South Korean support for the U.S. mission in Iraq. Opposition was fierce; aid was niggardly and reluctant. The vast majority of the South Korean population opposed coming to the aid of the United States, despite 50 years of military protection.[79]

Third, the relationship between the two countries will never be equal so long as South Korea is dependent on Washington for its defense. For instance, Chung Jin-young, a professor at Kyung Hee University, writes: "Recently, South Koreans have become much more sensitive about the unequal nature of the ROK–U.S. alliance."[80] He points to the SOFA, U.S. limits on the range of South Korean–made missiles, and "rising cost sharing without a commensurate increase in South Korea's responsibility and power."[81] Kim Jin-wung makes much the same case.[82] The inconvenience of training exercises and even pollution from American bases also draw complaints.[83]

But if a country wants America's protection, it cannot complain when Washington calls the shots. How could it be any other way? The United States cannot be expected to risk war on another nation's terms, nor to deploy its forces to please its dependents.

Thus, so long as America protects the ROK, it will rightly demand special treatment for its soldiers. The SOFA has long been a matter of controversy, with revision talks stemming back to November 2000.[84] In late 2002 the two governments set up a task force to review the current agreement, which covers a variety of issues involving the investigation and custody of U.S. soldiers accused of a crime.[85] In January 2004 Washington for the first time turned over a soldier to South Korean authorities before his trial, on drunken driving charges in a fatal accident.[86]

However, even assuming that South Korean courts are fair and that rampant anti-Americanism will not spill over into the judicial system, it would not be fair to U.S. soldiers to station them in another land to protect others while leaving them vulnerable to the vagaries of foreign injustice. David Scofield, a lecturer at Kyung Hee University, points to "what observers call South Korea's penchant for the rule by law rather than the rule of law."[87] Moreover, fairness cannot be guaranteed: for instance, it was the three soldiers victimized by a Korean mob, and not those who beat them and kidnapped one of them, who were charged with assault by the South Korean police.[88] Put bluntly, the SOFA is part of the price a country pays when it is a de facto protectorate.[89]

THE NORTH KOREAN FACTOR

Placing even greater pressure on this unequal arrangement is the disagreement about how to deal with the DPRK. Explains Seongho Sheen, "Differences between the United States and South Korea over North Korea policy have exacerbated anti-American sentiment in South Korea. Many South Koreans have come to view the United States as a spoiler of the inter-Korean reconciliation process."[90]

For decades the South has been drawn north by obvious cultural, ethnic, and family ties, even as it was repelled by a brutal totalitarian dictatorship that impoverished its own people while threatening those in the South. Violent skirmishes along the DMZ, terrorism in the air and on land, and virulent denunciations of the ROK and America were constant features of Pyongyang's conduct. The Cold War lasted longer on the Korean peninsula than anywhere else.

Yet the DPRK periodically seemed to consider warming relations with the South. For instance, in 1972 the two Koreas signed a reconciliation agreement and halted hostile propaganda. The accord, which endorsed unification, promised inter-Korean exchanges, and provided for a bilateral telephone hot line, soon collapsed. A decade later the North Koreans attempted to assassinate South Korean President Chun Doo-hwan during a state visit to Rangoon.

In 1990 the two nations' prime ministers met; soon thereafter they inked weapons disarmament and economic cooperation agreements. (The latter was even more detailed than the pledges made by the two Kims following their June 2000 summit.[91]) But the first nuclear crisis soon followed, with the United States threatening—and, by some accounts, coming close to—war.

In 1994 Washington and the North reached the Agreed Framework to freeze the latter's nuclear program. North Korea's Kim Il-sung and South Korea's Kim Young-sam then planned a summit, only to have the former die of a heart attack 17 days before the meeting. Relations rapidly soured—in the

North's view, the ROK did not pay sufficient respect to the deceased Kim, for instance—with the DPRK returning to threats and aggressive action. Differences also arose with Washington, which was, ironically, at that time more conciliatory than South Korea in its attitudes toward North Korea.[92]

However, Kim Dae-jung, who was elected in December 1997, initiated his so-called sunshine policy emphasizing dialogue with and aid to the North, which was generally supported by the Clinton administration. Progress was slow, but in 2000 what seemed like the breakthrough summit occurred. Three years later the peninsula was engulfed by the nuclear crisis.

Pyongyang's behavior, though ever erratic and usually hostile, had been better between 1997 and 2000—with the DPRK, everything is relative. The North actually had apologized for a submarine infiltration incident in 1996, inaugurated the first phone and fax lines with the South, pursued various bilateral discussions, and allowed international humanitarian groups to operate in the North Korean countryside and South Korean technicians to construct the nuclear plants under the Framework accord.[93] Inter-Korean trade rose 4.6 percent, to $250 million, in 1997.[94] An International Monetary Fund delegation visited, and the World Bank reportedly was considering offering technical assistance to Pyongyang.[95]

Most stunning of all was the summit. The two Koreas ended propaganda broadcasts across the DMZ and came to speedy agreement on an initial experiment in family reunification. Aid and investment flowed North.

Euphoria was the response of many Koreans. Polls found that 90 percent of people said they had a positive view of the North, and a majority believed the possibility of war to be remote.[96] Nine of ten also believed that North Korea would change, improve its relations with the West, and continue to expand its ties to South Korea. The vast majority considered the North to be a partner and said they would welcome a visit by Kim Jong-il.[97]

The magazine *Korea Now* emblazoned its cover with a photo of the two Kims shaking hands, entitled "Gateway to Peace and Unity."[98] Article titles included "Hope Floats in the Air," "Embracing the Future," "Dawn of a New Era," "With Wide Open Arms," "Epoch History in the Making," "A Monumental Step Forward," and "Meeting of Unified Minds."[99] One would have thought that the magazine was published in Pyongyang. Exulted President Kim Dae-jung: "the danger of war on the Korean peninsula has disappeared."[100]

The summit seemed more successful than most observers imagined to be possible. Kim Jong-il confounded his image, appearing to be more intelligent, well informed, and charming than anyone had believed.[101] The DPRK engaged in a widespread diplomatic offensive throughout Asia and Europe.

Moreover, Kim Jong-il endorsed Chinese economic reforms during a visit to Beijing.[102] Pyongyang attempted to create a more inviting investment climate and encourage tourism, and some North Korean officials evidenced surprising knowledge of the outside world.[103] The DPRK created special economic zones, somewhat akin to those in China, to encourage foreign investment.[104] Many of the reforms directly contradicted a half century of *Juche,* or self-reliance: seeking foreign investment, granting discretion to managers of state companies (and urging the former to make *profits*), raising salaries, and lifting some price controls.[105]

There is evidence on the streets of Pyongyang that at least a few people have benefited from these changes.[106] Recent American visitors report a vibrant market for food and other goods in the capital.[107] Indeed, Sungwoo Kim of Northeastern University argues that "the market place is the only force which prevents total collapse of the North Korean economy."[108]

Nevertheless, this program is obviously not nearly enough. Introducing a few rational economic incentives into a system that remains utterly irrational cannot transform the North Korean economy. The implementation of the development zones has been disappointing.[109] Many companies that once intended to invest in the North have abandoned their plans. The DPRK lacks a rule of law, convertible currency, productive industry, and transportation network; DPRK and foreign business customs differ wildly.[110] Agricultural land, transportation infrastructure, and industrial plants all are in decay.

Foreign investment in selected areas, using inexpensive—and obviously well-"disciplined"—labor will bring in hard currency but will not revive indigenous industries.[111] Still less is the DPRK ready to compete independently with other nations in global markets. Today trade with nations such as Japan appears more like charity than commerce.[112] European companies have set up a chamber of commerce in the North, but Jean-Jacques Grauhar, secretary-general of the European Union Chamber of Commerce in Korea (based in Seoul), admits: "At the moment, there is no real market in North Korea."[113]

Some analysts even believe the North continues to move backward. Instead of jump-starting the economy, the reforms, a series of half-measures, may have disrupted what little production was occurring. Chinese economist Cui Yingjiu explains: "They can't do this half-way. They risk social chaos and economic collapse."[114] Similarly, writes Dominique Dwor Frecaut, of Barclays Capital in Singapore, "avoiding a systematic collapse would probably require the DPRK to move to full-fledged price liberalization."[115] Some observers thought that the DPRK was continuing to lose economic ground in the early

2000s.[116] In early 2004 the UN World Food Program warned of the continuing threat of starvation.[117]

If there is good news, it is that, as Marcus Noland of the Institute for International Economics argues, further reforms are inevitable: "the train has left the station."[118] Nevertheless, success is far from guaranteed. So disastrous has been Pyongyang's mismanagement of the DPRK's economy that even the most rational transition to the marketplace will be painful. Writes Yang Moonsoo, a professor at Kyungnam University's Graduate School of North Korean Studies, "It is inevitable that North Korea will suffer even worse decline in production and employment than were experienced by the more typical Soviet Union and Eastern Europe, not to mention China."[119]

Thus, in practice, South Korean government policy is predicated on large and continuing aid transfers to the North.[120] "The survival of the Kim Jong-il regime is in no small part conditioned on its relations with the rest of the world," argues Noland.[121]

Although North Korea's necessity and desire for reform seemed obvious, even at the time of the 2000 summit some critics warned of "sophisticated extortion."[122] However, the United States remained hopeful, if not as exuberant as many were in the South. America's ambassador to Seoul, Stephen W. Bosworth, felt that rapprochement "could take less time than many of us wise pundits on the outside now believe. North Korea does not have a vested interest in delay and will be interested in moving this process forward."[123] The Clinton administration responded with what Pentagon spokesman Kenneth Bacon called "controlled exuberance," lifting some economic sanctions.[124] One official told the Los Angeles Times: "It's not a reward, because we don't know if there's anything to reward yet. It's the U.S. trying to do what it can to support this positive movement by North and South Korea."[125] Secretary of State Madeleine Albright traveled to Pyongyang, and the administration unsuccessfully attempted to arrange a summit between President Bill Clinton and Kim Jong-il before the former left office.

However, the Bush administration took a very different view. Although Pyongyang seemed to be complying with the 1994 Agreed Framework, there were some indications that it might be conducting a secret nuclear enrichment program. At the same time, the North complained that the United States was failing to meet its commitments—to normalize relations and construct the replacement nuclear reactor, which was well behind the schedule envisioned by the agreement. Observed Jonathan Pollack of the Naval War College, "As the Bush administration took power, U.S.–North Korean relations remained uncertain, incomplete, and far from satisfactory for either country."[126]

Nevertheless, Secretary of State Colin Powell seemed generally comfortable with the Clinton administration's support for Kim Dae-jung's sunshine policy. Others in the Bush administration were not, however, and the secretary was forced into a very embarrassing public retreat. President Bush ensured a frigid summit with the ROK president in March 2001 by publicly distancing the United States from South Korea's policy toward the North.[127] Bush later announced that he loathed Kim Jong-il; after an internal policy review, the administration eschewed negotiations with Pyongyang.[128] Then came the events of September 11, which, explains Pollack, "further reaffirmed the diminished U.S. policy priority attached to engaging North Korea and strengthened the administration's predisposition to view Pyongyang as a looming danger, not a negotiating partner."[129] The president's celebrated inclusion of the DPRK as a member of the "axis of evil" was routinely noted in the North Korean press.[130]

U.S.–DPRK relations remained essentially nonexistent. Washington also seemed to obstruct Seoul's attempts to improve relations with the North. For instance, American objections over procedures regarding the DMZ long held up the project to connect a rail line and road between the two Koreas. Seoul asked the Bush administration to relax the UN Armistice rules, but initially received no response.[131] The road was finally opened without evident U.S. enthusiasm. In early 2002 South Korean presidential aide Lim Dong-won said he planned to visit Pyongyang to stave off a "rumored crisis on the Korean peninsula in 2003," widely attributed to delays in the construction of the reactors under the Agreed Framework, the Bush administration's characterization of the DPRK as a member of the axis of evil, and Washington's listing of the North as one of seven possible targets for America's nuclear forces.[132]

Momentum in the North Korea–ROK relationship also stalled because of DPRK intransigence. Kim Jong-il failed to reciprocate with a visit to Seoul. Negotiations with the North proved ever difficult, even over seemingly simple topics, such as reopening the road between the two countries. Family reunions were canceled. Provocations, such as a naval shootout, occurred.

Still, a variety of cooperative initiatives proceeded, ranging from establishing a military hot line, to allowing separated family members to meet, to holding joint sports competitions.[133] Growing economic ties were even more important.

Trade among the two countries exceeded $600 million in 2002, making Seoul a close number two to China in economic ties with the North. On the same day that Pyongyang was restarting its nuclear plant, the two Koreas reopened a road between the two countries; ten buses carried South Korean tourists to the North's Diamond Mountain resort. As of 2001, 152 ROK firms were active in the DPRK.[134] The *Washington Post* reported that there are "many flows of money and goods that prop up the North Korean system" resulting from a complex "number of trade routes that snake in and out of North Korea."[135] All told, "South Korea's Unification Ministry on Jan. 2 [2003] tallied North-South interaction in 2002 overall as the most intensive ever since regular contacts started, haltingly, in 1989," observed Aidan Foster-Carter.[136] The overt hostility of five decades remained in abeyance.

Perhaps most important, although the Kim Jong-il regime's decision-making processes and foreign dealings remained opaque and often seemed irrational, senior North Korean officials, starting with Kim, knew that their nation was in desperate straits.[137] Former U.S. ambassador to South Korea and chairman of the Korea Society Don Gregg believes that Kim "demonstrates a willingness to learn from neighboring countries' economic policies and to differentiate his rule from that of his father, Kim Il Sung."[138] The point is not that Kim Jong-il has become a born-again democrat with a heart for the starving, but that he recognizes that small nations with collapsing economies and starving populations rate very little on the international scale, and he wants to do something about it.

Further, in September 2002, Japanese prime minister Junichiro Koizumi staged a surprise visit to Pyongyang. For a time hopes for a bilateral breakthrough surged, especially with Kim Jong-il's startling apology for the kidnapping of Japanese citizens in the 1970s and 1980s—ostensibly to teach North Korean agents Japanese language and culture. Some of the kidnap victims were allowed to visit Japan, but disputes over their future and that of their families, as well as Pyongyang's incomplete accounting of its victims, soon caused the relationship to sour. Talks over recognition and aid, initially expected to be simple, were called off amid mutual acrimony.[139] (The DPRK moved in January 2004 to reopen communication with Japan, presumably both to increase the likelihood of economic assistance and to win fuller Japanese participation in upcoming nuclear talks.[140])

WASHINGTON, SEOUL, AND NORTH KOREA'S NUCLEAR PROGRAM

The DPRK's public break with Washington came when Assistant Secretary of State for East Asian and Pacific Affairs James Kelly traveled to Pyongyang in early October 2002. The DPRK apparently expected talks on improving relations; Kelly instead informed his hosts that to allow any forward movement, they had to stop cheating on the Agreed Framework. Although the two sides dispute exactly what was said, Pyongyang apparently did not contest Kelly's charges.[141] Talks ended, South Korea and Japan cut off additional fuel shipments, and the North took a series of increasingly provocative steps. (See chapter 2.) Whether the DPRK was hoping to negotiate or gain acceptance for its nuclear plans was not, and still is not, clear.[142] Very quickly developed what everyone except the Bush administration—fixated on Iraq, which, ironically, possessed neither nuclear weapons nor a serious conventional capability—considered to be a dangerous crisis.[143]

Even if the Bush administration is not responsible for the North breaching the Agreed Framework, its inclusion of Pyongyang in the axis of evil seems to have been a counterproductive throwaway line in a speech rather than a rational policy.[144] Moreover, Bush officials were woefully unprepared for the consequences of unmasking Pyongyang's deception.[145] Their subsequent fumbling turned the dispute into a far bigger and more serious one. Complains Walter C. Clemens, Jr., a professor of political science at Boston University: "The George W. Bush team generated the worst of possible worlds for U.S. security: it suspended what had been promising negotiations with the DPRK while it fostered a defiant self-reliance in Pyongyang. Washington proffered neither carrots nor sticks."[146]

Most dramatic was the controversy's impact in Seoul, which was in the midst of a divisive presidential election. President Kim Dae-jung was bedeviled by scandal; his Millennium Democratic Party's candidate, Roh Moo-hyun, had a leftist pedigree; and the party suffered an embarrassing breakup of its electoral alliance with an independent candidate on election eve. Most important, conservative candidate Lee Hoi-chang targeted the seeming growing unpopularity of Kim's sunshine policy.

However, contrary to most expectations, Roh won. His margin, though narrow, was larger than Kim's edge five years before. One factor in Roh's victory was the softening of many South Koreans' opinion of the North, noted earlier.[147] It seems that when forced to decide whether the North Korean glass was half full or half empty, more voters chose the former.

Despite all of the difficulties in dealing with North Korea, the situation is different from what it was in the past. Moreover, many ROK voters in the 2000 presidential election apparently saw no alternative strategy to engagement. In Roh they chose as president someone firmly committed to engagement. One of Roh's advisors said, "Negotiating with Kim Jong Il is the easiest way to change North Korea."[148] Roh emphasized the importance of avoiding "mistrust," which raised questions of whether he is naive about dealing with the totalitarian North.[149] *New York Times* columnist Nicholas D. Kristof, for one, judged that President Roh was "simply trying to send a conciliatory message to Pyongyang."[150] The truth of Kristof's assessment will undoubtedly be tested many times during Roh's term.

But an equally important election factor was the United States. Roh was an opposition lawyer who had fought military rule and called for the withdrawal of U.S. forces.[151] He ran on an explicit peace platform that sharply diverged from U.S. policy: "We have to choose between war and peace," he told one rally.[152] His candidacy captured rising popular antagonism to the United States and particularly to the presence of American troops.[153] American officials made no attempt to hide their preference for the more conservative Lee Hoi-chang; a U.S. intelligence analyst related to one of the authors that no military or political officials with whom he dealt would even acknowledge the possibility that Roh might win. Some Americans baldly demanded that the Bush administration intervene to try to elect Lee.[154]

Even the Clinton administration had some reservations about Kim Dae-jung's sunshine policy.[155] Tensions, however, obviously were greater between the Bush and Kim administrations.[156] Relations grew still worse after Roh's victory. The South Korean president-elect denounced "blindly following U.S. policy."[157] He said the ROK should take an "independent and autonomous line" in dealing with the North.[158] An unnamed U.S. official returned the favor by denouncing Roh as "an appeaser."[159] Edward Olsen delicately observed: "Washington's uneven track record on consulting with Seoul regarding these sensitive issues [U.S. deployments in the South and policies toward the North] exacerbates for the Roh administration the Bush administration's reputation for not being well endowed with empathetic Korea expertise at the highest levels."[160]

Perhaps it was not surprising that so poisonous had become the bilateral atmosphere that many Koreans suspected Washington of arranging the nuclear crisis to boost Lee's candidacy. Similarly, the seizure of the North Korean vessel carrying Scuds for Yemen in late 2002 was seen as an attempt to manipulate South Korean voters by diverting attention from the accident involving the two ROK teenagers.[161] Such claims were all extremely unlikely, of course, but paranoia and nationalism create a potent brew.

Most South Koreans worried about the North's nuclear course, but not nearly as much as did Americans. Moreover, people and especially policymakers in the two nations operated from different frames of reference. Security analysts Gregory F. Treverton, Eric V. Larson, and Spencer H. Kim note the importance of the events of September 11 on U.S. support for military action to eliminate adversaries that might threaten the United States.[162] In contrast,

South Koreans worry far more about the possibility of a war arising from miscalculation or clumsy U.S. policy than they worry about a premeditated attack. An aggressive misstep toward Pyongyang would be bothersome for the United States; it would be disastrous for the South. Policymakers in Seoul, within easy reach of North Korean artillery and Scud missiles, remember their vulnerability on a daily basis. Said President Roh: war "is such a catastrophic result that I cannot even imagine. We have to handle the North–South relations in such a way that we do not have to face such a situation."[163]

Even worse, many South Koreans believe that U.S. policy poses the greatest threat to their security. Observes Seongho Sheen: "North Korea's nuclear and other WMDs are perceived as deterrence measures against the United States rather than offensive weapons aimed at South Korea. South Korea increasingly regards an unprovoked attack by North Korea as unlikely and tends to emphasize North Korean 'intention' as opposed to 'capability' with regard to its WMD and missiles. Many South Koreans think that it is impossible for North Korea to use WMD on fellow Koreans."[164]

Yet, former president Bill Clinton admitted that he prepared military options for use against the North a decade ago to eliminate the DPRK's nuclear program, with nary a nod to the South Koreans (or the Japanese).[165] Roh understandably complained, "We almost went to the brink of war in 1993 with North Korea, and at the time we didn't even know it."[166] Roh has even more reason to worry today; the Bush administration is far more belligerent than its predecessor.

In late January 2003 President Kim Dae-jung sent an envoy to North Korea to discuss the nuclear issue and offered veiled criticism of the United States: "Sometimes we need to talk to the other party, even if we dislike the other party."[167] President Bush reportedly abstained from endorsing military coercion only because Kim personally related the horrors of the Korean War.[168] But at the same time Washington was pushing the issue toward the UN Security Council, which, in Seoul's view, would short-circuit the diplomatic process. Shortly thereafter the Bush administration pointedly observed that military action remained an option for dealing with the North, generating a near-hysterical response from Seoul.

Although the administration later downplayed possible military strikes as it engaged in multilateral talks that included the DPRK, few analysts believed that coercion had disappeared from consideration.[169] A decade ago many American policymakers, politicians, and columnists blithely talked about military options, most obviously the destruction of the nuclear reactor in Yongbyon and any other known atomic facilities.[170] Throughout 2003 similar proposals were advanced. (See chapter 3.)

The more outspoken American hawks believed that coercion was inevitable.[171] Some advocated that the United States simply bide its time. Explained columnist Charles Krauthammer: "It is obvious that, at least until Iraq is settled, nonbelligerence is warranted. We simply cannot handle two military crises at once."[172]

This may essentially be the Bush administration's position. President Roh, for one, charged that "at the time of the [Korean] elections, some U.S. officials who held considerable responsibility in the administration talked about the possibility of attacking North Korea." Only later, he said, had "opinion in the United States started to change to resolving the matter peacefully."[173] Anonymous Bush administration officials denied the report, and Roh himself claimed that he had been misinterpreted, that he was referring to media reports.[174] Yet his original claim was plausible, if impossible to verify.

In fact, in early 2003 President Bush indicated that "all options are on the table," including military action.[175] Defense advisor Richard Perle, who was suggesting military preemption back in 1991, predicted: "The Bush administration will consider all the alternatives, because the dangers involved are so substantial."[176] War is, after all, the logical outgrowth of the administration's doctrine of preventive war, first used against Iraq. Defense Secretary Donald Rumsfeld commented that the United States is "capable of fighting two major regional foreign conflicts."[177] He also called North Korea a "terrorist regime," perhaps the most obvious justification for attack, given the administration's overarching "war on terrorism," which included the preventive strike against Iraq.[178]

And there is no reason to believe that the administration ultimately would be persuaded by what it saw as an "appeasement-minded" ROK government. (More likely, though still uncertain, might be the disincentive effect arising from the postwar mess in Iraq that seemed likely to bedevil the U.S. government for years.) Indeed, some hawks explicitly dismissed Seoul's views. Opined Senator John McCain (R-Ariz.): "while they may risk their populations, the United States will do whatever it must to guarantee the security of the American people. And spare us the usual lectures about American unilateralism. We would prefer the company of North Korea's neighbors, but we will make do without it if we must."[179] Frank Gaffney, head of the Center for Security Policy, similarly stated: "the desire of dangerous nations' neighbors to accommodate, rather than confront, them is understandable. But it should not be determinative of U.S. policy. Such pleading today from South Korea and Japan is reminiscent of the Cold War advocacy for detente by leftists in the West German government."[180]

Stephen J. Morris of the Johns Hopkins University School of Advanced International Studies argued that coercive regime change "may be the only solution, no matter how horrible the costs might be."[181] Perhaps most chillingly, David Frum and Richard Perle write: "A North Korean nuclear warhead that might be sold to al-Qaeda or some other terrorist group is more dangerous to us than a war on the Korean peninsula."[182] Such sentiments are not likely to reassure nervous South Koreans.

There is no more important issue for Seoul than the prospect of a U.S. preemptive strike against North Korea. As Roh explains, "It is impossible not to have differences [with the United States], and I cannot agree to attacking North Korea."[183] During a campaign debate, candidate Roh declared:

> We must not tolerate North Korea's development of nuclear weapons, no matter what. In relation, there have been many discussions on exactly how we should prevent it; whether by dialogue or by force. Personally, I feel resorting to force is too much of a risk. During the first nuclear crisis in 1994 our nation failed to play our rightful part in the conflict between the North and the United States. That's part of the reason we have come so close to this second crisis. The issue should be resolved through dialogue with close coordination with the United States. However, it is still our nation that should take the main role to make the difference. Seoul and Washington basically differ in view. For Washington, their prime interest lies in getting rid of weapons of mass destruction to restore the world order, but for us it's a matter of survival.[184]

After President Bush indicated that military action was an option, Chang Chun-hyong, deputy spokesman for the ruling Millennium Democratic Party, complained in early 2003 that "we cannot help expressing concern as to whether emotions have interfered with U.S. efforts to resolve the North's nuclear problem."[185] Howard French of the *New York Times* described South Korean officials as being "shocked" by Secretary Rumsfeld's rhetoric.[186]

DRIFTING APART

Both governments have attempted to patch over their differences. The 2003 ROK defense white paper announced: "In the past, the domestic affairs of the U.S. or changes in the international security environment resulted in one-sided policy decisions, which in turn caused the ROK-U.S. alliance to undergo certain fluctuations. However, both countries agree that the alliance between the two sides should be coordinated in accordance with the common interests achieved through close cooperation."[187]

When visiting the U.S. military headquarters in South Korea after the election, Roh argued that "there are some voices of anti-Americanism in Korea, but the number of those voices is small, and the chances of their leading public opinion is even smaller."[188] He went so far as to say that the alliance "was precious, is now still precious and will continue to be important in the future."[189] There are many possible reasons for his flip-flop: criticism of the sunshine policy and charges that the Kim Dae-jung/Kim Jong-il summit was bought with bribes, concern over the cost of replacing U.S. forces, normal maneuvering toward the political center, and a concerted effort to restore overall U.S.–Korean relations.[190]

Yet around the same time Roh complained that "so far, all changes in the size of U.S. troop strength here have been determined by the United States based on its strategic consideration, without South Korea's consent."[191] (On what, one wonders, would he expect Washington to base its force deployments?) Moreover, Roh reportedly ordered the ROK military to prepare for a reduction or withdrawal of U.S. forces.[192] He explained in one speech: "Although we don't know if it might take 10, 20 or 30 years, someone has to consider an independent defense. Senior military officials have to prepare a plan for a special emergency situation when the U.S. Army moves away."[193]

And that time is not likely to be decades away. After all, proposed "reforms" of the relationship—adjusting the SOFA, moving America's Yongsan base out of Seoul, marginally reducing force levels, changing the joint command (which envisions an American general commanding Korean troops in war)—are inadequate. The Bush administration reportedly is considering shrinking the number of American installations in the ROK from 41 to 25 over the next decade—too little change too slowly. Also divisive was Secretary Rumsfeld's decision to pull back U.S. forces from the DMZ: America's forces are too few to be anything but a tripwire, and a tripwire in, say, Pusan is one with no value. The move even raised fears in both South and North that Washington was preparing for a possible preemptive strike on the DPRK by moving its forces out of range of a retaliatory response.[194] That might not be the administration's plan, but the South Koreans could be forgiven for thinking so: "as we reposition troops, we should develop detailed plans for a preemptive strike against North Korea's nuclear facilities," advocate Frum and Perle.[195] Frum is a former Bush speechwriter and inveterate administration cheerleader;

Perle is a friend, colleague, and mentor to several Bush administration figures, such as Deputy Defense Secretary Paul Wolfowitz.

Roh's decision to force the resignation of Foreign Minister Jeong Chan-yong in mid-January 2004 seemed, despite public denials, to reflect Seoul's desire to adopt a more distant relationship with the United States—at least, to strike an independent stance. But that course would degrade relations with an American administration that takes perceived disloyalty badly.[196] In any case, the basic problem of unequal, unnecessary military dependence in the midst of changing public opinion persists. Worry Lee Nae-young and Jeong Han-wool of Korea University, "the anti-Americanism in South Korea is likely to remain for a long time as a source of conflict within Korean society, and may pose an obstacle to ROK–U.S. relations in the future."[197]

Striking is the change in Korean attitudes. For instance, favorable-unfavorable/like-dislike ratings for the United States have fallen from 64–15 percent in 1994 to 53–37 percent in 2002 to 43–50 percent in 2003. The generational shift makes it likely that these trends will continue, promoting increased opposition to Washington's military presence. Lee and Jeong contend that much of the anti-Americanism is directed at changing "the institutions and procedures of the alliance," rather than "the legitimacy of the ROK–U.S. alliance."[198] Nevertheless, they also find a sharp generational polarization that they believe could threaten the relationship.[199]

Stephen J. Morris complains: "Over the past decade, South Korea's political culture has gradually adopted a left-wing, pacifist and appeasement-oriented attitude toward the North and an increasingly virulent hostility toward the United States."[200] He points out that the problem in Korea is anti-Americanism in general, and not hostility toward the Bush administration, unlike Europe, where the large majority of critics of the United States blame the administration.[201] Even the good news cited by Lee and Jeong—a drop from 57 percent to 40 percent from January to June 2003 in the number of South Koreans who want to reduce or eliminate the U.S. forces in the ROK—means that four of ten desire to downgrade the relationship despite the looming danger from the North.[202]

Friction between Korean civilians and American forces also will continue: for example, on average, 200 to 300 crimes are committed annually by U.S. soldiers. No longer are they likely to be overlooked. Lee and Jeong contend that the two governments should "pursue equal bilateral relations" to forestall another round of anti-Americanism, but there are no easy institutional fixes to yield genuine equality.[203] Thus, any new incident seems likely to inflame sentiments that have only temporarily gone dormant. After all, observed Sam

Stratman, a spokesman for the House International Relations Committee, "I saw 150 troops in front of the American embassy. We need 150 troops to guard our embassy from our friends."[204]

Roh's election simply accelerated an inevitable reevaluation of the alliance. Observed Nicholas Eberstadt of the American Enterprise Institute, a strong proponent of a continuing ROK–U.S. alliance, before the last election: "If Lee Hoi Chang wins, maybe there will be a stay of execution for the relationship. But in five years' time, there will be an even bigger problem."[205]

That problem will be not only the burden of dealing with U.S. troops. It will be policy differences. Report Norman D. Levin and Yong-Sup Han of the RAND Corporation, "Whatever their expectations, South Koreans overwhelmingly want to maintain control over the unification process. By a nearly three-to-one ratio . . . they prefer negotiating unification matters directly with North Koreans themselves rather than allowing other countries to participate."[206]

Yet the South Korean and U.S. governments remain far apart on how best to deal with North Korea. The ROK is committed to negotiations and believes, publicly at least, that Pyongyang can be dissuaded peacefully from becoming a nuclear power (or "bought off," in more informal parlance).

For instance, Seoul's Ministry of Unification has argued that the North Koreans' "true aim is not to continue the nuclear development program, but to seek a breakthrough in relations with the United States."[207] Chang Young-dal, a member of President Roh's ruling party, contends that "at heart, the North would like to have their regime guaranteed. I think the actions they have taken lately have come because they fear for their survival."[208] Roh says that "North Korea wants to escape from its status as a rogue state." In his view, "once those things [from a conciliatory approach] are guaranteed, North Korea will abandon its nuclear ambitions."[209]

Another DPRK goal is perceived as cash, given what Chang delicately calls "the difficult economic conditions" afflicting the DPRK.[210] Similarly, argues Lim Chae-jung, the leader of Roh's transition after his election: "North Korea's nuclear program is an economic, not a military, question."[211] Ha Young-sun of Seoul National University says simply: "This is nothing new. It's just a continuation of the North Korean scenario. We are engaged in a game of bluffing."[212]

Even in the midst of the nuclear deadlock and criticism over the $500 million payment by the powerful Hyundai corporation, including substantial South Korean government funds, to the DPRK in advance of the 2000 summit, the South was moving ahead to engage North Korea.[213] For instance, the two nations opened air links between Seoul and Pyongyang. Railways are being connected through the DMZ. South Korean firms began building an industrial park in the northern city of Kaesong. In the fall of 2003 the two countries opened a large sports complex, which, explained *Korea News,* was "expected to accelerate sports exchanges between the two countries and contribute to overall reconciliation."[214] Domestic criticism of aid to the North has risen because of Pyongyang's nuclear brinkmanship.[215] Nevertheless, Foreign Minister Yoon Young-kwan explains that "the key of our North Korean policy is helping North Korea adopt market mechanisms."[216] DPRK–U.S. hostility was seen as an impediment to improved relations: "There has been growing concern recently over the potential negative impact on inter-Korean relations that may stem from the North's harsh rhetoric to escalate its nuclear standoff with the United States."[217]

Washington policymakers, and especially those in the Bush administration, were much less convinced that negotiation could resolve the issue.[218] (Of course, there are optimists, but few seemed to be in the government.[219]) Nor is it obvious that the United States has the patience necessary to persevere with negotiations that will be inevitably tortuous and torturous. Certainly its previous behavior leaves little cause for optimism.[220] To the contrary, as noted earlier, Washington seems much more prepared to resort to coercion, including military force.

Over the objection of South Korea, the United States pushed the International Atomic Energy Agency to forward the issue of the North's noncompliance to the UN Security Council, which could issue a warning or move directly to impose economic sanctions. Pyongyang has threatened to regard sanctions as a declaration of war; that is likely a bluff, since it would lose the most in any conflict.[221] Nevertheless, the threat remains a worry.

Whether sanctions would work is another question. The DPRK remains one of the world's most isolated nations, but it is weaker and more vulnerable than it was a decade ago.[222] It is more heavily reliant than ever on outside support—aid, remittances, and trade—and thus is susceptible to economic pressure. Nevertheless, sanctions usually hurt the poor, vulnerable, and powerless the most. Increased suffering would be decisive only if it roused the disorganized and disheartened rural masses to revolt, which is unlikely, or inconvenienced a critical faction of the communist party and military, which is only slightly more plausible. Believing that another squeeze would bring the regime to heel probably represents the triumph of hope over experience.

Moreover, sanctions would not work without support of the surrounding countries. Yet none of the DPRK's neighbors is eager to destabilize the North. Although the PRC has pressed Pyongyang to negotiate and evidenced annoyance at the latter's behavior, that might not translate into a willingness to potentially destroy the regime. South Korea is even more strongly opposed to sanctions. It worries about undercutting the range of improved ROK–North Korean relations, including business opportunities.[223] A return to a cold war on the peninsula is not in its interest.

More important, notes Edward Olsen, "Seoul does not want a North Korean hard landing any more than Pyongyang does."[224] The collapse of the DPRK could spark internal armed conflict that spills into the ROK. Even absent violence, refugees would undoubtedly flood south. During meetings with Deputy Secretary of State Richard Armitage, an American observer reported that "one South Korean official said they'd prefer a nuclear North Korea to a collapsed North Korea."[225] Similarly, a delegation of South Koreans sent by President-elect Roh reportedly shocked their Washington hosts when they stated that it would be better for Pyongyang to acquire an atomic bomb than to collapse.[226]

In fact, the South fears an early peaceful reunification almost as much as war. It watched German reunification with horror, recognizing that a similar Korean experience would be extraordinarily costly. Goldman Sachs Group Inc. has figured that the cost of "fixing" the DPRK would run up to $1 trillion, more than wealthier West Germany spent on reunification with a wealthier East Germany (and more than twice the ROK's annual gross domestic product [GDP]).[227] One estimate is that the price of absorbing the North, where the per-capita GDP is little more than 5 percent of South Korea's, would reduce the living standard in the ROK by 10 percent.[228] For understandable reasons, the goal of President Kim Dae-jung's sunshine policy was not only to reduce the chance of conflict; it also was to help the North muddle along and reduce the cost of eventual reunification. Even many conservative critics of the specifics of Kim's approach agree with that goal. To that end, Seoul's government-funded Korea Development Institute proposed spending $2 billion annually to upgrade the North's economic infrastructure and feed its population, with a target of increasing per-capita GDP to $1,000 by 2008.[229]

Even more divisive is the possibility of military action. Some Americans predict that the North would not respond; others simply do not care. Few South Koreans desire to try the experiment.

Even if the military action remained limited and did not escalate to full-scale war, the alliance would be dead. The perception that South Koreans died because the United States acted against the wishes of the ROK government would create a divisive, and probably decisive, split between Seoul and Washington. North Korea's siren song of the two Koreas uniting against America would sound more plausible if Washington initiated a conflict that left Seoul in rubble: for instance, in January 2003 the North declared that the two Koreas should "pool their efforts and condemn and frustrate the U.S. nuclear policy for aggression."[230]

There is another ROK consideration, although seldom is it voiced publicly. If the North Korean regime is doomed, any nuclear arsenal would fall into the hands of the South through reunification. And inheriting nuclear weapons is a lot easier than building them.[231] In fact, a recent novel published in the ROK, *The Rose of Sharon Has Blossomed,* centers on a South Korean aiding the North in building nuclear weapons that are used jointly to defeat Japanese aggression.[232]

On other issues Washington and Seoul also are likely to grow apart. IFANS scholar Kim Sung-han speaks of a "convergence of interest" between the ROK's desire for survival and America's commitment to leadership.[233] But while these goals coincided during the Cold War, they may not in future years. Korean survival could be threatened by an assertion of U.S. leadership to contain China militarily, for instance. Nor, without a tie to larger threat, is South Korea's survival important for American security today.

Moreover, at a time when Washington's military resources are stretched in meeting threats of terrorism and occupying Afghanistan and Iraq, real leadership requires discretion in choosing among priorities. In today's world, South Korea—less threatened by other nations and more able to cope with any dangers—is no longer the priority that it once was for American security. But the most important issue remains the North. "South Korea and the United States face different threats from the advent of North Korean nuclear power," writes Stephen Morris. "As such, American and South Korean priorities have begun to diverge fundamentally."[234]

The policy in both Seoul and Washington has been "That which is must always be." Even in the midst of recent alliance divisions, many officials contend that the only problem is public relations. In December 2003 Secretary of Defense Rumsfeld and ROK defense minister Lee Jun issued a joint communiqué stating that "the members of the alliance need to do a better job of communicating the value of the alliance to the people of both countries."[235] But what is the value? The benefits are just assumed. "The U.S.–South Korean alliance is simply too important for both countries," says Hyung Kook Kim, director of the Center for Asian Studies at American University.[236] But important to whom? And why?

Alliances exist to serve a purpose. Unfortunately, for Washington the means have become an end. America has defended the ROK for 50 years. Why not do so another 50 years? But U.S. interests no longer are served by this arrangement. Washington pays the bill but gains little benefit from doing so. Indeed, it is finding ingratitude replacing appreciation. "Sometimes I wonder which one is really our adversary" was the sardonic comment of one American officer in discussing the two Koreas.[237]

America's one-time protectorate has grown up, causing angst in Washington. President Roh's election is "a big headache," complained one U.S. official to the *Economist*.[238] A U.S. military official in South Korea described "a real sense of mourning" after Roh's victory.[239] But the ROK is entitled to elect its own leaders, assess its own interests, and chart its own course.

At stake is much more than the right to try American personnel for crimes committed in Korea or the location of U.S. forces. It is the future of the Korean peninsula. It should come as no surprise, then, that South Korea increasingly is insisting that not only should it be consulted, but it also should be involved in shaping policy toward the North. And as the approaches of the two nations diverge, tensions between them will grow. "Absent a compelling new rationale for its continuation, this alliance will come under mounting pressure for revision," admits Nicholas Eberstadt.[240] As well it should. Even if the countries avoid a crisis today, they will only delay the inevitable. Washington's security guarantee has lost its raison d'être, leaving no reason for the United States and the ROK not to seek an amicable divorce.

Chapter Two

THE NORTH KOREAN
NUCLEAR CRISIS

THEN AND NOW

North Korea's interest in nuclear weapons is not a recent development. The Democratic People's Republic of Korea (DPRK) began its nuclear effort as far back as the mid-1950s and was originally assisted by the Soviet Union, which helped establish an atomic energy research center in 1962, and China, which aided the North's uranium mining effort.[1] South Korea was sufficiently concerned about these developments that it pursued its own covert nuclear-weapons program in the early and mid-1970s. When U.S. leaders discovered what Seoul was doing, they put immediate and intense pressure to get South Korea to renounce its efforts. Washington's campaign was successful, although Republic of Korea (ROK) dictator Park Chung-hee was none too happy about adopting that course. Efforts to revive the program occurred again in the mid- and late 1980s, and it was not until 1991 that Seoul finally abandoned the goal.[2]

Although South Korea ultimately ended its flirtation with a nuclear-weapons development program, the DPRK did not follow suit. In fact, its efforts intensified. True, North Korea insisted all along that its nuclear efforts were entirely for the peaceful purpose of power generation, but each step brought the DPRK ever closer to a nuclear-weapons capability. North Korea joined the International Atomic Energy Agency (IAEA) in 1974, giving the country's scientists access to technical assistance in the peaceful use of nuclear energy. Over the years the DPRK constructed a 5-megawatt reactor and began building a 50-megawatt reactor at a complex at Yongbyon. North Korea even started construction on a 200-megawatt reactor in 1985.

North Korea also signed the Nuclear Nonproliferation Treaty (NPT) in 1985. But even at that early date there were questions about the sincerity of Pyongyang's commitment. As Mohamed ElBaradei, the current director general of the IAEA (the enforcement arm of the NPT) notes, North Korea took seven years to sign the obligatory verification agreement with the IAEA, a process that takes most signatories about 18 months. The ink was barely dry on the inspection agreement, ElBaradei recalls, before IAEA inspectors in May 1992 "discovered plutonium discrepancies in North Korea's nuclear-waste streams—indicating nuclear activity that had not been reported."[3] When North Korean officials blocked a more intrusive inspection the following year, the IAEA declared the DPRK to be in noncompliance with its obligations under the NPT and alerted the United Nations Security Council. Thus officially began the first North Korean nuclear crisis.

In reality, there was evidence that North Korea was cheating on its nonnuclear commitment long before May 1992. As early as 1989 the United States learned from satellite images and other data that Pyongyang might be processing nuclear material in violation of its commitments under the NPT, as U.S. satellite photos revealed what appeared to be a reprocessing plant. The evidence grew stronger the following year when it became clear that the North had tested bomb components, opened a plutonium processing plant, and inaugurated a new uranium processing plant.

As calls for international inspections became more insistent, North Korea denied that it had a nuclear-weapons program and resisted any oversight. Pyongyang even rejected a Japanese offer of diplomatic recognition in exchange for an inspections agreement. When evidence of an ambitious nuclear facility at Yongbyon seemed irrefutable, the issue began to get more attention from the United States and its East Asian allies. Northern intransigence led to proposals for more than negotiations. Among the options discussed at the annual U.S.–South Korean security talks in November 1991 were economic sanctions and a naval blockade.[4]

Meanwhile, the North began a maddening pattern of often contradictory diplomatic maneuvers. Originally the DPRK used the presence of U.S. tactical nuclear weapons in South Korea to justify its refusal to allow IAEA inspections. Then in October 1991 DPRK foreign minister Kim Yong-nam stated that inspections would be allowed if "such a nuclear threat is removed."[5] Typically, though, after Washington announced its intention to withdraw the bombs and warheads stationed in South Korea, Pyongyang quickly added new conditions—that the ROK renounce nuclear protection by the United States and forbid the overflights of planes and docking of ships carrying nuclear weapons.

But in December 1991 the North's zigzag policy took another zag. Pyongyang concluded an agreement with Seoul pledging to keep the Korean peninsula nuclear free. The agreement also provided for even more intrusive inspections than those typically conducted by the IAEA. Hope of détente between the two Koreas blossomed, and there was a surge in optimism that the nuclear issue could be resolved in the near future.

Although the two Koreas subsequently deadlocked on bilateral inspection procedures, the IAEA made its first inspections in May 1992, and by the end of the year the agency had conducted six examinations of North Korean nuclear facilities. The agency's conclusions were mixed but generally favorable: the DPRK appeared to have produced more than the 90 grams of plutonium that it admitted possessing, but the regime had generally been cooperative. Although the IAEA was skeptical of some of Pyongyang's explanations of the purpose of its apparent reprocessing facility, the North took IAEA investigators to sites not on the formal inspection list and offered to allow the agency to make additional special visits on demand. By November 1992 Ronald Lehman, head of the U.S. Arms Control and Disarmament Agency, reversed his earlier pessimistic assessment and concluded that the international efforts had stopped the DPRK's nuclear program and "blocked" its ability to amass "a sizable number of nuclear weapons over time."[6]

Throughout this period, the administration of George H. W. Bush was surprisingly passive.[7] It greatly scaled back the annual Team Spirit military exercises with South Korea in both 1990 and 1991. In late 1991 the United States announced the withdrawal of all U.S. tactical nuclear weapons from South Korea, and in January 1992 Bush announced that the Team Spirit exercises scheduled for that year would be suspended. Finally, the administration agreed to a high-level meeting with North Korean officials, and a meeting between the U.S. undersecretary of state and his North Korean counterpart occurred in February 1992.[8] That was the highest-level contact that had ever taken place between the two governments. All of these steps accommodated long-standing North Korean demands. Although President Bush denied that such concessions were a quid pro quo for Pyongyang's willingness to conclude an agreement to allow IAEA inspectors to examine its facilities, the conciliatory gestures certainly seemed to take that form. Unfortunately, the lesson that North Korean leaders may have learned is that nuclear blackmail gets results from the United States.

THE 1993–94 CRISIS

Just when it appeared that the concerns of the international community about the North's nuclear program could subside, Pyongyang again turned uncooperative. In January 1993 the DPRK refused the IAEA access to two suspected waste depositories, and tests showed that the North had lied about how much plutonium it had extracted.[9] When the IAEA made an unprecedented demand for a special inspection of the two sites, North Korea denounced the agency as a front for the United States and stated that it was refusing to allow any more IAEA inspections. Even more dramatic, the DPRK announced on March 12 that it was withdrawing from the NPT (an action that no other nation had ever taken) and abrogating the inspection agreement. The IAEA responded by declaring North Korea out of compliance, and the international crisis flared again.

It was not clear why the North took such actions. The most likely explanation is that it feared that IAEA inspectors would discover additional evidence that it had lied about its production of plutonium. Selig Harrison, a longtime expert on North Korea, speculates that DPRK leaders may have underestimated the intrusiveness and effectiveness of IAEA inspections.[10] Another possibility is that the regime decided that it had received too few tangible benefits from its decision to forgo nuclear weapons. Perhaps DPRK leaders decided to test the newly elected governments in the United States and South Korea by fomenting a crisis. Or perhaps the decision reflected internal political maneuvering within North Korea's political elite. Given North Korea's closed, secretive system, we may never know for certain why the regime adopted a confrontational course in early 1993.

Even as they pursued such a course, however, North Korean officials held out hope for an amicable settlement. Privately, DPRK diplomats stressed that Pyongyang was receptive to three-way talks with the United States and the ROK about nuclear inspections on the peninsula, and they hinted that their country was willing to return to the NPT if such talks got under way. At the same time, the North pressed for a permanent end to the Team Spirit military exercises between the United States and South Korea that the Bush administration had suspended earlier.

Such nuances were ignored in the United States, where fears about the DPRK's nuclear program reached a fever pitch. As the IAEA's March 31 deadline for the resumption of inspections approached, Secretary of State Warren Christopher told a congressional committee that, if the North did not relent, "there will be enforcement action taken within the UN Security Council."[11] Christopher emphasized the likelihood of economic sanctions. But there were some problems with that approach. It was not clear that such measures would have much impact on North Korea's autarkical economy. Moreover, sanctions authorized by the Security Council required the approval of China—long the North's closest ally. It soon became apparent that Beijing was in no mood to penalize Pyongyang in that fashion. "We support patient consultations to reach an appropriate solution," explained Chinese foreign minister Qian Qichen. "If the matter goes before the Security Council, that will only complicate things."[12] Those who saw economic sanctions as an alternative to military action also had to confront the reality that Pyongyang had warned that the imposition of sanctions would mean war.

As the new Clinton administration grappled with the crisis, a growing number of analysts and pundits advocating resorting to military action. Referring to Israel's 1981 attack on Iraq's Osirak reactor, columnist Paul Greenberg argued that "America and its allies should be readying an Israel-style strike against North Korean facilities now."[13] Similar was the analysis of former deputy assistant secretary of defense Frank Gaffney, now head of the Center for Security Policy. "The choice," he contended, "is not between possibly going to war with North Korea and not going to war. Rather, it is a question of risking going to war *now*, when U.S. military capabilities are relatively strong and North Korean nuclear forces are minimal (or not yet completed), rather than later when such advantageous conditions will almost surely not exist."[14] "Rather than trying to appease" a Stalinist dictatorship, Heritage Foundation scholar Larry DiRita wrote, the administration should set a firm deadline for North Korea to allow international inspections. If the North did not comply, not only should the United States and its allies impose comprehensive economic sanctions, but they should consider "destroying military headquarters, ballistic missile launch sites, or command and control facilities."[15]

John McCain embraced a rationale disturbingly close to that expressed by Gaffney: "To all those apologists for the Administration's appeasement policy who argue that we must refrain from responses that might provoke the North into launching a military attack, I ask one question: Would an attack be more or less likely after North Korea acquires a nuclear arsenal and after it has completed its production of ballistic missiles capable of delivering nuclear warheads to Tokyo? I think the answer is obvious."[16] Although McCain did not favor resorting to military action immediately (advocating instead the imposition of rigorous sanctions), he warned that "stronger measures" might be needed if sanctions did not achieve the desired goal. He then described in considerable detail how the United States might destroy North Korea's nuclear program using aircraft and cruise missile strikes.

More worrisome than the warlike statements of pundits and even opposition politicians, Clinton administration officials declined to rule out the military option. At one point Secretary of Defense Les Aspin stated bluntly, "We will not allow the North Koreans to develop a nuclear bomb."[17] His statement left open the possibility of using military force to prevent that outcome.

The second half of 1993 was marked by a series of maneuvers by both North Korea and the United States and its allies, while tensions ebbed and flowed. Pyongyang made a conciliatory gesture by "suspending" its withdrawal from the NPT. A little later in the year the United States and South Korea responded by agreeing to suspend their Team Spirit military exercises for that year. The DPRK accepted restricted IAEA visits to maintain the continuity of safeguards by replacing batteries and film in the monitoring cameras in the North's nuclear facilities. Bilateral talks between the United States and North Korea continued amid periodic threats (by both sides) and mutual recriminations.

The situation again turned ominous in early 1994. After the IAEA found its seals on the suspected reprocessing plant broken and indicated that it could not certify North Korea's compliance with the inspection agreement, the United States broke off bilateral talks. Pyongyang again threatened to leave the NPT, and there were additional indications that the DPRK was proceeding with its nuclear-weapons program. North Korea appeared to be speeding up construction on its 200-megawatt reactor, and in May 1994 Pyongyang indicated that it had begun removing the 8,000 fuel rods from the 5-megawatt reactor without allowing international inspectors to take test samples. (Removing these spent fuel rods is the first step in processing the spent fuel into plutonium for nuclear weapons.)

A showdown again seemed imminent. The United States began to enhance its naval and air power in the vicinity of the Korean peninsula, upgraded military readiness, and shipped several batteries of Patriot antiballistic missiles to the ROK. Washington and its allies also began to move toward imposing sanctions on North Korea. The first step was to include a ban on North Korean arms exports and UN development aid. Those measures were to be followed, if necessary, by a prohibition on all trade and financial flows.[18] The administration received strong bipartisan support from congressional leaders for imposing economic sanctions.[19]

Moreover, talk of war again filled the air, and this time it did not come solely from armchair warriors. General John Shalikashvili, chairman of the Joint Chiefs of Staff, warned that the "culprits" running North Korea "do not lend themselves to the kind of deterrent action that we were able to apply to the Soviet Union during the Cold War."[20] He implied that military action might be needed to eliminate the threat. The political leadership also was becoming more belligerent. Senate minority leader Robert Dole (R-Kan.) argued that the "military option must be kept open."[21] Aspin's successor as secretary of defense, William Perry, acknowledged that sanctions "might provoke the North Koreans into unleashing a war" but indicated that the United States might have to pursue them anyway.[22] Perry went on to echo Frank Gaffney's argument of the previous year: "I would rather face that risk [of war] than face the risk of even greater catastrophe two or three years from now," if the North continued its nuclear program.[23]

There is no question that the Clinton administration seriously considered using military force during the 1993–94 crisis. Perry and former assistant secretary of defense Ashton B. Carter candidly admit it: "Eight years before the Bush administration issued its national security strategy espousing a doctrine of preemption, the United States came to the brink of initiating war to stop North Korea from acquiring nuclear weapons. Faced with Pyongyang's threat to divert plutonium from a nuclear reactor to its weapons program, the Clinton administration contemplated its own act of preemption against the strange, isolated regime then considered the greatest threat to U.S. national security. The two of us, then at the Pentagon, readied plans to strike at North Korea's nuclear facilities and for mobilizing hundreds of thousands of American troops for the war that probably would have followed."[24]

Clinton has confirmed that not only were such plans drawn up, but the United States informed North Korea of those plans. In a December 2002 speech, the former president stated that "we told them we would attack unless they ended their nuclear program."[25] The United States and North Korea may have been much closer to war in the spring of 1994 than Congress and the American people realized.

THE 1994 FRAMEWORK AGREEMENT AND AN AVALANCHE OF CRITICISM

War was averted by a series of diplomatic initiatives in the summer and fall of 1994. First came an unpublicized June 1994 trip by Selig Harrison, then a senior associate at the Carnegie Endowment for International Peace, during which the North Koreans hinted that they might be willing to freeze their nu-clear "power generation" program in exchange for certain concessions by the United States and its allies. Days later came the better-known visit by former president Jimmy Carter to Pyongyang, at which time North Korean dictator Kim Il-sung explicitly offered to freeze the program if such an agreement could be reached.[26] U.S.–DPRK negotiations resumed, despite Kim's death on July 8. The result was the Framework Agreement signed in October.[27]

The Framework Agreement was a classic exercise in compromise diplo-macy. It committed the DPRK to remain within the NPT and freeze opera-tions at its 5-megawatt reactor, radio-chemistry laboratory, and fuel fabrication plant, as well as halt construction on the 50- and 200-megawatt reactors. The IAEA was to resume inspections, including ad hoc visits to other sites. Pyongyang agreed to satisfy "IAEA needs for access to data and sites to resolve discrepancies concerning the DPRK's production of pluto-nium" (i.e., the two waste disposal facilities) within five years. North Korea also agreed to begin shipping abroad the 8,000 spent fuel rods (currently stored in cooling ponds) within seven years and dismantle its nuclear plants within ten years. Finally, Pyongyang promised to conduct bilateral talks with South Korea on economic and political relations as well as on implementa-tion of the 1991 North–South Joint Declaration on the Denuclearization of the Korean Peninsula.

In return, the United States, South Korea, and Japan were to create a new entity, the Korea Peninsula Energy Development Organization (KEDO). Rep-resenting KEDO, the United States agreed to provide the North with 500,000 tons of fuel oil annually—officially to offset the DPRK's loss of power gener-ation capacity supposedly caused by the shutdown of its nuclear program. Washington also promised that KEDO would construct two "proliferation re-sistant" light-water reactors to replace North Korea's older gas-graphite mod-els.[28] Finally, the United States pledged not to use nuclear weapons against North Korea as long as the latter remained a member of the NPT, to eliminate economic sanctions against Pyongyang, and to move toward the establishment of diplomatic relations.[29]

A good many hawks were disappointed that the Clinton administration chose to resolve the crisis through negotiations rather than pursuing the Osirak option. The Framework Agreement came in for immediate and harsh criticism. Charles Krauthammer was merciless. North Korea got all the sub-stantive benefits, he fumed. Under the agreement, "the oil flows, the diplo-matic isolation ends, the North Korean economy is revived by Western trade—and its nuclear program remains intact! It is to be 'frozen,' meaning ready to restart anytime in the next 10 years when Pyongyang decides it has got all it wants from the West." He was scornful of the administration's defense: "The Administration defends this investment in peace by saying that the only alternative is war. This is simple capitulation to blackmail." Pyongyang had "rattled its saber," Krauthammer concluded. "Clinton caved."[30]

Hoover Institution scholar Angelo M. Codevilla was equally caustic: "Mr. Clinton's deal with North Korea is straightforward: Up front, we pay $4 billion as well as provide free oil, technology and diplomatic recognition that the world's nastiest regime could not otherwise obtain. In return, Kim Jong-il permits us to pretend to believe that North Korea has given up the acquisition of nuclear weapons."[31] He urged the Senate to repudiate the deal.

Gaffney may have surpassed Krauthammer and Codevilla by denouncing the Framework Agreement as act of "appeasement" ranking with Neville Chamberlain's abandonment of Czechoslovakia to the Nazis in 1938.[32] Paul Greenberg epitomized the views of many conservative critics when he said that the agreement amounted to giving "a devious dictator bent on wielding nuclear weapons" what he wanted and then declaring an illusory "victory."[33] Former secretary of defense James Schlesinger dismissed the Agreed Framework as a "negotiated surrender."[34]

Republican political leaders lost no time in criticizing the administration's handiwork. Indeed, even before the agreement was formally signed, a group of Republican senators including Alfonse D'Amato (R-N.Y.), Mitch McConnell (R-Ken.), Jesse Helms (R-N.C.), and Frank Murkowski (R-Ala.) sent Clinton a letter urging him to back away from the deal. They argued that the agreement would merely "paper over the crisis and delay its resolution." The senators expressed uncertainty about "how to distinguish such a deal from U.S. submission to North Korean blackmail."[35] Senator Dole complained that the accord "shows that it is always possible to get an agreement when you give enough away."[36] Dole's sentiments were echoed by a number of Republican House and Senate members, especially after the GOP took control of Congress in the November 1994 elections.[37]

The criticism did not abate in the coming months and years. A year and a half later, Heritage Foundation senior fellow Daryl M. Plunk urged the Clinton administration to take a harder line with Pyongyang about its belligerent attitude toward South Korea. The president should "remind Pyongyang that the U.S.–North Korea nuclear accord explicitly links tension reduction with the political and economic benefits offered to the North," Plunk opined. "Mr. Clinton should warn Pyongyang that if it continues to violate both the spirit and the letter of the Agreed Framework, it will put at risk further implementation of the deal."[38] James Lilley, former ambassador to both South Korea and China, concluded simply that attempts to implement the 1994 accord had become a black hole down which U.S. tax dollars disappear.[39] In 1997 Hoover Institution scholar Victor Galinsky described the agreement as an example of successful nuclear blackmail by North Korea. He urged the United States to insist on changes to the agreement, specifically a requirement that North Korea engage in a phased dismantlement of its nuclear facilities as construction progressed on the light-water reactors.[40]

Criticism of the administration's strategy became even more pronounced after a high-ranking defector, Hwang Jang-yop, told South Korean and U.S. intelligence agencies in the spring of 1997 that the North already had a small number of nuclear weapons. Hwang further stated that Pyongyang had planned to conduct an underground nuclear test but postponed it when the North Korean foreign ministry warned that the international reaction to such a development would be excessively troublesome.[41] Since Hwang was the highest-ranking North Korean defector to date, U.S. officials—and conservative opponents of the administration—took his allegations quite seriously.

Worse than the vitriol that conservatives periodically directed toward the administration, the Republican-controlled Congress repeatedly engaged in legislative harassment, threatening (and in some cases voting) to delay or slash funding to implement provisions of the 1994 accord.[42] On several occasions KEDO's funding shortfalls threatened to halt scheduled delivery of fuel oil shipments to North Korea.[43]

Nearly a decade after the signing of the Framework Agreement, many hawks are more convinced than ever that the Clinton administration made a tragic blunder in not resorting to military force or at least imposing comprehensive economic sanctions. Author and syndicated columnist Martin Gross excoriates the administration for its handling of the 1993–94 North Korean crisis: "Contrast that courageous [Israeli] action with that of our former President, Bill Clinton. In 1994, he faced a similar dilemma, but acted without either foresight or courage. When North Korea showed it was on the path to developing nuclear weapons, Mr. Clinton was faced with two choices: either follow the Israeli precedent and bomb North Korea's nuclear facility before it was too late, or engage in diplomacy with Kim Jong-il, the leader of that distorted totalitarian nation. He chose diplomacy, much as Neville Chamberlain did with Adolf Hitler, a fruitless route when dealing with evil governments."[44]

Washington Post columnist Steven Mufson aptly summarized the attitude of conservative Republicans in Congress and elsewhere toward the Agreed Framework: "To many Republicans, remedying the flaws in the accord represented more than a matter of bargaining. It became a moral crusade. With reports trickling out about repression and starvation in North Korea . . . many Republicans decided that the United States should view the Kim Jong Il regime as one of unmitigated evil. Rather than look for a reason to reengage North Korea and renegotiate the Agreed Framework, they wanted to rip it up completely, not only ending the construction of the new, somewhat safer reactors but also cutting off fuel oil shipments to the North. After all, they were only propping up an immoral regime." Mufson concludes: "Beware what you wish for."[45] He has a point. The Agreed Framework is no longer in effect, but that development has led to a crisis even more dangerous than the one in 1993–94.

YEARS OF SUSPICION, DISSENSION, AND TURBULENCE

The 1994 agreement hardly ushered in a new cooperative relationship between North Korea and the United States and its allies.[46] Tensions surfaced repeatedly. In June 1995 Pyongyang threatened to rip up the 1953 armistice that had ended the fighting in the Korean War. Even more provocatively, the following spring DPRK troops entered the northernmost portion of the DMZ, in violation of provisions of the armistice. Later that year Pyongyang was caught red-handed in the act of landing special forces teams by submarine on the east coast of the Republic of Korea. Efforts by the United States to improve its relationship with the DPRK during the mid-1990s were rebuffed or went unanswered. For example, in April 1996 Washington and Seoul proposed four-party talks (involving the United States, South Korea, North Korea, and China) to replace the armistice with a treaty officially bringing the Korean War to an end. It was not until the end of June 1997 that Pyongyang responded favorably to that proposal.[47] Talks finally opened in August.

For its part, the United States was slow to implement its commitments under the Agreed Framework. Not until August 1997 were there firm plans for construction of the light-water reactors, and it was not until December 1999 that the final contract was signed by KEDO.[48] That meant that the first reactor could not be completed until at least 2007—some four years behind schedule. The delays were not entirely Washington's fault. America's partners in KEDO were chronically slow in providing funding for the project as well as money for the fuel oil shipments.[49] And as Selig Harrison points out, the Clinton administration was so intimidated by congressional opposition to the Agreed Framework, the president never asked Congress for even a token U.S.

financial contribution to the reactor project. That, in turn, annoyed the South Koreans and Japanese, who felt that they were being expected to carry a disproportionate amount of the financial burden.[50] Whatever the principal cause, such delays intensified North Korean suspicions about U.S. duplicity.

Movement on the normalization of political and economic relations was even more torpid. Much of that hesitation was apparently because of timidity on the part of the Clinton administration. According to Robert Gallucci, the chief negotiator of the 1994 accord, the administration was especially apprehensive about domestic political opposition. "Congressional and press skeptics and critics did lead us to take the minimum interpretation of sanctions lifting," Gallucci admitted.[51] Washington also was reluctant to proceed rapidly to lift sanctions since the government of South Korea wanted a more measured pace. Seoul's view on that issue did not change until Kim Dae-jung became president in early 1998.

True, the U.S. administration periodically considered lifting economic sanctions on North Korea.[52] Yet there always seemed to be new conditions attached to that move. For example, Winston Lord, assistant secretary of state for East Asian affairs, stated in June 1996 that the United States would end sanctions—but only if Pyongyang halted the development and sales of ballistic missiles.[53] (During this period, the United States did provide food aid to alleviate the famine that was already beginning to devastate the North Korean people.[54]) Again in March 1998, the administration hinted that it would be prepared to lift sanctions—but only if the North took immediate steps to reduce tensions with South Korea.[55] In theory, that may not have been an unreasonable expectation for a quid pro quo, but from Pyongyang's standpoint it was evidence of U.S. insincerity. North Korean leaders assumed that lifting sanctions and establishing normal diplomatic ties was an appropriate quid pro quo for the concession that Pyongyang had already made in the Agreed Framework by freezing its nuclear program.

Pyongyang's frustration at what it regarded as U.S. foot-dragging on its obligations under the Agreed Framework surfaced repeatedly. In April 1996 a North Korean official stated that it was "high time" for North Korea and the United States to strengthen their bilateral ties. He specifically called on the United States to honor its commitment to remove restrictions on trade with his country.[56] Two years later Pyongyang accused the United States of not living up to its commitment to build the light-water reactor and threatened to restart its nuclear program if Washington did not comply soon. "There is a limit to our patience on this matter," stated a Foreign Ministry spokesman.[57] Again in spring 1999 the North Koreans threatened to withdraw from the pact. "The U.S. has not faithfully implemented any of its commitments. This compels the DPRK to expect nothing any longer from the Agreed Framework," stated North Korea's official newspaper, *Rodong Sinmun*.[58]

But Pyongyang's own conduct repeatedly interfered with prospects for improved relations. North Korea's ballistic missile program became a matter of major concern to the Clinton administration during the mid- and late 1990s. Two North Korean defectors, army colonel Joo-hwai Choi and former diplomat Ko Young-hwan, informed U.S. officials in October 1997 that Pyongyang was building several types of medium- and long-range missiles. According to the defectors, not only would those missiles be able to target U.S. forces stationed in Japan, but eventually they would be able to strike U.S. territory.[59] In addition, evidence emerged that North Korea was earning as much as $1 billion a year from missile sales to such anti-American regimes as those in Libya and Iran.

Tensions on the missile issue became decidedly more acute at the end of August 1998, when North Korea conducted a test of an extended-range ballistic missile. At first U.S. experts believed the missile tested was a two-stage Taepo Dong 1 missile with a range of about 1,500 kilometers.[60] Later U.S. intelligence sources concluded that the episode had been a failed space satellite launch involving a three-stage missile with an even longer range.[61] The most provocative aspect of the test was the trajectory of the missile; North Korea had fired it directly over Japan. Not only did that development upset the Japanese public and government, but Pyongyang had demonstrated in a none-too-subtle fashion that it now had the capability to strike U.S. forces stationed in Japan.

To the administration's critics, the missile test was another compelling piece of evidence that North Korea was an incorrigible rogue state and that agreements with it were not only useless but dangerous. Representative Robert Livingston (R-La.), chairman of the House Appropriations Committee, stated, "I just don't see any reason to proceed with this failed policy." He added that funding for the Agreed Framework "should be discontinued."[62] In another interview he was even more negative: "I think we ought to stop talking to them, stop appeasing them. I see this as a pretty good excuse just to get out of this agreement."[63]

The missile issue interacted with concerns about possible North Korean violations of the Agreed Framework for the next several months. In November U.S. intelligence sources concluded that North Korea was building at least two new launch facilities for the Taepo Dong missile and was stepping up its production of short-range missiles. Reports circulated that Pyongyang was also planning to conduct a second test of the Taepo Dong.[64] The following spring

U.S. intelligence sources concluded that the North was developing the Taepo Dong 2—an intercontinental ballistic missile (ICBM) capable of reaching the western portion of the U.S. mainland. Even worse, some of those intelligence sources feared that the DPRK might be able to deploy that missile without having to flight-test it first.[65]

Critics of the Clinton administration, already skeptical of the Agreed Framework, seized on the missile test issue as another piece of evidence why U.S. policy toward North Korea needed to be changed. In May 1999 a bipartisan group of legislators introduced a bill, the Korean Threat Reduction Act of 1999, that attached firm conditions for the continuation of aid under the 1994 agreement. Not only did the bill demand verification that North Korea's nuclear program remained frozen, but it stipulated that the U.S. economic embargo must remain in effect "until North Korea terminates its long-range missile program and ceases all efforts to export such missiles."[66]

Although the Clinton administration was reluctant to take coercive measures, officials warned North Korea repeatedly that there would be serious consequences if the North conducted another test of the Taepo Dong.[67] Conversely, the United States and its allies offered benefits—specifically, an easing of the economic embargo—if Pyongyang adopted a moratorium on tests. North Korea responded by giving a verbal pledge to freeze its missile tests, although it declined to sign a formal agreement to that effect.[68] President Clinton then announced that he would issue an executive order relaxing the embargo. Clinton's order would permit trade in a wide range of both commercial and consumer goods, and individuals in the United States would be allowed to transfer funds to North Koreans. Moreover, American companies would be allowed to invest in North Korea's raw materials industries, including agriculture, petroleum, and timber. An administration spokesman warned, though, that the sanctions could be reimposed at the stroke of the presidential pen if North Korea resumed testing missiles.[69]

Although there was widespread relief that another East Asian crisis had been averted, even supporters of the administration's willingness to make concessions to get an agreement expressed uneasiness about the implications of that strategy. A *Washington Post* editorial admitted: "There is something distasteful in this transaction, which fits neatly into a pattern of North Korean behavior that, anywhere outside diplomatic circles, would be known as blackmail. North Korea's Communist leaders threaten to do something inimical to world peace (build a nuclear weapon, sell arms to war zones, launch missiles over Japan). If it then restrains itself, it is rewarded for not doing what it shouldn't have done in the first place."[70]

The administration's opponents exhibited no such mixed emotions. They lost no time in savaging the new U.S.–North Korean understanding. Frank Gaffney predictably denounced the decision to soften the embargo as the administration's "latest act of appeasement" toward Pyongyang. He echoed the views of other conservatives in calling for an alternative policy aimed at overthrowing the North Korean regime.[71] Future under secretary of state John Bolton accused the White House of being "unable to muster even a modicum of resoluteness to contain, let alone roll back, the North Korean threat."[72]

The ferocity of the attacks was puzzling. In reality, easing the embargo had far more symbolic than substantive importance. North Koreans lacked the hard currency to buy more than a trickle of U.S. goods, and the North produced little that American consumers wanted. And the DPRK was hardly an attractive arena for American investors.

The most serious issue of contention in the U.S.–North Korean relationship during the mid- and late 1990s was the continuing suspicion that the North might be cheating on the 1994 agreement. In the early months of 1998 Pyongyang again refused to allow international inspectors full access to nuclear sites. This led a General Accounting Office (GAO) report to conclude that the North Koreans might be trying to hide evidence that they had stockpiled a much larger quantity of plutonium than they admitted possessing at the time the agreement was signed. That report led to a scathing assessment by Senator Murkowski, chairman of Senate Energy and Natural Resources Committee. Murkowski said that the report showed that the 1994 agreement was "folly." He added that the GAO report confirmed that "we may never know how much bomb-grade plutonium the North Koreans have diverted" to their weapons program. "Our carrot-and-stick approach is all carrots and no stick," he said. "We were too quick to provide North Korea with the goodies before we knew the truth."[73]

Matters became even more testy in August 1998 when U.S. spy satellites detected indications of suspicious construction activity at a mountainous site at Kumchang-ri, approximately 25 miles northeast of Yongbyon. U.S. intelligence agencies concluded that the North Koreans were probably at work on a vast underground nuclear facility. Intelligence analysts surmised that the DPRK was building either a nuclear reactor or a reprocessing plant.[74] Although the development did not pose an immediate danger, since U.S. experts estimated that it would take two to six years to complete the construction, it did raise questions about Pyongyang's willingness to abide by the 1994 accord.

The Clinton administration immediately conveyed its strenuous objections about the construction to North Korea. According to a senior administration official, the North Koreans were told that the tunneling "is not acceptable to the United States, and that activities intended to permit them to start [their nuclear program] on a moment's notice are not acceptable." But the administration rejected calls from domestic critics to abrogate the 1994 agreement. "Terminating the agreement gives them the ability to restart existing facilities, which could begin producing nuclear weapons within months," explained the senior official. "These new ones will take a half a decade or more" to complete.[75]

The suspicious construction, combined with North Korea's August 31 missile test, provoked calls from the usual conservative sources to repudiate the Agreed Framework.[76] This time, however, such calls were not confined to staunch right-wingers. Even Benjamin Gilman (R-N.Y.), the moderate Republican chairman of the House International Relations Committee, took a very hard line. Describing the 1994 agreement as "fatally flawed," Gilman called for the creation of a bipartisan commission to conduct "a zero-based policy review and propose a course of action that takes into account realistic perspectives on the nuclear and missile threats." The recent incidents, he concluded, "demonstrated the bankruptcy of the administration's effort to moderate North Korea's behavior."[77] A year later, as the crisis continued to fester, Representative Christopher Cox (R-Cal.) stated bluntly: "U.S. policy is conducting a one-sided love affair with the regime in North Korea."[78]

North Korea did not help matters when it demanded a cash payment of "reparations" before U.S. inspectors would be given access to the site.[79] Administration officials reacted angrily to that demand. When asked if the United States would accept Pyongyang's conditions, a senior State Department official responded: "Hell, no."[80] The official warned North Korea that persisting in refusing to allow inspections would put the Agreed Framework in jeopardy. Just days later, though, Secretary of State Madeleine Albright reaffirmed Washington's commitment to the agreement and defended it from mounting attacks.[81]

Despite Albright's assurance, the Agreed Framework seemed on the brink of collapse in late 1998 and early 1999 as Pyongyang persisted in its demand for a $300 million payment before it would allow an inspection of the Kumchang-ri site.[82] Indeed, hard-liners in Congress and the U.S. foreign policy community were demanding not just a right to inspect the one suspect site but regular inspections of nearly a dozen other sites that the Defense Intelligence Agency had identified as suspicious. Defenders of the Agreed Framework pointed out that no provision in the agreement gave the United States the right to conduct such fishing expeditions, but the mood in Washington seemed increasingly confrontational.[83]

In was in this atmosphere that President Clinton appointed former secretary of defense William Perry as a special envoy on the North Korean issue. Perry conducted a nine-month review of U.S. policy with the aim of averting another crisis on the peninsula. The fruit of that review effort was the informal agreement under which North Korea pledged to continue a moratorium on its missile tests, both sides reaffirmed their commitment to the Agreed Framework on the nuclear issue, and the United States then eased its economic sanctions against the North.

Even before the deal involving the missile test moratorium and the lifting of sanctions, tensions between the United States and North Korea had begun to abate. In March 1999 Pyongyang finally agreed to let U.S. inspectors see the site at Kumchang-ri, in exchange for "improved political and economic relations" with Washington—specifically, increased shipments of food and fuel.[84] When the inspectors were finally admitted to the site in May, they found only a system of empty tunnels.[85] Administration officials pronounced themselves cautiously satisfied with the results, believing there was no hard evidence that North Korea had been violating the 1994 accord. Critics scorned that conclusion. The editorial page of the *Washington Times* excoriated the White House for being naive: "White House spokesman Jamie Rubin said the inspection served to 'remove fully U.S. concerns about the nature of the site and about the activities there.' Now that is embarrassing. The North Koreans, exploiting Clintonesque delaying tactics, were given enough time to cart away all but the kitchen sink from the site. It is dangerous to trumpet the inspection as a success when the United States should be trying to secure comprehensive proof that North Korea is nuclear-weapons free—which it is overwhelmingly likely that it is not."[86]

By late 1999 criticism of the administration's policy toward North Korea had reached especially ferocious levels—especially after President Clinton announced the lifting of some economic sanctions in September. Moreover, the criticism had a more organized, systematic quality. In November 1999 a special House Republican task force appointed by Speaker Dennis Hastert (R-Ill.) issued a report alleging that North Korea had become a more serious military threat even as the White House continued to pursue a policy of engagement. Describing the 1994 agreement as "deeply flawed," the report cited evidence of North Korean sales of missiles and illegal drugs. More to the point, it charged that the DPRK was continuing to develop nuclear weapons.[87] Representative Floyd Spence (R-S.C.), a task force member and chairman of the House Armed Services Committee, called the administration's policy one of "appeasement and bribery" that simply had not worked.[88]

Although opponents of the Clinton administration's cautious policy became more vocal in their denunciations, during the last year of Clinton's presidency the North Korea issue was marked by relative calm. At the end of April 2000, the administration even leaked reports to the media that the United States might take North Korea off the list of states that supported terrorism.[89] In June Clinton's executive order easing U.S. economic sanctions went into effect.[90] During this same period, evidence emerged that North Korea had stopped construction at the Kumchang-ri complex, a conclusion verified during a second visit to the site in May by a U.S. team of inspectors.[91] Following Washington's easing of sanctions, Pyongyang announced that it would continue its moratorium on missile tests indefinitely and expressed hope of a normal political and economic relationship with the United States.[92]

North Korea took several other steps that suggested that the insular Stalinist state might be seeking better relations with the outside world. The entire tone of Pyongyang's diplomacy changed. Gone was the kind of rhetoric employed by a North Korean negotiator who, during the 1993–94 crisis, proclaimed that DPRK forces would turn Seoul into "a sea of fire" in the event of war. Instead, northern leaders now turned on a charm offensive toward their southern counterparts as well as the United States. The DPRK's reclusive leader, Kim Jong-il, also traveled to Beijing and seemed receptive to quiet but insistent Chinese calls for economic reform. During this same period, North Korea took the first hesitant steps toward domestic economic reforms. Such developments led a number of Korea experts in the United States to call for a new and more conciliatory U.S. policy toward the North.[93]

Even as the U.S.–North Korean relationship experienced a series of ups and downs, South Korea began to play a much more active role in the process. That point became apparent in December 1997 when President-elect Kim Dae-jung proposed direct talks between the two Koreas and even indicated a willingness to meet personally with Kim Jong-il. The following spring he roiled the environment further when he called on the United States and other countries to lift their economic sanctions against the North. It soon became apparent that lifting sanctions was merely one step in what Kim regarded as a comprehensive policy of economic engagement with North Korea, which he had begun to describe as a "sunshine policy."[94] By September 1999 Kim was vowing to end the cold war with North Korea by the end of his term in office.[95]

Contacts between the two Koreas accelerated during the early months of 2000. That rapprochement culminated in a June summit meeting between Kim Dae-jung and Kim Jong-il in Pyongyang, where the two leaders signed a vague but historic accord, vowing to resolve their differences peacefully and to effect a reconciliation of the Korean peoples. They also discussed the creation of liaison offices in each other's capitals and establishing a hot line between Seoul and Pyongyang to defuse any future crises. More substantively, the agreement provided for cultural exchanges, the commencement of exchange visits by members of families that had been divided by the Korean War, and initial steps toward the reestablishment of rail links between the two states.[96]

The summit meeting was the high point of Kim Dae-jung's sunshine policy. Although some of the measures have gone forward, others have been stillborn, just like so many previous signs that relations might improve between North and South Korea. The summit itself has been sullied by evidence that the South Korean government paid a thinly disguised bribe to induce Pyongyang to agree to that meeting.[97] But in the final months of 2000, it looked as if the long cold war on the Korean peninsula might be coming to an end, and even the usual American advocates of a hard-line policy toward North Korea were uncharacteristically quiet.

After an initial hesitation, the Clinton administration expressed support for the sunshine policy and was especially supportive after the June summit. During the final months of Clinton's term of office, relations between Washington and Pyongyang were far friendlier than they had ever been. The most tangible sign of the thaw was a visit by Secretary of State Albright to the North Korean capital in October, where she met with Kim Jong-il. The talks went surprisingly well, and there was considerable speculation about a further improvement in relations.[98] From Albright's memoirs, we now know that her visit was designed in part to pave the way for a visit by President Clinton.[99] Had it not been so close to end of his term—and had the administration not been so sensitive to criticism that dramatic policy initiatives should not be undertaken by a lame-duck president—that visit might have taken place. Already, though, there were signs that Washington's policy was likely to be different under Clinton's successor, George W. Bush.

There were no dramatic changes in U.S. policy toward North Korea during the first year of the Bush administration, but there was a noticeable difference in tone. That point became evident during a visit to Washington by South Korean president Kim Dae-jung in March 2001. Kim sought Bush's backing for the sunshine policy, continuing the support he had received from Clinton. Instead, during a photo op with Kim seated next to him, Bush stated bluntly that there was nothing to talk to North Korea about at this point. Dialogue with the North would be productive, Bush added, only when Pyongyang lived up to the commitments it had already made, especially on the nuclear issue.[100] Kim sat grim-faced during this implicit repudiation of the sunshine policy. He later described his summit with Bush to a longtime friend, William Taylor of the Center for Strategic and International Studies, as nothing short of a "disaster."[101] (Eventually the Bush administration did respond somewhat to South Korean pressure, conducting talks with the North Koreans in the summer of both 2001 and 2002, but those discussions were fruitless even by the meager standards of normal episodes of U.S.–North Korean dialogue.)

The Bush administration took no substantive actions to repudiate U.S. commitments to KEDO regarding either the delivery of fuel oil shipments or construction of the light-water reactors, even though many conservative Republicans were pressing for such action.[102] Yet progress toward normal political and economic relations, which seemed so promising during the last year of the Clinton administration, ground to a halt. Meanwhile, North Korean officials were issuing ever more pointed warnings that, if Washington did not take more serious steps to implement its commitments under the 1994 accord, the North would be under no obligation to honor its commitments.[103] The North had made similar statements before, but those of 2001 and early 2002 seemed more serious.

The subtle signs of escalating tensions between Washington and Pyongyang became decidedly more obvious in January 2002. In a now-famous passage in his State of the Union address, President Bush linked North Korea to Iraq and Iran in an "axis of evil."[104] Kim Jong-il's regime responded with shrill denunciations and warned ominously that if the United States persisted in pursuing a threatening policy toward the DPRK, it would have no choice but to acquire a nuclear-weapons capability.

Nevertheless, in the summer and early autumn of 2002, the North again seemed to embark on a policy of trying to achieve a more normal relationship with its neighbors in East Asia and with the United States. Pyongyang's outreach effort including making the startling admission to Japan that it had kidnapped Japanese citizens during the 1970s and brought them to North Korea. The DPRK also made conciliatory gestures to South Korea, announced new economic reforms, and renewed calls for negotiations with the United States. It was in that context that Assistant Secretary of State for East Asia James Kelly went to Pyongyang for talks in October. But Kelly was carrying with him information that would trigger a new North Korean nuclear crisis.

THE CRISIS RESUMES

Kelly ostensibly was in Pyongyang to thaw the icy relations between the two countries, but his trip would soon have the opposite effect. During a meeting with DPRK officials, Kelly presented evidence from U.S. intelligence sources that North Korea had been pursuing a secret uranium enrichment program. Such a program violated at least the spirit, if not the letter, of the 1994 Agreed Framework as well as Pyongyang's other commitments on nuclear issues. Indeed, it appears that the North had been pursuing the uranium enrichment program for several years, apparently assisted in that effort through a barter arrangement with Pakistan. North Korea sent Pakistan missile components that helped Islamabad build a nuclear-capable force to match India's. In turn, Pakistan supplied North Korea with designs for gas centrifuges and much of the machinery needed to make highly enriched uranium for a nuclear-weapons program.[105] It is not certain when the enriched uranium program began, but several prominent experts on North Korea believe that it started as early as 1997 or 1998.[106] If true, that is a very important point, for it suggests that the resumption of Pyongyang's nuclear ambitions was not merely a response to Washington's chilly policies and belligerent rhetoric since George W. Bush became president.

Much to Kelly's surprise, the North Koreans seemed to admit the existence of the uranium enrichment program and sought to justify it because of Washington's hostile posture toward their country.[107] (The North Korean regime now insists that it made no such admission.) In any case, the incident brought the talks to an abrupt halt, but it was not the end of Pyongyang's moves on the nuclear front. In mid-November the North sent conflicting signals about whether it already possessed nuclear weapons.[108]

Up to this point, the Bush administration's reaction to the evolving crisis was surprisingly mild. President Bush's initial response was to stress that he intended to use diplomacy to resolve the issue, and a few administration officials even suggested privately that the North Koreans' alleged admission concerning the uranium enrichment program might be an opportunity for productive negotiations on a range of issues. Even at that early date, however, some policymakers favored a harder-line policy, and hints of retaliatory U.S. actions were already present. One anonymous senior official told the *Washington Post* just days after Pyongyang's apparent admission that North Korea's deceit doomed the Agreed Framework. "I can guarantee you there won't be another dime for fuel oil," the official said. "Can you imagine taking the Agreed Framework back to Capitol Hill for funding?" The North Koreans "lied to us. They treated us with contempt. What kind of deal are you going to cut with a country like that?"[109]

The official's comments proved to be prophetic. In mid-November the United States and its East Asian allies announced that they were "suspending" all future shipments of fuel oil to North Korea.[110] A few weeks later the DPRK announced that it was restarting work at the three-reactor complex at Yong-byon.[111] At this point both sides effectively considered the Agreed Framework to be a dead letter. As if all this were not enough, during the course of talks with the Japanese in early November, the North Koreans threatened to end their moratorium on missile tests—a threat that they renewed in January.[112]

Matters on the nuclear front escalated in late December, when North Korea began to remove seals and surveillance cameras installed by the International Atomic Energy Agency at Yongbyon and ordered the IAEA monitors out of the country.[113] Then, on January 9, the DPRK announced that it was withdrawing from the NPT.[114] In marked contrast to the 1994 crisis, when Pyongyang later "suspended" its withdrawal, Kim Jong-il's regime made good on that threat in April. That action set a very important precedent, since no previous signatory of the NPT had ever repudiated it.

A few weeks after the announcement that it was withdrawing from the NPT, the North announced that it was restarting the 5-megawatt reactor, supposedly to generate electricity—a step allegedly made necessary by the U.S. cutoff of fuel oil shipments.[115] The credibility of that claim was somewhat suspect since the reactor is not linked to North Korea's electrical power grid, making its usefulness for power generation low. By early March there was evidence that the North Koreans might be moving the spent fuel rods out of storage—a possible prelude to processing the spent fuel into plutonium for bomb production.[116] This was the central element of the nightmare that the United States had tried to avoid in 1994 with the Agreed Framework. By early May U.S. satellite photos provided additional evidence that the DPRK had reactivated the nuclear-processing facility, although there was not yet any hard evidence that the spent fuel rods actually were being processed.[117]

In that same month Pyongyang repudiated the joint declaration with South Korea, thus removing the last legal restraint on the DPRK's nuclear activities. North Korea's official news agency stated that the agreement had to be nullified because of "a sinister and hostile U.S. policy." Accusing the United States of planning to attack their country, the North Koreans stated, "We have realized that as long as the United States does not abandon its hostile policy against the North, efforts to keep the Korean Peninsula nuclear free is [sic] nothing more than an illusion."[118]

As the crisis escalated, there was a curious political and ideological role reversal in the United States. Conservative hawks who had demanded a hard-line policy toward North Korea throughout the 1990s, when Bill Clinton was in office, seemed generally subdued. Although they urged the Bush administration not to make the same "mistakes" as its predecessor in offering North Korea concessions or in accepting an unverifiable agreement, they regarded Iraq as the primary enemy and appeared content to keep the North Korea issue on the back burner and defer to the administration's judgment. Conversely, prominent liberal Democrats chastised Bush and his advisors for not taking the North Korean situation seriously enough and not being sufficiently firm with Pyongyang.[119] True, liberals were divided on the latter point. Some urged dialogue and concessions (see chapter 4), but others took a surprisingly hard line.

While the crisis continued to percolate, there was some activity on the diplomatic front. During the initial months of the confrontation, Washington's position was unyielding: there would be no talks whatsoever with Pyongyang until the DPRK ended its violations of the Agreed Framework and allowed outside inspections to verify that it was complying with the provisions of the agreement. When it became evident that North Korea was accelerating the revival of its nuclear-weapons program, China, Russia, Japan, and South Korea all urged Washington to relent and agree to talk to Pyongyang.[120] The United States finally responded to such pressure (especially the pressure exerted by its allies) and relented in January 2003. Following a meeting with Japanese and South Korean diplomats, the State Department announced that it would agree to direct talks with Pyongyang. U.S. officials stressed, however, that such "talks" would in no way constitute "negotiations."[121]

Most experts believed that that was a distinction without a difference. And there was some truth to that assumption. The Bush administration soon proceeded cautiously to offer Pyongyang inducements that might jump-start negotiations toward resolving the crisis. The most significant gesture was a comment by Secretary of State Colin Powell that, if the DPRK agreed to a verifiable end to its nuclear-weapons program, Washington would consider offering formal assurances that the United States had "no aggressive intent."[122] Shortly thereafter, Assistant Secretary Kelly indicated that private investment in North Korea's energy sector from U.S. and allied sources might flow following a settlement.[123] On another occasion, administration officials stated that Washington did not intend to seek sanctions against North Korea from the United Nations in the immediate future, despite Pyongyang's announced withdrawal from the NPT.[124] (The United States did, however, press the UN Security Council for a formal statement condemning North Korea's withdrawal from the treaty and the expulsion of IAEA inspectors.[125]) As the prospect of sanctions had greatly intensified the crisis in 1994, Washington's reassurance was not a trivial gesture. In addition, "unofficial" low-level talks were held between U.S. and North Korean diplomats in Germany in February.

Otherwise, though, there appeared to be little movement on the diplomatic front until April.[126] The one exception was a bizarre episode in mid-January when North Korean diplomats in the United States bypassed the Bush administration to meet with New Mexico governor Bill Richardson, who had served as ambassador to the United Nations during the Clinton administration. The North Koreans had dealt with Richardson on several occasions at the UN and apparently trusted him far more than they did Bush administration officials. But their decision to meet with a state official rather than a national official—and one from the opposition party at that—showed how little they understood the workings of the American political system. Richardson emerged from those peculiar talks and stated that the North Korean government was serious about wanting negotiations with the United States.[127] The Bush administration took due note of his observation but refrained from making any meaningful comments.

Throughout the winter and early spring of 2003, the United States insisted that any negotiations with North Korea must be conducted within a multilateral framework. The North's nuclear-weapons program menaced all of its neighbors, Washington argued, and all should play a role in any diplomatic sessions with Pyongyang. Conversely, North Korea insisted that it was interested only in bilateral talks with the United States. It was the United States, Kim Jong-il's regime argued, that threatened the DPRK's security, and only the United States could remove that threat. Until the threat was removed—and until Washington fulfilled all of its commitments under the Agreed Framework—North Korea would have no choice but to move forward with its nuclear-weapons program. The North reiterated its now-familiar demands that the United States sign a nonaggression pledge, normalize political relations with Pyongyang, and stop "interfering" with the DPRK's economic development—that is, end all economic sanctions and stop blocking possible loans from the World Bank and the Asian Development Bank. North Korea's insistence on bilateral talks and Washington's insistence on multilateral talks produced an impasse that lasted until April.

North Korea finally broke the diplomatic impasse on April 12 by dropping its demand for one-on-one negotiations with the United States. Pyongyang stated that it would "not stick to any particular dialogue format," but would test whether "the U.S. has a political willingness to drop its hostile policy."[128] President Bush welcomed the shift in the North Korean position, but the tone of his comments threatened to undo that gain when he implied that Pyongyang's concession had occurred because the U.S. attack on Iraq had shown that "we are serious about stopping the spread of weapons of mass destruction."[129] In reality, it appears that pressure by Beijing induced Pyongyang to give up its insistence on bilateral talks.[130] The talks that opened in Beijing later in April were actually closer to the format that North Korea wanted than the comprehensive, six-nation format the United States was pushing. Although the Beijing negotiations were technically trilateral (North Korea, the United States, and the People's Republic of China [PRC]), the Chinese acted more as hosts and moderators than full-fledged parties to the proceedings.

In any event, the talks did not turn out well. Even before the discussions got underway, both Tokyo and Seoul were sending signals that they were miffed about being left on the sidelines.[131] And when the sessions finally began, the atmosphere was anything but cordial. Indeed, the sessions degenerated into little more than an exchange of already familiar demands by the two sides, with the Chinese uncomfortably caught in the middle. The acrimony culminated when the North Korean delegation reportedly informed their American counterparts that the DPRK already had nuclear weapons and was prepared to test them or sell them to other parties if the United States did not back away from its threatening, confrontational policy.[132] The talks ended after three days with no visible signs of progress. The Chinese did their best to portray the outcome in a reasonably favorable light, arguing that the North Koreans had put a serious offer on the table and that this move was encouraging.[133] Despite Beijing's attempt at spin control, however, it was clear that the negotiations had not alleviated the confrontation between the United States and North Korea over the nuclear issue.

Indeed, the crisis deepened in the summer of 2003. Two assessments by U.S. intelligence agencies were especially alarming. A Central Intelligence Agency (CIA) assessment in June concluded that North Korea was developing the technology to make nuclear warheads small enough to put atop the DPRK's growing fleet of ballistic missiles.[134] If true, that development would soon enable North Korea to threaten targets in South Korea and Japan, including U.S. bases in those countries, with nuclear as well as conventional strikes.

The furor from that conclusion had barely subsided when news stories reported that the CIA had revised its conclusions about whether Pyongyang had begun to reprocess the spent fuel rods from the Yongbyon reactor. CIA analysts had concluded in April and early May that North Korea had made no move as yet to reprocess the rods. In early July, however, the agency reportedly changed its assessment, indicating there was a possibility that reprocessing was already under way, although it had not yet been completed. South Korean intelligence sources reached an even more definitive conclusion that Pyongyang had likely processed at least "a small portion" of the 8,000 spent fuel rods. The South Koreans also reported that the North had recently conducted some 70 conventional explosive tests on devices that could be used to trigger nuclear explosions.[135] North Korea then informed the United States that it had reprocessed enough fuel rods to produce plutonium for at least six bombs.[136] That claim may have been bluster, but U.S. and South Korean officials were increasingly nervous about Pyongyang's statements and actions. These various developments suggested that the DPRK was proceeding at a brisk pace to carry out its nuclear-weapons program.

As if all that were not enough, evidence began to emerge in July 2003 that North Korea might have a second, clandestine plutonium processing plant. The most telling sign that the DPRK was processing plutonium was that sensors began to pick up elevated levels of krypton 85, a gas emitted as spent fuel is converted into plutonium. What bothered U.S., South Korean, and Japanese intelligence analysts is that the pattern of the gas as it blew across the Korean peninsula appeared to rule out the Yongbyon complex as a source. That fact suggested the existence of a second, as-yet-unidentified plant. And because U.S. satellites had not discovered such a facility, the most likely explanation is that it was an underground installation somewhere in the mountains.[137]

Various moves by Pyongyang ratcheted up the tension, but Washington was hardly inactive during the spring and summer of 2003. Washington's principal move was to line up support from its allies in East Asia and elsewhere for a policy to interdict North Korean ships and aircraft to prevent commerce in weapons of mass destruction or other contraband (including Pyongyang's increasingly active trade in narcotics). That Proliferation Security Initiative (PSI) was officially directed against all rogue states, but U.S. officials left little doubt that North Korea was the main target. The North Koreans needed "to understand that they will not be allowed to ship weapons of mass destruction free of risk," said Undersecretary of State for Arms Control and International Security John Bolton.[138]

There also were press reports that the Pentagon was preparing a variety of contingency plans for war with North Korea. As described by U.S. News & World Report, some of those plans (especially Operations Plans 5026 and 5027) outline potential phases of the war and specific provisions for deploying large numbers of troops, aircraft, ships, and other force requirements. The magazine also learned details of the prewar phase of the latest draft (known as Operations Plan 5030), which apparently seeks to blur the line between war and peace. One provision of that plan reportedly envisages flying RC-135 surveillance flights closer than ever before to North Korean airspace, forcing Pyongyang to scramble aircraft and burn scarce jet fuel. Another provision envisages staging a surprise military exercise lasting several weeks to force North Koreans to relocate to bunkers and deplete stores of food and other resources. The apparent logic behind such ploys is to put excruciating pressure on the North Korean military and perhaps cause it to turn against Kim Jong-il's regime.[139] Such initiatives suggest that the Bush administration is at least contemplating the prospect of a showdown—and perhaps even a full-scale war—against North Korea if the crisis cannot be resolved by other means.

There also were some important developments on the diplomatic front. China and Russia continued to pressure North Korea to agree to a new round of multilateral talks, and in July Pyongyang finally relented. The new round of talks took place in Beijing at the end of August, and this time they were six-party talks involving Japan, South Korea, and Russia as well as North Korea, the United States, and China. Washington did make a limited concession, however; it agreed that "informal" bilateral talks between U.S. and DPRK diplomats could take place within the context of the multilateral negotiations.[140]

As the talks approached, there was not much optimism about a breakthrough. Indeed, the Bush administration went out of its way to leak comments to the press that it did not intend to make any concessions to the DPRK and would instead emphasize the need for North Korea to agree to a verifiable and irreversible end to its nuclear-weapons program.[141] U.S. officials conceded that progress toward that goal was likely to be slow and that they did not expect many tangible results from the initial round of negotiations. Administration officials also chose the day before the opening session to leak information that KEDO was prepared to suspend construction on the light-water reactors indefinitely at the consortium's next meeting in early October.[142] That report was not designed to convey an impression to the North Koreans that the United States was in a mood to be conciliatory.

Any doubts that the administration was adopting a hard-line position were erased when the State Department's top expert on North Korea, Charles ("Jack") Pritchard, abruptly "retired" just days before the talks in Beijing were scheduled to begin. Pritchard was known to be an advocate of offering the North Koreans incentives as well as threatening them with penalties to get them to relinquish their nuclear-weapons program.[143] His departure indicated that the hard-liners were firmly in control of the administration's policy.

The six-party talks lived down to their expectations, producing yet another impasse. North Korea again threatened to test a nuclear weapon if the United States did not change its negotiating posture. The U.S. delegation indicated that it was not about to respond to efforts at blackmail.[144] About the only achievement at the talks was an agreement to meet again at some un-specified point in the future, although days later Pyongyang cast doubt on whether even that meager result would hold. (Ultimately, though, the North Koreans attended another round of six-party talks in May 2004.) Predictably, North Korea and the United States blamed each other for the lack of progress. More significantly, Beijing seemed to place most of the blame for the failure at Washington's doorstep. Vice foreign minister Wang Yi, who had been China's chief negotiator at the talks, stated bluntly: "America's policy toward the DPRK—that is the main problem we are facing."[145]

The negotiating environment deteriorated further in the weeks following the six-party talks. Barely a week later, the Bush administration pressed ahead with the PSI, announcing that the United States and 10 allies would stage a series of land, sea, and air exercises within the next six months to begin im-plementing the initiative.[146] At the beginning of October, Pyongyang an-nounced that it had completed processing the spent fuel rods at the Yongbyon reactor and intended to build additional nuclear weapons.[147] Some U.S. intel-ligence sources expressed doubt about Pyongyang's claims, but a new intelli-gence estimate in mid-October concluded that North Korea probably had built one or two additional bombs in recent months, and the IAEA informed East Asian governments that it was likely that the DPRK had at least extracted enough plutonium to build such bombs, even if the actual construction had not yet taken place.[148]

Then President Bush unexpectedly offered a proposal to break the diplo-matic impasse. During his trip to East Asia in late October, he indicated that the United States would be willing to guarantee North Korea's security if Py-ongyang gave up its nuclear program. Bush stressed that he was not talking about a bilateral nonaggression treaty but rather a less formal multilateral se-curity agreement made by North Korea's neighbors as well as the United States.[149] The model Bush apparently had in mind was the trilateral security pledges given by Russia, Britain, and the United States to Belarus, Kazakhstan, and Ukraine when those countries gave up the nuclear weapons they had in-herited from the defunct Soviet Union.

Although the new U.S. proposal fell considerably short of North Korea's demand for a bilateral, binding nonaggression pact with the United States, it went at least part way toward meeting Pyongyang's concerns on that issue. Yet the DPRK's initial reaction was dismissive. North Korea's official news agency denounced Bush's initiative as "laughable."[150] After some rather intense dis-cussions with Chinese officials, however, the North Koreans altered their atti-tude. Pyongyang agreed to take part in a new round of six-party talks, and it indicated that it would consider Bush's offer of a written multilateral security pledge. But ominously, the DPRK also stressed that a security pledge was merely one component of a number of actions it expected from the United States in exchange for renouncing its nuclear program. And Pyongyang emphasized that it was not about to freeze its program in advance of such concessions; any agreement would have to be a package deal.[151]

Prospects for a diplomatic solution to the burgeoning crisis were uncertain during the early months of 2004. Although there were a few signs of flexibility on both sides, a large gap still existed between their respective positions. In the meantime, North Korea's nuclear program continued with no apparent reversal on the horizon.

Signs remained ominous when Pyongyang surprised the outside world by allowing an "unofficial" delegation of U.S. experts (which included Pritchard) to visit the Yongbyon complex in early January 2004. Although the delegation could not confirm that North Korea was building nuclear weapons, it could confirm that the cooling pond that had contained 8,000 spent fuel rods was now empty.[152] That development seemed to support the regime's earlier claim that it had been busy reprocessing those fuel rods to extract the plutonium for the construction of nuclear weapons. Indeed, it is highly probable that the North Koreans approved the visit to show the U.S. government that its nuclear program was proceeding without delay.

Unless Pyongyang is bluffing (which is a possibility but an increasingly unlikely one), the DPRK might well present the United States and the nations of East Asia with a nuclear fait accompli within a year or two. Pritchard, for one, came away from his visit to Yongbyon convinced that the program is not a bluff. Since the new crisis began, he concluded, "North Korea may have quadrupled its arsenal of nuclear weapons."[153] The next phase could be decisive. If North Korea builds an arsenal of a dozen weapons or more, few analysts believe that it would be possible to get Kim Jong-il's regime to give up those weapons and return to a nonnuclear status.

WHERE DO WE GO FROM HERE?

One should not mince words. North Korea's actions in the current crisis have confirmed a long record of perfidy on nuclear issues. True, the United States and its allies had fallen behind schedule in building the light-water reactors, and Washington had been even slower to implement other provisions aimed at creating a less hostile U.S.–North Korean relationship.[154] Nevertheless, there was no justification for North Korea to pursue a secret uranium enrichment program, much less to restart the Yongbyon reactor and to begin processing the spent fuel rods. It also should be noted that Pyongyang did not disclose the uranium enrichment program until Kelly confronted North Korean officials with evidence from U.S. intelligence agencies about its existence. All of this suggests that Pyongyang was not serious about honoring the Agreed Framework or any of the other agreements it had signed. There is some evidence that the North may have begun to cheat on the Agreed Framework as early as 1997. Indeed, IAEA director general Hans Blix charged in May 1997 that the North Koreans probably had more plutonium than they admitted possessing at the time they signed the 1994 agreement.[155]

The reality is that the 1994 Agreed Framework was a gamble from the outset. In essence the Clinton administration adopted a strategy to bribe North Korea to end its violations of previous agreements to renounce nuclear weapons. On balance, it was probably a gamble worth taking, especially since the alternatives appeared to be to watch helplessly as Pyongyang built a sizable nuclear arsenal or to launch military strikes to take out the reactor at Yongbyon, with all the horrid risks that such a course would entail. Responding to increasingly harsh criticisms, a 1999 report by the Clinton administration noted that, had the Yongbyon complex been operating, the North Koreans could have produced 50 nuclear weapons in the intervening years.[156] That they did not do so "is a solid achievement," the report concluded. Defenders of the 1994 accord had a point. The agreement to freeze the North's program produced tangible benefits, albeit by setting the dubious precedent of bribing a would-be nuclear proliferator.

The framework agreement also bought time. Clinton administration officials and other proponents of the agreement apparently hoped that, as the years passed, the North Korean regime would either collapse or transform itself into something other than an aggressive, totalitarian dictatorship.[157] An assessment by the Defense Intelligence Agency in 1996 concluded that, given the country's growing economic problems, the communist regime was unlikely to survive.[158] The following year the U.S. military reportedly began planning for participation in a possible international relief operation following the collapse of the Pyongyang regime.[159] Given that hundreds of thousands of North Koreans were dying of starvation at the time, it was not a far-fetched assumption that the communist system was on the verge of collapse.[160] Wendy Sherman, a North Korea specialist in the Clinton administration, notes just how pervasive was the belief that the days of the communist regime were numbered: "At the beginning of the second Clinton administration, we had a meeting to discuss our agenda. Everybody in the room thought that North Korea would collapse within two years. We were all wrong."[161]

One of the few points on which the Clinton administration and many of its critics agreed during the mid- and late 1990s was that the communist regime was not likely to endure. But they reached very different conclusions about the appropriate policy prescription. The administration assumed that its policy of accommodation would maximize the chances of a "soft landing." Advocates of a hard-line policy believed that the DPRK's bleak prospects made "appeasement" both unnecessary and ill-advised. Indeed, they feared that providing energy aid to North Korea—much less lifting economic sanctions— would prop up the tottering system and help it remain in power.[162]

The actual developments have not matched the hopes of a North Korean collapse or political transformation. There have been signs, over the past two years or so, that North Korea is moderating its hostility toward South Korea, Japan, and other countries and that it is beginning to open up to the outside world economically. Nevertheless, North Korea is still governed by a secretive, ruthless, and unpredictable totalitarian system. And the developments in late 2002 and early 2003 show yet another massive violation of North Korea's promises not to pursue the goal of developing nuclear weapons.

Writing in the spring of 2003, former Clinton administration advisors Samuel R. Berger and Robert Gallucci ably summarized the probable consequences if the current trends continue. "If the North proceeds with reprocessing, it could produce enough plutonium for six additional bombs in six months; if it resumes construction of the two uncompleted nuclear reactors, in a few years it could be producing enough plutonium for roughly 30 bombs a year—or the bombs themselves."[163] Brookings Institution scholars Michael O'Hanlon and Mike Mochizuki estimate that it would take North Korea about two years to complete the 50-megawatt reactor and three years or so for the 200-megawatt reactor.[164] In other words, North Korea could become within a few years not just a state with a few nuclear weapons, but a significant nuclear power.

Those are most unsettling prospects. The pertinent question is: Where should we go from here? In the autumn of 2002 Gallucci and another former Clinton national security advisor, Anthony Lake, expressed the conventional wisdom about America's options: "The choices in 1994 were the same four we have today: We could launch a military strike against the unidentified nuclear facilities; we could refuse negotiations and go to the United Nations for sanctions to isolate and contain the North's nuclear program; we could essentially accept the nuclear weapons status of North Korea and try to contain the damage to international nonproliferation efforts, as well as to our alliances with South Korea and Japan; or we could negotiate with the North to stop the nuclear weapons program that creates the problem."[165] Those are indeed the most obvious choices, but the United States also has some other options. The problem is that none of the available options is especially appealing.

Chapter Three

OPTIONS FOR DEALING WITH NORTH KOREA

A key question—perhaps *the* key question—about the ongoing crisis is: Why is North Korea pursuing a nuclear-weapons program? It is a difficult question to answer. There are a number of possible explanations, and Pyongyang may have multiple motives for its actions.

One possibility is that North Korea may be using the specter of nuclear weapons as a way to extort concessions from the United States and its neighbors in East Asia. Given the agitation that Washington and the other relevant capitals have shown every time Pyongyang rattles the nuclear saber, it is not a far-fetched expectation. North Korea received substantial concessions in the 1994 Agreed Framework for the mere promise to freeze (not, it must be emphasized, abandon) its nuclear-weapons program. Perhaps Kim Jong-il's regime believes it can get even more concessions this time around.

And there is a precedent for such expectation in addition to the 1994 agreement. Ukraine and Kazakhstan, for example, used the nukes they inherited from the defunct Soviet Union as bargaining leverage to extract loans and other important economic concessions from the United States and the other western powers in the early 1990s. History shows that Washington and its allies will pay a lot to induce a country not to go nuclear.

Another possibility is that North Korea may be seeking the weapons for prestige. The handful of powers in the international system that possess nuclear weapons have a status quite different from the bulk of the nations that do not possess them. All five permanent members of the UN Security Council (the United States, Russia, China, Britain, and France) are nuclear-weapon states. Although it is true that a few nonnuclear powers, most notably Germany and Japan, have significant prestige and influence in the international community, the possession of those weapons is a route into a rather exclusive club. It is no coincidence that China was treated with greater respect and caution by the United States and other countries after it acquired nukes than before it achieved that breakthrough. Similarly, Washington and other capitals now treat India as a serious player—in marked contrast to the tendency to view that country as a Third World underachiever before its 1998 nuclear tests. Pakistan also went from being regarded as a problem state (and in some quarters a potential failed state) before its tests in 1998 to being a significant factor in the war on terrorism and other important security issues.

True, factors other than the nuclear issue help explain the change in U.S. policy. Pakistan borders Afghanistan and has aided the United States in its struggle against al Qaeda and the Taliban. India's economic growth rate has reached impressive levels in recent years, a development that has contributed to Washington's evolving perception of that country. But the nuclear factor is certainly not trivial in altering the way that Pakistan and India are now treated, and Pyongyang may believe that possession of nuclear weapons is the admission ticket to the club of major powers.

Yet another motive may be cost. Nuclear weapons are far less expensive than expanding the size of the army or trying to build high-tech conventional weapons. Indeed, North Korea insisted at one point that it was pursuing a nuclear-weapons program to *cut* the size and expense of its conventional forces. The bulletin from KCNA, North Korea's official news agency, added that the government hoped "to channel manpower resources and funds into economic construction and the betterment of people's living."[1] Although one should view any North Korean statement with skepticism, that rationale makes a fair amount of sense. North Korea currently devotes a burdensome 11.6 percent of GDP to the military, and a large portion of the working-age population is in uniform.[2] Given that the DPRK's economy has been in an alarming downward spiral since the mid-1990s, cutting the cost of the military may be an essential step to prevent the system from imploding.

Finally, North Korea may have a strategic motive for its actions. What U.S. officials do not wish to admit is that Pyongyang's nuclear program is a logical, perhaps even inevitable, response to the foreign policy the United States has pursued since the end of the Cold War. Consider the extent of U.S. military coercion since the opening of the Berlin Wall in 1989. The United States:

- invaded Panama and overthrew the government of Manuel Noriega
- devastated Iraq in the first Persian Gulf war
- occupied Somalia
- forced the government of Haiti from power by threatening to invade the country
- bombed the Bosnian Serbs into accepting a peace agreement
- bombed Yugoslavia into relinquishing control over its province of Kosovo
- invaded Afghanistan and overthrew the Taliban government
- attacked and occupied Iraq in the second Persian Gulf war

In all, the United States has conducted eight *major* military operations in 14 years (not including such incidents as the periodic bombing of Iraq during the years between the Gulf wars or the cruise missile strikes on Afghanistan and Sudan in 1998). That is an extraordinary record of belligerence.

Moreover, in his 2002 State of the Union address, President Bush explicitly linked North Korea to Iraq (a country with which the United States was apparently headed to war) in an axis of evil. The North Koreans probably noticed as well that Bush had stated, "I loathe Kim Jong Il. I have a visceral reaction to this guy because he is starving his people."[3] Although he did not explicitly call for forcible regime change, Bush added that he did not understand how the world continued to "coddle" Kim's regime.

It is hardly surprising if Pyongyang concluded that it might be next on Washington's hit list unless it could effectively deter an attack. Yet the DPRK cannot hope to match the conventional military capabilities of a superpower. The most reliable deterrent—perhaps the only reliable deterrent—is to have nuclear weapons.[4] DPRK officials told a visiting delegation of U.S. congressmen in June 2003 that they were building nuclear weapons precisely so their country would not suffer the same fate as Saddam Hussein's Iraq.[5] Even a few American hawks acknowledge the possibility that North Korea may have reached that conclusion. The *Wall Street Journal's* Karen Elliott House notes, "the lesson Kim Jong Il almost surely has deduced from the impending war with Iraq is that all that stands between his fate and Saddam's is his credible confession that he has a nuclear capability and a credible fear abroad that he might use it."[6]

In other words, U.S. behavior may have inadvertently created a powerful incentive for nuclear-weapons proliferation—the last thing in the world Washington wanted to occur. American officials dismiss the fears of North Korea as manifestations of paranoia. That is true to a point. When the Creator passed out paranoia, the North Korean political elites got in line twice. But as Henry Kissinger once pointed out, even paranoids have real enemies. And there is little doubt that the United States is the enemy of the DPRK.

Washington's conduct toward nonnuclear powers such as Iraq and Yugoslavia likely has stimulated Pyongyang's worst fears. The lesson that North Korea (and Iran and other countries may be learning as well) is that possessing a nuclear arsenal is the only way to compel the United States to exhibit caution and respect. That is especially true if the country has an adversarial relationship with the United States.

U.S. leaders need to face the reality that America's foreign policy may cause unintended (and sometimes unpleasant) consequences. Those people who cheered such initiatives as the expulsion of Iraqi forces from Kuwait, the ouster of the dictatorship in Haiti, the nation-building crusades in the Balkans, and the overthrow of Saddam Hussein need to ask themselves whether increasing the incentives for nuclear proliferation was a price worth paying. Because greater proliferation is the price we are now paying with North Korea. As syndicated columnist Steve Chapman notes, nuclear weapons "are the best way to assure a government's survival. Any government that has serious disagreements with the U.S.—and particularly any on our 'axis of evil'—knows that if we may decide who rules Iraq, we may later decide who rules other nations. There is only one protection: going nuclear."[7]

The wide range of possible motives for North Korea's actions underscores a crucial point: it is difficult to determine whether Pyongyang merely is using the specter of nuclear weapons to force negotiations or whether it is serious about becoming a nuclear-weapons power. The first scenario means that there is a good chance that the crisis can ultimately be resolved.[8] The second scenario means that the crisis will almost certainly intensify.

CALLS FOR DIALOGUE

Many Americans who are convinced that North Korea is using its nuclear program primarily as bargaining leverage issue increasingly urgent calls for dialogue. Clinton-era diplomat Nancy Soderberg argues: "Today, President Bush faces a crisis eerily similar to the one faced by President Clinton in 1993—and the one his own father faced four years earlier. If he has learned from history, Mr. Bush will negotiate directly with the North Koreans. In exchange for an end to both of North Korea's nuclear programs and tougher inspections, he will need to put new incentives on the table, like more food aid, a resumption of the light-water reactor construction, a nonaggression pact, and the possibility of normal relations." She concedes that such concessions might be difficult to stomach, but insists that they are better than the alternatives: "As President Bush's predecessors learned, negotiation is the best option in each new North Korean crisis."[9] Like many other members of the American foreign policy community who base their hopes on dialogue, Soderberg fails to see the irony in her last sentence. The United States has negotiated with North Korea several times before, but each understanding or formal agreement merely seems to pave the way for a new round of cheating and a new crisis.

But she is hardly alone in advocating dialogue and a new agreement as the only way to halt North Korea's nuclear-weapons program.[10] Former president Jimmy Carter stresses that the North Koreans "must be convinced that they will be more secure without nuclear weapons, and that normal diplomatic and economic relations with the United States are possible."[11] Senator Joseph Lieberman (D-Conn.) has chastised the Bush administration for its reluctance to negotiate with Pyongyang. Like so many others, he contends that the United States should be willing to offer "political recognition and regional investment" to North Korea if it agrees to give up its ambitions to build nuclear weapons.[12]

Some calls for dialogue come from rather surprising sources. Former national security advisor Brent Scowcroft argues that the United States should be prepared to enter into discussion with the North Koreans "in any forum, multilateral or bilateral." Moreover, if North Korea is willing to agree to an enhanced version of the 1994 Agreed Framework, the United States should "be willing to provide the kind of security assurances North Korea seeks, as well as other steps to bring North Korea into the community of nations."[13] Republican Senator Richard Lugar, chairman of the Senate Foreign Relations Committee, insists that the only reasonable way of resolving the crisis requires "creative diplomatic solutions," which hold out the hope of better ties between North Korea and the United States if the North again puts its weapons development program on hold.[14] On another occasion, Lugar criticized the Bush administration for refusing bilateral negotiations with North Korea. "The stakes are simply too high" to maintain such a rigid stance, Lugar concluded. "We do not have the luxury to be this absolute."[15]

Curt Weldon (R-Penn.) presented a similar view after leading a congressional delegation to North Korea in late May and early June 2003. Following that visit, Weldon and his colleagues were surprisingly receptive to negotiations with Pyongyang. The lawmakers stated that they were optimistic that Washington could get North Korea to dismantle its nuclear program if U.S.

officials were prepared to offer economic incentives and security guarantees. Weldon said that he discussed with senior North Korean officials the prospect of Washington's providing energy, food, and economic aid if Pyongyang scrapped its nuclear-weapons program. The response, he reported, was "overwhelmingly positive."[16] That a conservative Republican ally of the Bush administration would hold out such a prospect was more than a little surprising.

Shortly after his return, Weldon circulated a 10-point plan to resolve the crisis. The plan was to be implemented in two stages. In the first phase, the United States would sign a one-year nonaggression pact with North Korea, recognize the Pyongyang government, and offer economic assistance jointly with Japan and South Korea. In exchange, the North would be required to renounce any intentions to pursue the development of nuclear weapons, give a full inventory of its nuclear facilities, and agree to outside inspections of all such facilities. North Korea also would have to rejoin the NPT.

The second phase would begin immediately after the first year or on the completion of the inspections of the North's nuclear installations. In the second phase, the nonaggression pact would become permanent, North Korea would sign the Missile Technology Control Regime (thus renouncing its trade in ballistic missiles and missile technology), agree to observer status in the Helsinki Human Rights Commission, and set a timetable for improving its human rights record. In exchange, the United States and its East Asian allies would open new avenues for investment in agriculture, energy, and other sectors of the North Korean economy.[17]

An even more comprehensive blueprint for dialogue is a 2003 report from a task force on U.S. Korea policy cosponsored by the Center for International Policy and the University of Chicago's Center for East Asian Studies.[18] Chaired by Selig Harrison, the task force consisted of 28 leading scholars on East Asia, although it should be noted that the membership had a noticeable left of center tilt. The task force report recommended "urgent diplomatic initiatives" by the United States "to test whether North Korea is in fact prepared for a verifiable end to all aspects of its nuclear weapons development." Those negotiations should include both multilateral and bilateral formats. The report cautioned that negotiations would likely succeed only if the United States acted in concert with the East Asian powers (as well as the European Union). Equally important, negotiations to halt Pyongyang's nuclear program would succeed "only if the resolution of the nuclear issue is addressed together with the pursuit of four other directly related issues: normalizing U.S. economic and political relations with North Korea; guaranteeing the security of a non-nuclear North Korea; promoting the reconciliation of North and South Korea; and drawing North Korea into economic engagement with its neighbors."[19]

Not only was the task force rather accommodating to North Korea, it clearly placed blame for the ongoing crisis on the United States as well as the North. "In North Korean eyes, the United States got up front what it wanted from the 1994 accord, the suspension of a North Korean plutonium project that could otherwise have produced up to 30 nuclear weapons a year, while North Korea got only unfulfilled promises, with the exception of the 500,000 tons of heavy oil annually pledged" in the agreement. From this assumption, the task force concluded that "without condoning North Korean duplicity" in violating the agreement, the breach did not, by itself, prove that North Korea cannot be trusted to fulfill a new accord.[20]

The report went on to offer detailed proposals for resolving the crisis. One recommendation was that the United States should "offer to negotiate directly with North Korea on all issues of concern to both sides." That would mean addressing not only the nuclear issue, but North Korea's food and energy needs and the full normalization of political and economic relations if Pyongyang agreed not to process the spent fuel rods, to allow the return of IAEA inspectors, and to end its uranium enrichment program.

The task force also proposed a joint declaration by Colin Powell and North Korean foreign minister Paik Nam Soon. In that declaration, North Korea would pledge to negotiate the verified dismantlement of all aspects of its nuclear capabilities. Both sides would pledge not to use force against the other during negotiations, and upon the conclusion of dismantlement, "they would categorically rule out the use of force against each other thereafter. The United States would also pledge to respect North Korean sovereignty and not to hinder its economic development."[21] In short, the task force proposed meeting all of Pyongyang's demands in exchange for verified dismantling of the North's nuclear weapons program.

In addition to those specific issues, the task force recommended resuming negotiations to continue North Korea's 1999 moratorium on missile testing and proposed a peace agreement to bring the Korean War officially to an end. It also suggested lowering the U.S. military profile in South Korea by moving forces away from the DMZ and gradually reducing the number of troops stationed in South Korea. Finally, the report proposed U.S. support for North Korea's economic aspirations and reforms.

Although the task force recommendations are more detailed than those contained in other proposals for negotiations, they accurately reflect the views of the pro-dialogue camp. In essence, the members of that faction propose to give North Korea a good many concessions in exchange for a verifiable freeze of Pyongyang's nuclear program. That North Korea's track record of honoring its previous agreements on nuclear matters is less than impressive does not discourage them from making such proposals.

A STRATEGY OF DIPLOMATIC AND ECONOMIC PRESSURE

The Bush administration has been decidedly more skeptical about the efficacy of negotiations. Indeed, when the crisis first broke, the administration seemed to reject negotiations with the North until Pyongyang resumed honoring the commitments it had made under the Agreed Framework. Assistant Secretary of State Kelly made that point when he noted that the North Koreans wanted a nonaggression declaration from the United States, a peace treaty formally ending the Korean War, and Washington's diplomatic recognition of the DPRK government. North Korea had suggested that "when all of these wonderful things were done, then we might be able to talk about their uranium enrichment program. That in my mind has it upside down," Kelly stated.[22] On another occasion, the State Department stated bluntly: "We will not bargain or offer inducements for North Korea to live up to the treaties and agreements it has signed." The United States "will not enter into dialogue in response to threats or broken commitments."[23]

President Bush softened this approach slightly in January 2003, when he indicated that the United States might consider providing agriculture and energy aid to North Korea if Pyongyang dismantled its nuclear-weapons program. Even on that occasion, though, Bush insisted that the United States would not be "blackmailed."[24] Moreover, it has become clear that the administration has no interest in merely restoring the Agreed Framework. Washington's condition for any concessions to North Korea is an agreement that would include comprehensive "on demand" inspections of all possible nuclear-weapons sites.[25]

The logic of Washington's dual-track strategy of multilateral diplomacy combined with economic pressure was expressed candidly by Douglas Feith, undersecretary of defense for policy. "It's important that the North Koreans understand that there is a price to be paid for violating their commitments and pursuing a capability that threatens the peace and security of the region," Feith stated. "The challenge is devising a way of imposing a price so that diplomacy can work."[26]

One of the administration's first steps to exert coordinated economic pressure on Pyongyang was to get agreements from South Korea and Japan to cut off shipments of fuel oil to the DPRK. Although the two allies initially were reluctant to take that action, by mid-November 2002 they were on board.[27] Washington's decision to lobby Tokyo and Seoul on that issue won plaudits from the administration's hawkish domestic political allies. A *Wall Street Journal* editorial endorsed the cutoff and suggested that it be expanded to include a comprehensive embargo on all trade and investment and a ban on remittances to the North from offshore Koreans (primarily those living in Japan).[28]

Administration leaders have been especially hostile to bilateral talks with Pyongyang, viewing the North Korean demands for such talks as a ploy to split the United States from its East Asian allies and to disrupt a united diplomatic front against the DPRK. U.S. officials have repeatedly insisted that any negotiations with North Korea must be conducted within a multilateral framework.

Washington did deviate from its policy slightly in April 2003 when it agreed to trilateral talks hosted by China. The disappointing results from that session, however, have caused the administration to resume its insistence on the multilateral approach. When North Korea again floated the suggestion of bilateral negotiations in June 2003, Secretary Powell spurned the suggestion. Speaking to a meeting of the security forum sponsored by the Association of Southeast Asian Nations (ASEAN), Powell stated: "There is nothing the North Koreans can say to us that we will not have to share with our partners. And there is no proposal that will come from us without the concurrence of our partners. There is, therefore, no need for a bilateral dialogue."[29]

The administration's attempt to achieve a united diplomatic front against North Korea has been only partially successful. The prevailing attitude of the East Asian nations was summed up in the resolution passed in June 2003 by the 23-member ASEAN Regional Forum, which passed a resolution calling for the denuclearization of the Korean peninsula and urging North Korea to reverse its decision to withdraw from the NPT. But the resolution also emphasized the need for negotiations to "pursue peaceful resolution of outstanding security concerns."[30] That phrasing suggested that North Korea might have some legitimate security concerns regarding the United States. Given the intense lobbying effort by Secretary Powell, such a balanced resolution was something less than a definitive endorsement of U.S. policy.

In addition to its efforts at the ASEAN forum, the United States has sought to put pressure on North Korea in other ways. Also in June U.S. officials pressed the UN Security Council to issue a statement declaring that North Korea is "out of compliance" with its obligations to have its nuclear energy program inspected by the IAEA.[31] Although a Security Council statement is one step short of a formal resolution, Washington appeared to be laying the legal foundation for a resolution authorizing coercive measures against North Korea, if that should become necessary.

But the bulk of the administration's efforts to pressure North Korea have focused on joint measures with Pyongyang's neighbors in Northeast Asia. Barely a week after North Korea's alleged admission about the enriched uranium program, Assistant Secretary Kelly and Under Secretary of State Bolton were engaged in a flurry of diplomacy in East Asia. Both men met with high-ranking officials in Beijing. Bolton then continued on to Moscow for meetings with Russian leaders while Kelly performed a similar mission with stops in Tokyo and Seoul. Their agenda at every stop was to get the host government to put pressure on Pyongyang.[32]

They received generally supportive words but not all that much in the way of action. Yet the administration has never wavered in its effort to enlist the support of North Korea's neighbors for concerted pressure on the DPRK. In February 2003 Secretary of State Powell embarked on a four-day trip to East Asia to continue the lobbying campaign that Bolton and Kelly had started the previous autumn. Thomas Hubbard, the U.S. ambassador to South Korea, succinctly expressed the administration's rationale. "Because other nations have much to lose from North Korea's dangerous actions, the challenge to regional and global peace concerns us all," Hubbard stated in a speech on the eve of Powell's arrival. "It must be met by a combination of concerned states."[33]

Indicative of the U.S. attempt to enlist support for escalating the pressure on North Korea was the statement that Bush and Japanese prime minister Junichiro Koizumi issued following their summit meeting in Crawford, Texas, in late May 2003. "The prime minister and I see the problem the same way," Bush asserted. "We will not tolerate nuclear weapons in North Korea. We will not give in to blackmail." Although the two leaders were confident that diplomacy would bring a peaceful solution, Bush added ominously that "we agreed that further escalation by North Korea will require tougher measures from the international community."[34] Koizumi repeated Bush's warning about tougher measures almost verbatim.

Japan's position on the North Korean nuclear problem has been reasonably close to Washington's, although Tokyo has always stressed the need for dialogue as well as pressure. North Korea's other neighbors have been decidedly more out of sync with Washington's approach. Russia, for example, has been extremely reluctant to pressure Pyongyang. When urged by Washington to exert such pressure in December 2002, Russian officials flatly refused and indicated that they "would not do so in the future" either. "History has shown that pressure on North Korea has pitiful results rather than solving a problem," said Deputy Foreign Minister Alexander Losyukov. "We are not going to unite with anyone to pressure North Korea. That is absolutely ruled out."[35] Although (as usual) Moscow has since wavered as the U.S. demands for such a policy have escalated, it is clear that Russia believes that diplomatic and economic coercion is a counterproductive approach.

South Korea also is wary of putting too much pressure on Pyongyang. At a June 2003 summit meeting with Koizumi, President Roh pointedly declined to endorse his call for a tougher response if North Korea escalated tensions by continuing work on its nuclear-weapons program. Instead, Roh chose to emphasize the need for continuing dialogue with the North.[36] Seoul has conveyed that same tone to Washington on numerous occasions.[37] And on several occasions Roh and other South Korean leaders have flatly ruled out the use of military force to resolve the crisis. Moreover, although the ROK is not willing to rule out using economic pressure, it is clearly apprehensive about adopting that course.

At the same time it has tried to mobilize support for economic pressure on North Korea from that country's neighbors, Washington has resisted their calls for a greater willingness to negotiate with Pyongyang. The joint statement issued after a meeting with South Korean and Japanese officials in January 2003 illustrates the Bush administration's attitude: "The U.S. delegation explained that the United States is willing to talk to North Korea. However, the U.S. delegation stressed that the United States will not provide quid pro quos to North Korea to live up to its existing obligations."[38]

The administration's strained distinction between "dialogue" and negotiations won the plaudits of hard-liners in the American foreign policy community. Former secretary of state James A. Baker called for a policy of "armed containment" of the North and criticized those who call for far-reaching negotiations with Pyongyang as being naive. "The Bush administration, to its great credit (and unlike its predecessor) has simply refused to play the role of Alice in Pyongyang's wonderland of pretend diplomacy," Baker stated. "Events since the naive and ill-considered 1994 framework agreement that the United States entered into with North Korea have convinced Pyongyang that crime can pay. So now: talk, yes; extortion, no." Diplomacy, Baker concluded, "works best when it is proffered in a mailed fist."[39]

The administration has continued to pursue the dual-track approach of talks and economic pressure. That strategy was formalized at a meeting of President Bush's top foreign policy advisors in early May 2003.[40] The administration's approach incorporates a willingness to engage in multilateral talks combined with a determination to, in the words of one official, "tighten the screws" economically. That dual-track strategy appears to be a compromise between those in the administration who favor broader talks with Pyongyang and those who want to escalate the pressure. Said one official who favors more dialogue, "We signed up for the hard side in order to get the soft side." The official added: "Some people only want the hard side."[41]

The most critical component of Washington's strategy to forge a united diplomatic and economic front that will pressure North Korea to give up its nuclear-weapons program is the role of China. Bush administration officials believe that China is by far the most crucial participant in that coalition. Indeed, the administration apparently expects China to exert whatever diplomatic and economic leverage is needed to get North Korea to abandon its nuclear ambitions.

U.S. leaders have not had their hopes fulfilled. During his trip to East Asia in February 2003, Powell privately expressed disappointment that China had not done more to pressure its neighbor.[42] But the Chinese did not seem overly sympathetic to the secretary's objectives. Indeed, in the midst of Powell's trip, Chinese foreign minister Tang Jiaxuan and Kim Yong-nam, president of North Korea's Supreme People's Assembly, issued a joint statement pledging to boost the ties between their two countries.[43] China's cooperation in attempting to get Pyongyang to back away from its nuclear ambitions has improved only modestly since then. China does seem more alarmed about North Korea's actions than it did during the early stages of the crisis.[44] Nevertheless, PRC officials have proceeded cautiously about bringing pressure to bear on the DPRK.

Washington may be overrating both Beijing's willingness and ability to get North Korea to remain nonnuclear. True, China does have significant economic leverage over the DPRK. Seventy to 90 percent of North Korea's annual energy supplies, approximately 30 percent of its total outside assistance, and an estimated 38 percent of its imports come from China.[45] But it is leverage that Beijing so far is reluctant to use.

Chinese leaders may be willing to exert some diplomatic, and perhaps even economic, pressure on Pyongyang to keep the Korean peninsula nonnuclear. China, in fact, insists that it has been working hard on the issue through quiet diplomacy.[46] But that position illustrates an important point. China sees itself as an intermediary between the United States and North Korea, not as Washington's partner in a campaign of isolation and coercion. China has repeatedly urged the United States to negotiate with Pyongyang without preconditions.[47] It is revealing that Beijing's most visible role to date has been to facilitate the April 2003 trilateral talks involving the United States, North Korea, and China, and the subsequent six-party talks in August.

A few Sinophobes in the United States charge that China is in league with the North Koreans and would not mind seeing a nuclear-armed North Korea. Former congressional staffer William C. Triplett II states bluntly that "the idea that Beijing shares our desire for a nuclear weapons free Korean Peninsula is nothing more than a dangerous self-delusion." Triplett alleges further that if the Chinese "disapproved of North Korea's WMD activities, they could end them with a telephone call."[48]

Such criticism contains at most a kernel of truth. Beijing may not be overly upset that Pyongyang's behavior discomfits the United States and allows China to play the role as essential diplomatic broker in the region. Some Chinese officials also may be enjoying how the North Korean issue has sowed dissension in the U.S.–ROK relationship. If Seoul begins to loosen its close ties with the United States, China is likely to be the principal beneficiary. (Given the historical Korean antipathy toward Japan, the ROK is unlikely to look to that country as a substitute for its partnership with the United States.)

Most evidence suggests, however, that while China may not be above fishing in troubled waters, Beijing is not eager to see nuclear weapons introduced on the Korean peninsula. Among other drawbacks, such a development would increase the chance that Japan would respond by building a deterrent of its own, and a nuclear-armed Japan is the last thing China wants to see.

But while maintaining the nonnuclear status quo on the peninsula may be a significant Chinese objective, it is not the most important one. Beijing's top priority is to preserve the North Korean state as a buffer between China and the U.S. sphere of influence in Northeast Asia, although it also clearly wants Kim Jong-il's regime to reform.[49] As North Korea's economy has languished in recent years, resulting in mass famine, China has worried that the North Korean regime might implode, much as the East German system did in 1989. Such a development would lead to the sudden emergence on China's border of a unified Korea allied to the United States. It might also lead to a massive flow of North Korean refugees into China. As two prominent experts on East Asia note: "To guard against this event [China] will ultimately allow fuel and food (sanctioned or unsanctioned) to move across its border with the North."[50]

The overriding objective of keeping North Korea as a viable country probably places a limit on the amount of pressure that Beijing is willing to exert on Pyongyang.[51] In theory, China might be able to use its economic leverage as North Korea's principal source of energy and other vital commodities to compel Kim Jong-il's regime to put its nuclear-weapons program back into the deep freeze. In reality, though, China fears the possible consequences of using that leverage.

And as far as diplomatic influence is concerned, the United States tends to overrate Beijing's clout. China may be North Korea's closest ally, but that is only because most other countries (with the partial exception of Russia) have utterly frosty relations with the reclusive Stalinist state. The North Korean elite is not especially fond of China. In addition to the wariness with which a small state typically regards a much larger neighbor, Pyongyang considers the Beijing government a communist apostate for its extensive flirtation with market-oriented economic reforms and its tolerance of a considerable amount of social pluralism for the Chinese people. The North Koreans may listen to China's diplomatic message that it is dangerous and counterproductive to pursue the nuclear option, but it is not at all certain that they will heed that message. *New York Times* columnist Nicholas D. Kristof correctly concludes, "China's influence on North Korea has always been wildly exaggerated. North Koreans speak openly of their contempt for Chinese officials."[52]

In short, if U.S. officials are counting on China to "deliver" a nonnuclear North Korea, they may be making a miscalculation. Beijing probably will try to be helpful on the issue, but its willingness and its ability to influence Pyongyang are limited.

Indeed, with the partial exception of Japan, the Northeast Asian countries have not shown much enthusiasm for Washington's campaign for multilateral pressure on North Korea. Administration leaders react defensively when critics make that argument, but their counterpoints lack conviction. When asked by reporters about the apparent lack of Northeast Asian support for the U.S. strategy, Bush responded, "They may be putting pressure on and you just don't know about it."[53] Evidence of that phantom pressure, however, has yet to materialize.

Imposition of a naval blockade would be the most extreme form of putting diplomatic and economic pressure on North Korea.[54] Former assistant secretary of defense Richard Perle and neoconservative journalist David Frum openly advocate that course in their latest book, *An End to Evil*, stating: "Decisive action would begin with a comprehensive air and naval blockade of North Korea, cutting it off from all seaborne traffic, all international aviation, and all intercourse with the South." Frum and Perle acknowledge that South Korea would likely object to such a strategy, but they argue that Seoul "needs to understand that, as in Cuba in 1962, a blockade is its best alternative to war."[55]

By the late spring of 2003, there were some indications that the Bush administration was moving in the direction of a policy to interdict North Korean commerce. The initial action appeared to be aimed at imposing a selective blockade targeted against the North's nuclear and missile exports.[56] President Bush first proposed a "Proliferation Security Initiative" (PSI) to interdict suspect cargoes being carried to so-called rogue states during his European tour in early June 2003. Shortly thereafter, Under Secretary of State Bolton informed Congress that the United States was discussing with its allies a plan to interdict ships carrying militarily related goods to and from North Korea (and other rogue states that might be attempting to develop weapons of mass destruction).[57] Although the purpose of such a plan, according to Bolton, was to halt supplies for Pyongyang's nuclear program and to prevent the export of nuclear technology from the DPRK, it could be expanded easily to become an effort to strangle the North's already struggling economy. Washington quickly followed up Bolton's statement with a diplomatic effort to enlist the support of East Asian countries for a strategy to interdict suspect North Korean ships on the high seas. During his trip to attend the ASEAN forum in mid-June, Secretary of State Powell had that goal high on his agenda.[58] North Korea's response to the U.S. initiative was shrill and combative. The *Rodong Sinmun* newspaper blasted the measures as a premeditated war plan and warned that the DPRK "will take an immediate physical retaliatory step against the U.S. once it judges that its sovereignty is infringed upon by Washington's blockade operation."[59] Nevertheless, the United States has gone forward with PSI interdiction plans. Following the failure of the six-party talks in late August, the United States and 10 other countries announced plans to conduct land, air, and naval exercises to test the PSI.[60]

Imposing even a limited blockade would be a risky venture. North Korean leaders have already indicated that economic sanctions, similar to those imposed by the international community on Iraq, would be considered an act of war. And under long-standing principles of international law, a naval blockade certainly is considered an act of war. How Pyongyang would react is uncertain, but applying economic pressure to that extent would almost certainly escalate the crisis.

Moreover, it is not at all clear that even comprehensive economic sanctions would produce the desired policy changes. A few experts believe that pressure would cause Pyongyang to back down.[61] But others are quite pessimistic. UNICEF has concluded that, because North Korea already is so desperately poor, economic sanctions would have a slight impact. Former secretary of defense William Perry reaches a similar conclusion, arguing that the belief that the nuclear crisis could be defused by economic pressure "is optimistic to the point of being naive."[62]

Perhaps the most potent source of pressure would be to cut off food aid. Officially at least, Washington has refused to use such a cruel tactic.[63] Yet the amount of food donations flowing into the United Nations' World Food Program in North Korea has dropped, and relief groups are suspicious that the United States has quietly attached onerous conditions to future shipments and is quietly discouraging contributions from other countries.[64] In any case, the UN briefly stopped giving food to 3 million of the 6.4 million North Koreans it had been assisting.[65] Given the extent of the famine in North Korea the past few years, even a temporary reduction is no small matter.

But using economic coercion has limited prospects for success on the nuclear issue. Trying to further isolate one of the most economically isolated countries is a little like threatening to deprive a monk of worldly pleasures. A policy of tightening economic sanctions may cause additional suffering among North Korea's destitute masses, but such an approach is unlikely to alter the regime's behavior on the nuclear issue. The key question remains whether Pyongyang is using the specter of a nuclear arsenal merely as a bargaining tactic to secure concessions from the United States and its allies, or whether North Korea is intent on becoming a nuclear-weapons power. If it is the latter, the leaders of North Korea are not going to end their pursuit of that goal merely because its oppressed population may experience additional economic pain. A regime that has stood by while its policies have led to the starvation of 1 to 2 million of its citizens will not be bothered unduly if more of them perish.

WHAT IF NORTH KOREA IS SERIOUS ABOUT BECOMING A NUCLEAR POWER?

Ultimately, the competing strategies of dialogue and economic/diplomatic pressure are based on the same assumption: that North Korea is merely using the threat of a nuclear program as a bargaining chip. For all of their differences, the advocates of those competing strategies assume that the right policy mix will cause the North to give up its nuclear ambitions. "They are playing the same game they played in 1993, trying to force the U.S. to negotiate with them under the threat of proceeding with a nuclear weapons program," concludes Gary Samore, the former proliferation expert on President Clinton's National Security Council.[66] Selig Harrison, one of the most outspoken advocates of dialogue, asserts flatly that "North Korea is bargaining. The Bush administration should respond positively to its offer to negotiate by building on the 1994 U.S. nuclear freeze agreement with North Korea, not by abrogating it." Harrison adds: "Kim Jong Il's terms for ending his nuclear program are reasonable."[67] Leon V. Sigal, director of the Northeast Asia Cooperative Security Project of the Social Science Research Council, argues that North Korea "wants to end its lifelong enmity with the United States and has demonstrated its readiness to give up its nuclear, missile, and other arms programs in return." Sigal concludes, "Pyongyang now wants to make a deal with Washington."[68]

But what if the pervasive assumption that North Korea is merely using its nuclear program as an element in bargaining is wrong? During his testimony before the Senate Armed Services Committee, CIA director George Tenet tacitly conceded that North Korea may believe that there is no contradiction between continuing to pursue a nuclear-weapons program and seeking a "normal relationship" with the United States—a relationship that would entail substantial concessions from Washington. "Kim Jong Il's attempts to parlay the North's nuclear program into political leverage suggest he is trying to negotiate a fundamentally different relationship with Washington, *one that implicitly tolerates the North's nuclear weapons program*," Tenet concluded.[69] Robert Madsen, a fellow at Stanford University's Asia/Pacific Research Center, is even more blunt in his assessment, noting that conventional wisdom holds that North Korea is using the nuclear program solely as a bargaining chip to be cashed in at the appropriate moment. "The problem with this analysis is that Pyongyang probably does not intend to trade its nuclear weapons for foreign concessions. To the contrary, an examination of North Korea's national interests suggests the acquisition of a sizeable nuclear arsenal is a perfectly rational objective."[70]

Pyongyang's long-standing pattern of making agreements to remain nonnuclear and then systematically violating those agreements also casts doubt on the bargaining chip thesis. Such repeated cheating raises a very disturbing possibility: perhaps North Korea is determined to become a nuclear power and has engaged in diplomatic obfuscation to confuse or lull its adversaries. If that is the case, the United States and the countries of East Asia may have to deal with the reality of a nuclear-armed North Korea.[71] What are they going to do then?

THE OPTION OF PREEMPTIVE WAR

One frightening possibility is that the United States might decide to use military force to prevent North Korea from building (or, more likely, expanding) its nuclear arsenal. Hawks in the American foreign policy community are already broaching that possibility. Retired general John Singlaub, the commander of U.S. forces in Korea during the late 1970s, and Admiral Thomas Moorer, former chairman of the Joint Chiefs of Staff, avidly push the military option, citing Israel's successful raid on Iraq's Osirak reactor in 1981 as a model.[72] In the midst of the Iraq crisis, Robert Carstens of the Council of Emerging National Security Affairs mused, "What if, while everyone was looking towards Iraq, we turned on a dime and crushed North Korea's nuclear and military capability?"[73]

Richard Perle warns that no one can "exclude the kind of surgical strike we saw in 1981." Moreover, in what should sound alarm bells in Tokyo and Seoul, he makes it clear that America's allies should not expect to exercise a veto over that decision. "We should always be prepared to go alone, if necessary."[74] Surprisingly, even a moderate like Senator Richard Lugar refuses to rule out the use of force to resolve the nuclear crisis.[75]

Some advocates of preemptive military action are amazingly confident that such a course would not trigger a major war in East Asia. The *Wall Street Journal* asserted in November 2002 that any plutonium reprocessing by Pyongyang would be so dangerous as to constitute a "regime-ending event." Yet the *Journal* added: "That doesn't necessarily mean war."[76] Former State Department official Jed Babbin argues: "If the nuclear weapons program continues, we should consider an Osirak-like strike at the Yongbyon plant which is the center of North Korea's program. It is quite possible to do that without beginning a general war."[77] Ralph Cossa, head of the Pacific Forum Center for Strategic and International Studies, adopts a similar view, arguing that Kim Jong-il would not risk the destruction of his regime by retaliating for such an attack.[78]

The notion that America's overwhelming military might would discourage North Korea from responding to a limited strike on its nuclear facilities by escalating the crisis has a superficial plausibility. But deterrence works only when a regime concludes that it has something valuable to lose by taking rash action. If a regime concludes that it has nothing to lose, deterrence does not apply. Those who embrace optimistic scenarios regarding North Korean caution fail to explain why the North Korean elite would assume that a passive response to a U.S. preemptive strike would enhance prospects for regime survival. Given the way the United States treated Iraq, the North Koreans would more likely conclude that an attack on the country's nuclear installations would be merely a prelude to a larger military offensive to achieve regime change. The fact that some hawkish allies of the Bush administration already blithely talk about forcible regime change certainly does not reassure Pyongyang on that score.[79]

Most hawks do not yet openly advocate a military attack on North Korea. Instead, they argue that the military option must explicitly remain on the table, in case negotiations fail to get the desired result. Senator John McCain openly chastised the Bush administration for not making it more evident that it would consider using military force.[80] Similarly, former ambassador Dennis Ross, now a scholar at the Washington Institute for Near East Policy, opines: "The purpose is not to make the military option inevitable but to build the pressure to produce a diplomatic alternative."[81] Charles Krauthammer accused the Bush administration of taking the military option off the table. "This was a serious mistake," Krauthammer warned, adding that the administration had gone from a policy of "tailored containment" to one of "shoeless appeasement."[82]

But using military force to eradicate North Korea's nuclear program would be a high-risk venture that could easily engulf the Korean peninsula in a major war.[83] Indeed, it could be a war with nuclear implications. North Korea boasts that it already possesses nuclear weapons, and U.S. intelligence sources have long believed that Pyongyang already had built one or two nuclear weapons by the time it agreed to freeze its program in 1994.[84] The assessment by China's intelligence agency is even more alarming. Beijing reportedly believes that the North may have four or five such weapons.[85] Worse still, press reports contend that U.S. officials have told their Japanese counterparts that North Korea is working to develop "several" nuclear warheads that can be loaded onto ballistic missiles. U.S. intelligence agencies reportedly now believe that the DPRK has at least eight nuclear weapons.[86] If true, Pyongyang will soon have a deployable arsenal, not merely one or two crude nuclear devices.

If the United States launched preemptive military strikes against North Korea's nuclear installations, there would be an assortment of grave risks. It is not at all certain that the United States has identified all of the installations, much less that it could successfully eradicate them. The uncertainty about the number and sophistication of North Korean nuclear weapons illustrates the limits of U.S. intelligence capabilities.[87] Indeed, a few experts believe that Pyongyang's entire nuclear program is little more than bluff and bluster—that both the uranium enrichment program and the plutonium extraction effort are far less advanced than the North Koreans have led the world to believe.[88]

That is a possibility, but the opposite conclusion is even more likely. North Korea has had years to build installations deep underground and to disperse any weapons it has built. American Enterprise Institute scholar Joshua

Muravchik, a hawk on Korea policy, concedes that Yongbyon is not likely the only relevant facility. "The North Koreans have also built underground nuclear reactors, plutonium processing plants, and uranium-enrichment facilities—and who knows what else?"[89] An editorial in the equally hawkish *Washington Times* notes the limitations of U.S. intelligence capabilities: "Washington has yet to establish how many underground uranium enrichment plants the North has, where they are and whether they are operational. Nor can it confirm or refute North Korea's claim to have enriched plutonium from thousands of spent fuel rods."[90] The limitations of intelligence does not bother the more extreme hawks. Frum and Perle, for example, admit: "Of course, it is true that we do not know where all the facilities are. But we do know where the most important one is; and just as a surgeon will wish to remove a malignant tumor even if he suspects that there may be others that cannot be located, so we should not hesitate to hit the bomb factory we can find, even if other facilities may be hidden underground."[91]

Pyongyang's reaction to U.S. attacks obviously would be a matter of grave concern. It is unlikely that North Korea would passively accept such a blow against its sovereignty. At the very least, Washington would have to expect terrorist retaliation by North Korean operatives against U.S. targets overseas and, possibly, in the United States itself. North Korea might even retaliate by launching full-scale military operations against South Korea—a development that would put U.S. forces stationed in that country in immediate danger. Even if the DPRK tried to limit its actions to a tit-for-tat response (e.g., shelling one or two U.S. military installations in the ROK), the situation could easily spiral out of control into a full-blown war. Indeed, in a worst-case scenario, there is a risk that mushroom clouds could blossom above Seoul and Tokyo—or above U.S. bases in South Korea or Okinawa.

It is conceivable, of course, that Kim Jong-il's regime would fulminate about an Osirak-like strike but not escalate the crisis to full-scale war. Or perhaps North Korea's military would unravel under stress and not be able to mount a coherent offensive. But that is not the way to bet. Even a U.S. military buildup in the region designed to intimidate Pyongyang could trigger a catastrophe. Bold Sentinel, a war game organized by the Center for Strategic and International Studies in May 2003 and featuring a mock National Security Council comprised of individuals who held senior policy positions in previous administrations, concluded that North Korea would likely launch a preemptive strike.[92]

An account by a high-ranking North Korean defector, Cho Myung-chul, is especially sobering. According to Cho, in analyzing Iraq's defeat in the first

Persian Gulf war, North Korean military officials concluded that Iraq had been too timid and defensive. Cho characterized the North's approach growing out of the lessons learned from that conflict: "If we're in a war, we'll use everything. And if there's a war, we should attack first, to take the initiative." Cho estimates the chances of general war at 80 percent in response to even a limited strike on Yongbyon.[93]

The "everything" that Cho mentioned is more than a little daunting. Aside from its possible nuclear (and chemical and biological) weapons, Pyongyang possesses other impressive capabilities. In addition to its army of more than a million soldiers, North Korea deploys up to 600 Scud missiles and additional longer-range No Dong missiles. It must be remembered that the Seoul–Inchon metropolitan area (home of roughly half of South Korea's population) is less than 40 miles from the DMZ. Pyongyang is thought to be able to fire between 300,000 and 500,000 artillery shells *an hour* into Seoul in the event of war.[94] Even if the North were ultimately defeated in war, which would be almost inevitable, the destruction to South Korea would be horrific. Estimates of the number of likely casualties from a full-scale North Korean attack exceed 1 million. That fact alone should take the military option off the table.

Yet for all too many individuals in the American foreign policy community, it does not do so. Even normally cautious people such as Samuel R. Berger, former national security advisor in the Clinton administration, and Robert Gallucci, the chief architect of the Agreed Framework, sound increasingly bellicose regarding the current crisis: "[W]e must make clear that further separation of plutonium by the North will result in serious consequences, with all options, including military, on the table. This is the hardest part because the possibility of war here is not Iraq redux; it could be the Korean War redux."[95]

Most troubling of all, the Bush administration has not eliminated the military option. True, administration officials insist repeatedly that they want and expect the North Korean nuclear problem to be resolved by peaceful means.[96] Indeed, President Bush and Secretary of State Powell initially declined even to describe the matter as a crisis.[97] The president went out of his way to distinguish the Iraq and North Korea cases. With regard to the latter, he stated: "I believe this is not a military showdown; this is a diplomatic showdown. We can resolve this peacefully."[98]

But other statements by the president and his advisors are less reassuring. The president himself has stressed that "all options are on the table," including military action.[99] He has even gone so far as to say that if the administration's efforts "don't work diplomatically, they'll have to work militarily." In

May 2003 the administration publicly rebuffed an effort by South Korean president Roh Moo-hyun to get the United States to renounce the military option.[100]

There is also the troubling reality that the administration's new National Security Strategy (NSS) document, approved in September 2002, embraces the doctrine of preemptive military action to prevent so-called rogue states from acquiring weapons of mass destruction. The NSS states that goal succinctly: "We must be prepared to stop rogue states and their terrorist clients *before* they are able to threaten or use weapons of mass destruction against the United States and our allies and friends."[101] On another occasion the administration emphasized that the United States would not "permit the world's most dangerous regimes" to pose a threat "with the world's most destructive weapons."[102] That standard would certainly seem to apply to North Korea. Indeed, it would seem to apply to the DPRK even more than it did to Saddam Hussein's Iraq.

Actions taken by the Bush administration in 2003 also suggest that the military option remains quite viable. Early in the year Washington moved B1 and B52 bombers to Guam and relocated fighter planes and reconnaissance aircraft to the western Pacific. Some of those deployments were made supposedly in conjunction with joint military exercises with South Korean forces, but it is ominous that when those exercises ended, many of the newly deployed forces remained in place.

Journalists and others who speak with administration officials off the record come away very skeptical about the administration's publicly expressed pacific intentions. A prominent Asian academic told the *Far Eastern Economic Review* that "not one of the senior officials" he met with "would rule out military action to remove North Korea's nuclear threat."[103] *New York Times* columnist Nicholas Kristof interviewed numerous senior administration officials about war plans for Korea and concluded that there was "a growing possibility" that Bush might order military strikes.[104] According to an unnamed intelligence official who had attended White House meetings: "Bush and Cheney want [Kim Jong-il's] head on a platter." The official went on to say that talk about negotiations was a ruse. "There will be negotiations," he stated, "but they [Bush and Cheney] have a plan, and they are going to get this guy after Iraq."[105]

South Korean president Roh Moo-hyun believes that the Bush administration already flirted with the military option in December 2002. "At the time of the [December 19 South Korean] elections, some U.S. officials, who held considerable responsibility in the administration, talked about the possibility of attacking North Korea," Roh told a panel of scholars in Seoul. He did not say how he knew about the deliberations within the administration, but stated that "fortunately" U.S. officials decided to pursue a diplomatic strategy instead.[106]

Given that Washington has refused to eliminate the military option, questions arise about the motives for the administration's June 2003 announcement that it would reposition some of the U.S. troops stationed in South Korea. Currently most of those troops are deployed in the northern part of the country—between Seoul and the DMZ. The redeployment would entail moving those forces farther south.[107]

In announcing the decision, Deputy Secretary of Defense Paul Wolfowitz offered only a vague justification for such a move, contending that repositioning forces would make them more effective in meeting the threat posed by North Korea.[108] That is a curious argument. Since the end of the Korean War in 1953, the principal rationale for stationing the troops near the DMZ has been that they would serve as a tripwire in case of a North Korean attack, guaranteeing U.S. involvement in any conflict. North Korea, knowing that it would then face war not only with South Korea but with the United States, would be effectively deterred from taking such a reckless gamble, according to that logic.

Why is the Bush administration now abandoning the long-standing tripwire function? Perhaps it is merely to placate South Korean public opinion by consolidating the U.S. military presence in a smaller number of bases in less visible locations. Perhaps it is a quiet conciliatory gesture to North Korea. By moving troops away from the DMZ, Washington weakens Pyongyang's argument that the U.S. presence poses a threat to North Korea's security. There is, however, another, very unsettling, possibility: that the administration is considering a preemptive military attack on North Korea's nuclear installations and wants to move American troops out of harm's way as much as possible. The Bush administration may not be committed to a military course yet, but in deciding to move U.S. forces away from the DMZ, it is creating an important precondition for pursuing that option. There are indications that Pyongyang is interpreting the U.S. move in that fashion.[109] Therefore, Washington's decision to redeploy troops could make an already dangerous situation even more volatile. It also is not reassuring that some of the administration's most hawkish domestic political allies openly advocate a redeployment precisely so that the United States can have a free hand to pursue a military option against North Korea, if that becomes desirable.[110]

CONTAINMENT AND OTHER COUNTERMEASURES

Washington should pursue a two-pronged strategy for dealing with the North Korean nuclear issue. Two serious problems need to be addressed. One is the prospect that Pyongyang might be aiming to become a regional nuclear power with a significant arsenal that could pose a threat to its neighbors and, ultimately, to the American homeland. Hawks tend to exaggerate the danger of a direct attack on the United States, and by some of its statements, the Bush administration has fed a sense of panic. For example, some administration officials have mentioned the possibility that the North's Taepo Dong 2 rocket could hit the western United States. But North Korea is far from developing a credible capability to attack America—even if it were inclined to do so. There is no evidence that the North Koreans have ever successfully tested a Taepo Dong 2. The missile's range and accuracy are uncertain, and it is unclear whether it is capable of carrying a nuclear payload. It is also not clear whether the North has, or will soon have, nuclear weapons suitable for delivery via intercontinental ballistic missile (ICBM), although the most recent intelligence on that issue is not reassuring.

But countering the threat of an unprovoked attack on the United States is relatively straightforward. America retains the largest and most sophisticated nuclear arsenal in the world—as well as a decisive edge in all conventional military capabilities. The North Korean regime surely knows (although it might behoove U.S. leaders to make the point explicitly) that any attack on American soil would mean the obliteration of the regime. The United States successfully deterred a succession of aggressive and odious regimes in the Soviet Union from using nuclear weapons, and it did the same thing with a nuclear-armed China under Mao Zedong. It is highly probable that the United States can deter Kim Jong-il's North Korea—a country that would have a much smaller nuclear arsenal than those possessed by the former Soviet Union and by China. To protect the American population in the unlikely event that deterrence failed, Washington should continue developing a shield against ballistic missiles as an insurance policy. To counter North Korea's possible threat to the East Asian region, Washington ought to convey the message that Pyongyang may be making a serious miscalculation if it assumes that it will have a nuclear monopoly in Northeast Asia. North Korea's rulers are counting on the United States to prevent Japan and South Korea from even considering the option of going nuclear. U.S. officials should inform Pyongyang that, if it insists on crashing the global nuclear weapons club, Washington will urge Tokyo and Seoul to make their own decisions about whether to acquire strategic deterrents. Even the possibility that Japan and South Korea might do so would come as an extremely unpleasant surprise to North Korea.

The United States does not need to press Tokyo and Seoul to go nuclear; that would be inappropriate. A decision on nuclear weapons would be a difficult and politically sensitive issue in both countries, and the United States should not exert pressure one way or the other. Some experts are confident that at least Japan would overcome its long-standing nuclear allergy and embrace such weapons.[111] Others are equally confident that Tokyo would decline to do so even if it had to confront a nuclear-armed North Korea. There is no way to be certain how such a debate would turn out.[112]

Merely informing those governments that the United States would not object to South Korea and Japan developing nuclear weapons would be sufficient, and would in itself be a major change in U.S. policy. U.S. officials should also inform their Japanese and South Korean partners that, if they choose to remain nonnuclear, they cannot count on the United States to risk its own security to shield them from a nuclear-armed North Korea. Within a decade Pyongyang may have ballistic missiles capable of reaching targets in the continental United States.[113] Putting American cities at risk to deter attacks on East Asian allies by a volatile and unpredictable adversary would be far too dangerous, and we need to be candid with Japan and South Korea about that point.

Faced with those realities, Japan or South Korea (or perhaps both countries) might well decide to build their own nuclear deterrent.[114] The prospect of additional nuclear-weapons proliferation in Northeast Asia is obviously not an ideal outcome. But offsetting North Korea's illicit advantage may be the best of a set of bad options. Trying to renegotiate the Agreed Framework is unlikely to induce North Korea to return to a nonnuclear status. Diplomatic pressure and economic sanctions are not likely to achieve that goal either. And preemptive military strikes are clearly too dangerous. The one chance of getting the North to abandon its current course is if it becomes clear that Pyongyang may have to deal with nuclear neighbors and would, therefore, not be able to intimidate them. Indeed, Pyongyang might have to face the prospect of confronting more prosperous nuclear adversaries that could easily build larger and more sophisticated arsenals than North Korea could hope to do. The North may conclude that ending the cheating strategy and keeping the region nonnuclear would be a more productive approach. Even if it does not do so, a nuclear balance of power in the region would likely emerge instead of a North Korean nuclear monopoly.

The prospect of a nuclear-armed Japan is the one factor that might galvanize the Chinese to put serious diplomatic and economic pressure on Pyongyang to give up its nuclear ambitions.[115] Krauthammer expresses that thesis starkly: "We should go to the Chinese and tell them plainly that if they do not join us in squeezing North Korea and thus stopping its march to go nuclear, we will endorse any Japanese attempt to create a nuclear deterrent of its own. Even better, we would sympathetically regard any request by Japan to acquire American nuclear missiles as an immediate and interim deterrent. If our nightmare is a nuclear North Korea, China's is a nuclear Japan. It's time to share the nightmares."[116]

Even if one does not embrace Krauthammer's approach, the reality is that if the United States blocks the possible emergence of a Northeast Asian nuclear balance, it may well be stuck with the responsibility of shielding nonnuclear allies from a volatile, nuclear-armed North Korea. More proliferation may be a troubling outcome, but it beats that nightmare scenario. Yet oddly enough, some of the most hawkish members of the U.S. foreign policy community are terrified at the prospect of America's democratic allies in East Asia building nuclear deterrents. Neoconservative activists Robert Kagan and William Kristol regard such proliferation with undisguised horror: "The possibility that Japan, and perhaps even Taiwan, might respond to North Korea's actions by producing their own nuclear weapons, thus spurring an East Asian nuclear arms race . . . is something that should send chills up the spine of any sensible American strategist."[117]

That attitude woefully misconstrues the problem. The threat to the peace of East Asia is if an aggressive and erratic North Korean regime gets nukes. Nuclear arsenals in the hands of stable, democratic, and peaceable nations such as Japan and South Korea do not threaten the peace of the region. Kagan and Kristol—and other Americans who share their hostility toward Tokyo and Seoul having nuclear weapons—embrace a moral equivalency between a potential aggressor and its potential victims.

Although the prospect of North Korea possessing a nuclear arsenal is unsettling, the other component of the North Korean nuclear problem is the most troubling. The United States and North Korea's neighbors probably can learn to live with Pyongyang's possession of a nuclear arsenal. What the United States cannot tolerate is North Korea's becoming the global Wal-Mart of nuclear technology.[118] An especially acute danger is that Pyongyang might provide either a nuclear weapon or fissile material to al Qaeda or other anti-American terrorist organizations. The DPRK's record on missile proliferation does not offer much encouragement that it will be restrained when it comes to commerce in nuclear materials. North Korea earned $560 million in 2001 alone in missile sales—including sales to some of the most virulently anti-American regimes.[119]

Perhaps most troubling of all, Pyongyang has shown a willingness to sell anything that will raise revenue for the financially hard-pressed regime. In the spring of 2003, for example, evidence emerged of extensive North Korean involvement in the heroin trade.[120] It is hardly unwarranted speculation to worry that the DPRK might be a willing seller of nuclear weapons or materials to terrorist groups flush with cash. William Potter, director of the Center for Nonproliferation Studies at the Monterey Institute of International Studies, observes: "Certainly, groups such as al Qaeda must be attracted by the prospect of unsafeguarded nuclear material controlled by an impoverished and isolated regime which already has broken many of its international nonproliferation commitments."[121] Deputy Secretary of State Richard Armitage rightly argues that "the arms race in North Korea pales next to the possibility . . . that she would pass on fissile material and other nuclear technology to either transnational actors or to rogue states."[122]

Preventing that development will not be easy. Some people have proposed monitoring North Korean shipments around the world—and some have even suggested imposing a blockade on North Korea—to intercept suspect shipments. One example of an aggressive antismuggling policy was the joint U.S.–Spanish interception of a shipment of North Korean Scud missiles bound for Yemen in late 2002.[123] More recently, the United States has induced more than a dozen countries to join the PSI, which is designed to prevent trafficking in missile parts, unconventional weapons, and other contraband by various rogue states.

But successful interdiction as a general policy is a long shot at best. The utter failure to halt the trafficking in illegal drugs using that method does not bode well for intercepting nuclear contraband. It would be difficult to seal off North Korea in the face of a concerted smuggling campaign. That is particularly true without the active cooperation of Russia and China, and to date neither country has joined the PSI. Interdiction is especially daunting when one realizes that the amount of plutonium needed to build a nuclear weapon could be smuggled in a container the size of a bread box.

Since interdiction is not likely to prove successful except on fortuitous occasions, the United States needs to adopt another approach. First of all, it needs to communicate to the DPRK that selling nuclear material—much less an assembled nuclear weapon—to terrorist organizations or hostile governments will be regarded as a threat to America's vital security interests. Indeed,

U.S. leaders should treat such a transaction as the equivalent of a threatened attack on America by North Korea. Such a threat would warrant military action to remove the North Korean regime. Pyongyang must be told in no uncertain terms that trafficking in nuclear materials is a bright red line that it dare not cross if the regime wishes to survive.

There are subtle indications that the DPRK may understand that point already. In announcing that they were going to build a nuclear deterrent, the North Koreans also stated that they would not transfer that capability to other parties. Obviously, when assessing North Korean assurances on any subject, one ought to take them not only with a grain of salt but with the entire salt shaker in hand. Nevertheless, Pyongyang's statement does suggest that the regime understands that there are limits to how far it can provoke the United States.

An explicit warning about the transfer of nuclear technology or weapons should be the large stick in Washington's policy mix. The carrot should consist of a willingness to lift all economic sanctions on North Korea. If the North's economy becomes more prosperous, deriving sufficient income from legitimate sources, it may not be tempted to engage in nuclear proliferation. Prosperity, of course, will require extensive economic reforms by the DPRK along the lines adopted by China over the past quarter century. The lifting of economic sanctions is no guarantee that North Korean leaders will have the wisdom to adopt such reforms, but Pyongyang has shown some signs of recent years of modifying its policy of *Juche* (self-sufficiency) and opening itself to the outside world economically.

Susan Shirk describes some of the changes she saw during a visit to North Korea in September 2002: "Prices of goods in food markets and department stores have moved closer to international prices in what amounts to a drastic currency devaluation. Food rationing, except for rice, has been abolished. If you can afford eggs, you can buy as many as you want. Farmers are paid more for what they produce. For several years, they have been allowed to produce vegetables on small private plots and sell them on the free market. Now the collective also may grow profitable crops after meeting its grain quota, putting North Korea where Chinese agriculture was in 1977."[124] North Korea also sought to emulate China's early economic reforms by establishing its first special economic zone, where foreign investment would be permitted.

In the spring of 2003 Pyongyang went even further. It started building market halls around the country to encourage private merchants, and it loosened rules about who may do business and what may be sold. Surprisingly, even foreigners will be allowed to sell their products in the new markets. "Before, they were tolerating private business. Now, they are encouraging it," concluded Cho Myong-choi, a North Korea defector who once taught economics at Kim Il-sung University in Pyongyang.[125] Dartmouth College professor David C. Kang concludes: "There is growing evidence that North Korea is serious about opening to the West, and that it desires normal political and economic relations with the rest of the world."[126] Much as Taiwan has done with mainland China, South Korea is leading the way in developing economic ties with its northern sibling. In the first 10 months of 2003, South Korea's trade with the DPRK increased 40 percent from the previous year. South Korean firms are now building cars, roads, railroads, and a major industrial park in the North.[127]

True, North Korea's economic reforms to date are initial—and somewhat hesitant—steps on a long path. And Washington cannot do much to advance the DPRK's economic reforms; the North Koreans will have to do the bulk of the work. At the very least, though, the United States should not put obstacles in the path of reform.

In sum, the United States needs to pursue a two-tier strategy with regard to the North Korean nuclear crisis. At the most basic level, Washington should agree to negotiate with Pyongyang, without demanding that the North first return to the Agreed Framework and rejoin the NPT. Those negotiations should preferably be multilateral in nature, but U.S. officials should not rule out bilateral talks with the North, if that is the only way to make progress.[128] It would be in the best interests of the United States and the nations of East Asia if this crisis can be resolved through diplomatic means resulting in a comprehensive agreement.

Any diplomatic solution needs to have certain characteristics, however, to be worthwhile. It is not enough to get North Korea to promise to abide by the Agreed Framework and the NPT. North Korea has demonstrated repeatedly that its word means nothing. This time there must be intrusive "on demand" inspections of all known and suspected North Korean nuclear facilities. If North Korea truly abandons its nuclear-weapons program and agrees to such inspections, the United States should take a number of conciliatory steps. Those would include resuming the fuel oil shipments and construction on the light-water reactors, agreeing to North Korea's demand for a nonaggression pact (even though historically such agreements have rarely been worth the paper they are written on), signing a treaty officially bringing the state of war on the Korean peninsula to an end, normalizing diplomatic and economic relations with Pyongyang, and gradually withdrawing all U.S. forces from South Korea. (The latter two steps should have been taken years ago.) Indeed, Washington's ultimate goal should be to reduce its risk exposure in Northeast Asia and create conditions whereby North Korea's neighbors will have primary responsibility for dealing with any future destabilizing behavior by the world's last bastion of Stalinism.

The odds are not good, however, that North Korea will agree to a new accord that includes rigorous inspections—as opposed to a toothless, updated version of the Agreed Framework. The United States and North Korea's neighbors probably could get a rehash of the 1994 agreement from Pyongyang for the asking—if the concessions were sufficiently generous. But such an accord would not really resolve the crisis; it merely would pave the way for a new round of cheating a few years down the road.

The unpromising prospects for a meaningful, durable agreement ending the DPRK's nuclear-weapons program means the United States must have a second-tier (or backup) policy. Such a policy would involve allowing a nuclear balance of power in Northeast Asia to emerge, whereby Japan and South Korea would offset North Korea's nuclear arsenal with arsenals of their own. The United States should also make it clear to North Korea that any transfer of nuclear weapons to hostile states or terrorist movements will mean war and the end of the regime. A policy with those characteristics would hardly be an ideal outcome. It does, however, beat the alternatives of preemptive war or persisting in vainly trying to bribe Pyongyang as evidence mounts that North Korea may not be willing to abandon its goal of joining the global nuclear-weapons club.

Chapter Four

SOUTH KOREA AS A
SECURITY FREE-RIDER

Korean president Kim Young-sam visited the United States in 1995 to "cheer up" Americans, explained Prime Minister Lee Hong-koo. "This occasion celebrates what we've achieved together."[1] And, in fact, South Korea and the United States had achieved much together. Or, rather, the ROK had achieved much because of hard economic work carried out under Washington's military protection.

The United States became involved militarily on the Korean peninsula as an outgrowth of the end of World War II and the start of the Cold War. Had America not intervened, the South would almost certainly have been absorbed by North Korea. The Rhee Syngman regime was incapable of defending itself and viewed by many South Koreans as not being worth defending.

Thus, America's military presence and the subsequent "mutual" defense treaty invited ROK free-riding at the start, given the disparity in power of the two signatories. Such behavior was not only expected but arguably justified. By underinvesting in the military and focusing on economic development, Seoul set the stage for the eventual financial miracle that has transformed South Korea into a major international economic power.

But once that transformation was under way, it was time to increase the ROK's defense burden and decrease America's responsibility. That never happened. Shocked outrage greeted President Jimmy Carter's proposal to remove most U.S. troops, and that proposal eventually died. Carter's successor, Ronald

Reagan, reaffirmed the one-way U.S. commitment. Year after year of record economic growth did nothing to change American policy under presidents George H. W. Bush and Bill Clinton. Only pressure from the war on terrorism has prompted President George W. Bush to reconfigure, and perhaps finally reduce, Washington's force presence.

South Korea is one of America's most obvious security free-riders. The ROK vastly outstrips its northern antagonist, possessing about 40 times the GDP, enjoying a vast technological edge, and sporting a large economic presence around the globe. The South also has twice the population of the DPRK, is friendly with every major international and regional power, in contrast to the erratic North, and long ago won the diplomatic contest throughout the Third World.

However, argues Peter Huessy of GeoStrategic Analysis, a defense consulting firm, "the ROK's population, GDP and per capita income are all irrelevant to its defense."[2] That is true only in the sense of the South's military capabilities today. It says nothing about its potential defense capabilities. Moreover, simply citing the North's quantitative lead, 1.1 million to 686,000 armed services personnel, for instance (as defenders of the U.S. commitment to South Korea typically do), does not say much about actual combat capabilities either.[3]

In any case, the existing personnel and materiel imbalance is not inevitable, some immutable aspect of geography on the Korean peninsula. Rather, it results from past ROK free-riding. Seoul's failure to invest heavily in defense today to close the gap reflects current free-riding. The South can do so only because it relies on the U.S. presence as a supplemental deterrent to North Korean aggression. That the relationship is beneficial to the ROK is obvious. That it is in America's interest is not.

HISTORY OF THE U.S.–ROK RELATIONSHIP

There was little in the start of America's relationship with Korea that suggested Washington would ever have a security interest in the peninsula. Korea was forever a pawn in a larger regional game of power politics. Surrounded by China, Japan, and Russia, for centuries Koreans found themselves dominated by one imperial power or another. Washington attempted to assert itself commercially in China through the "open door" policy, but the United States lacked the proximity, ability, and commitment to impose its will in East Asia.[4]

America's first contacts with Korea were sporadic maritime visits. Little came of them until 1866, when the schooner *General Sherman* sailed up the Taedong River near Pyongyang. Allegedly intent on trade, the ship's crew was apparently planning on some profitable looting.[5] Alas, the ship ran aground and the crew was killed. Secretary of State William Seward proposed a joint punitive expedition to the French, who refused, and later proposed sending a naval task force to blast open the markets of the so-called Hermit Kingdom. In 1870 an expedition finally did set sail, modeled after Commodore Matthew Perry's famous "black ships," which had ended Japan's international isolation 16 years before. Another fight ensued, with the U.S. forces unable to impose a commercial treaty. The regent for King Kojong branded the Americans as "pirates" and "sea-wolf brigands," and called for resistance to any future invasions.[6]

As Japan increased its influence, however, King Kojong changed course. He concluded the Treaty of Peace, Amity, Commerce, and Navigation with America on May 22, 1882. In an accord modeled after the U.S.–Chinese agreement, Korea granted commercial privileges and extraterritorial status; the United States offered its "good offices" to help Korea resist foreign oppression. Reports Hahm Pyong-choon, former ROK ambassador to the United States, "The Korean leaders read into the Korean-American treaty of 1882 something that was not there: a strategic commitment on the part of the United States to intervene to preserve the sovereignty and political independence of the Kingdom of Korea."[7] As Tokyo tightened its grip, Korea's pathetic pleas for assistance grew ever more insistent.[8] Had Washington taken the latter seriously, Korea might have become a security free-rider seven decades earlier.

But Washington had no interest in fighting with China, Japan, or Russia to protect Korea. In 1905 Washington recognized Japanese predominance in Korea, terminated the two nations' treaty, and closed its Korean legation. For the next 35 years Korea essentially disappeared as an issue for Washington, except for the private campaign, waged by émigrés and American supporters, on behalf of Korean independence.

Then came World War II. Even then Korea, a Japanese colony, was not of much interest until the collapse of Japan became imminent. Then policymakers in Washington became concerned about the disposition of Korea—though, in one famous story, Secretary of State Edward Stettinius Jr. had to request a map to locate the nation. At Yalta in February 1945 Washington and Moscow agreed to a four-power trusteeship for the peninsula, but left the details to a committee; Harry Truman, who became president in April, was more skeptical of the proposal, which was subordinated to plans for the final defeat of Japan.

The United States was not prepared for Stalin's declaration of war against Japan, and, with Soviet troops racing for the peninsula, Washington requested that the USSR halt at the thirty-eighth parallel for what was to be a temporary division of the peninsula. The United States chose this line because it was as far north as policymakers thought Moscow would accept (in fact, there was some surprise when Stalin acceded to America's proposal).[9] The two occupiers agreed to establish a provisional government under a five-year trusteeship, reflecting Washington's view that the Koreans were not ready for full freedom, with independence to follow.

But the U.S.–Soviet partnership quickly broke down in Korea as well as in Europe once the Cold War began. Plans for peninsula-wide administration and elections went unfulfilled as both superpowers proceeded to create client states in their own images.[10] The USSR promoted communist and anti-Japanese guerrilla Kim Il-sung, while the United States relied on conservative nationalists, such as Rhee Syngman, to the exclusion of local leftist leaders. Observes Edward Olsen of the Naval Postgraduate School, "American haste to wash its hands of Korea induced a willingness to accept 'stability' at the cost of political pluralism."[11] Moreover, the division of the peninsula, although not intended by the United States to be permanent, stung. At the time many Koreans mouthed a popular slogan: "Don't rely on the United States, don't be deceived by the Soviets; Japan will rise again."[12]

Still, Seoul had little practical choice but to rely on America. The fact that the North refused to participate in UN-supervised elections with the South solidified the peninsula's partition. The ROK, with the repressive Rhee as president, was created in August 1948; the DPRK, led by the even more vicious Kim, emerged in December.[13] Both regimes claimed to represent the entire peninsula. "The ultimate result of great power rivalry . . . was to institutionalize the civil war in two contending states, both committed to the cause of unification," observes Callum MacDonald.[14] And that turned the ROK into another military client of the United States.

The two countries settled into a rather hot cold war, with frequent cross-border raids and formal military clashes. Moscow withdrew its troops from the North in late 1948; America's last forces left the South in July 1949.[15] Although Pentagon defense planners recognized that there was a risk of the North invading the South, they did not intend to unilaterally commit U.S. troops in the event of war. Given America's expanding military commitments in Europe and declining force levels, the U.S. reaction to any attack was to be an appeal to the United Nations.[16]

In his famous speech to the National Press Club on January 12, 1950, Secretary of State Dean Acheson excluded the ROK, along with the rest of the Asian mainland, from America's strategic "defense perimeter" and said that Seoul should look to the United Nations for help in deterring communist aggression. Although Acheson was only reiterating the stance of the Pentagon and even General Douglas MacArthur, he was widely blamed for having given the DPRK the go-ahead for war. The actual impact of his speech is difficult to gauge; President Truman appeared to tack away from its noninterventionist line shortly thereafter, and Acheson later denied that he had meant that Korea would not be defended, although Senate Foreign Relations Committee chairman Tom Connally had publicly taken much the same position just weeks after Acheson.[17]

In any case, the Pentagon had resisted proposals to increase military assistance to Rhee. The repressiveness of Rhee's administration (jailing political opponents and brutally suppressing media dissent) was one problem; moreover, Washington overestimated the ROK's military readiness.[18] Perhaps most important was Rhee's repeated threat to retake the "lost territories" in the North. As historian James Matray puts it: "Once Rhee had sufficient military power, there could be little doubt that he would attempt forcible reunification."[19] For this reason, Washington refused to equip the ROK's military with aircraft, tanks, and other heavy equipment, and the United States provided only limited ammunition stocks. Thus, Washington created a foolishly aggressive client but left it too weak to do anything but free-ride on the United States—while threatening war at America's expense.

On June 25, 1950, North Korean forces crossed the thirty-eighth parallel.[20] The Truman administration responded almost immediately. Although Washington had long believed that the ROK itself was not strategically significant, officials feared the impact on Japan (which was then seeking greater autonomy from the U.S. occupation authority), the implication for the global struggle between Washington and Moscow, and the possibility of a similar attack by East Germany on its western counterpart. As historian Glenn Paige puts it, "the President and his advisers had no doubt whatever that the North Korean invasion had been inspired and controlled by the Soviet Union."[21] That assumption was not true, but the United States reacted as if it were. President Truman attempted to contain the invasion first by supplying equipment to the ROK and then by launching naval and air strikes. However, the South

Korean army was overwhelmed by both surprise and tanks; it yielded Seoul in only three days. So Truman sent in American troops in what he termed a "police action."

The resulting three years of war are well known: America's race to the Yalu River, China's devastating entry into the war, and the lengthy stalemate near the original border. An armistice was signed on July 27, 1953. Yet Rhee, always a difficult wartime partner, resisted. Writes historian Clay Blair: "He never relented in his efforts to sabotage the armistice. Throughout the talks he had demanded that no concessions whatsoever be granted the Communists, that the [Chinese forces] be expelled from North Korea, that the [North Korean army] be disarmed, and that all Korea be united under the ROK government. [When] the armistice appeared to be impervious to sabotage, Rhee declared that South Korea would not honor its terms and that he might detach the ROK Army from the UN command and continue the war alone."[22] In the end, Rhee did not—without American participation he would have quickly lost any armed struggle—although along the way he freed North Korean prisoners of war and otherwise attempted to undermine the armistice negotiations.[23] But promises of a U.S. defense guarantee and financial aid mixed with threats to let the ROK face the North and China alone (buttressed by covert planning for an American-backed coup) ended his resistance. Still desiring to liberate the entire peninsula—while continuing to free-ride on American military power—Rhee refused to sign the accord.

WASHINGTON'S POST–KOREAN WAR COMMITMENT

No formal peace treaty was ever reached. As a cold peace descended on the peninsula, Washington negotiated a defense treaty with South Korea. Or as Youngnok Koo of the University of Michigan puts it, Rhee "extracted" the agreement, which the United States used to mollify him because of his dissatisfaction with the war's indecisive outcome.[24] The Mutual Defense Treaty, ratified in January 1954, does not explicitly guarantee U.S. military assistance to the ROK; rather, it states that each party "would act to meet the common danger in accordance with its constitutional processes," a caveat that later caused Seoul to request a strengthening of the clause.[25]

However, the continued presence of U.S. soldiers in the ROK acted as a tripwire that would make American participation in combat automatic. One infantry division—all the American ground forces likely to be present in the event of a surprise North Korean attack—adds little to the ability of the ROK's

560,000-man army in stopping an invasion. Observed General John Bahnsen, the chief of staff of the ROK/U.S. Combined Field Army during the early 1980s, "The wisdom of maintaining any U.S. infantry in a country so rich in manpower is purely political."[26] What those soldiers, wherever they are based in South Korea, do is guarantee immediate American casualties, making it unlikely that any U.S. administration would fail to order full-scale participation. It is equally unlikely that any Congress would challenge such a decision. Thus, while the treaty gives a perfunctory nod to the operation of America's constitutional processes, particularly the requirement that Congress declare war and fund military operations, the practical implementation of the treaty would effectively short-circuit these requirements.

It is no wonder, then, that South Korean officials opposed the Bush administration's decision to redeploy U.S. forces southward. It is the very visible tripwire to the treaty that has allowed the South to free-ride on America. Ironically, at least half of Korea has achieved the old kingdom's original objective of gaining the United States as regional protector.

As noted in chapter 1, after the war America continued to support the ROK despite Rhee's despotic and erratic rule. And although the United States drew down its troop levels, which had peaked at 360,000 during the war, it left two divisions, for a total of about 60,000 troops, after 1957. U.S. financial aid and military support continued after Rhee's fall and the rise of Park Chung-hee, because the peninsula was regarded as an integral part of the Cold War struggle. Explained John Spanier of the University of Florida: "The Asian balance depended upon the United States until the non-Communist states of the area became economically developed and possessed sufficient capabilities of their own. Commitments . . . were interdependent. The United States could not choose to defend West Berlin and Quemoy but not Matsu and South Korea."[27]

In 1963 Pentagon planners considered reducing U.S. forces but held off after South Korea dispatched some soldiers to Vietnam (in part to forestall any American drawdown). The United States continued to fund the bulk of South Korean's defense effort; it was 1969 before U.S. military aid accounted for less than 50 percent of the ROK's defense expenditures. In early 1970 President Nixon decided that additional troop reductions in Asia were desirable—reflecting a shift in U.S. strategy as Washington began to look to a post-Vietnam War era. He withdrew the Seventh Army Division the following year, leaving about 40,000 personnel stationed in Korea.

That decision horrified the ROK, which had grown accustomed to American protection. The Park government cited not only the North's military superiority, but also claimed that only an American presence could deter Chinese and Soviet support for a DPRK invasion.[28] However, Nixon helped purchase Korea's acquiescence, if not assent, to the pullout by authorizing a $1.5-billion, five-year military modernization program for ROK forces. (Additional U.S. force withdrawals were to begin in 1973, but were not carried out as the Watergate scandal consumed the Nixon presidency and North Vietnam conquered the Republic of Vietnam.[29]) Although Gerald Ford's administration admitted that Chinese intervention in any conflict was unlikely, it contended that the U.S. military commitment in the ROK remained necessary "to serve as a symbol of America's continued interest in the overall stability of that part of the world during a period of some tension."[30]

But President Carter proved far more concerned about Seoul's poor human rights record than had been his predecessors. In 1978 he pulled 3,600 soldiers out of South Korea, the first step of his plan to remove all ground forces (leaving 14,000 U.S. air force personnel and logistics specialists) by 1982. The defense guarantee would have remained in place, allowing continued ROK free-riding, but Seoul still resisted. Carter, too, attempted to buy Korea's sufferance to a troop reduction, through a $2.2-billion, five-year program of credit and weapons transfers. However, opposition to the president's plan emerged in the U.S. military, Congress, and even his own administration. Again, such critics linked Korea to the hegemonic threat to America in the larger Cold War. Under congressional pressure Carter put his plan "in abeyance."

Carter might have revived the program had he won reelection, for a military regime arose in the aftermath of the October 1979 assassination of President Park. The Carter administration attempted to use diplomatic and economic pressure to encourage political liberalization, but to no effect. Then in 1981 Carter was gone. President Reagan, who considered the ROK to be a front-line state in the struggle against global communism, immediately moved to improve relations with Seoul, reaffirming America's commitment to the South's defense and inviting South Korean president Chun Doo-hwan to be the first foreign head of state to visit during his administration. Although ROK defense free-riding was growing more evident in the midst of the South's rapid economic growth, in 1986 Secretary of Defense Caspar Weinberger pledged that American troops would remain there "as long as the people of Korea want and need that presence."[31] Amazingly, some conservative analysts were calling the alliance as important as ever and warning that China and the Soviet Union were still likely to back a northern attack, which could lead to both conquest of the ROK and "Finlandization" of Japan.[32]

Although South Korea was not inclined to take over its defense even as it emerged on the international stage as a significant economic player, its evident success led to domestic calls for winning a greater say in the operation of the alliance. The ROK army resented the fact that the Combined Forces Command, with nominal authority over most Korean forces, was headed by an American. Average Koreans—housewives and businessmen as well as radical students—disliked the inconvenience and cost of a U.S. base near the center of Seoul. And many Koreans were angered by the Status of Forces Agreement, which, as noted earlier, accorded American soldiers special treatment when accused of a crime. Not only was the ROK a free-rider; it was turning into an increasingly ungrateful one.

Yet nothing seemed to shake America's willingness to guarantee South Korea's security. Shortly after taking office, President George H. W. Bush promised to maintain America's troop presence "as long as they are needed and as long as we believe it is in the interest of peace to keep them there."[33] Assistant Secretary of State for East Asian Affairs Richard Solomon proclaimed in 1991 that "the United States intends to maintain appropriate forces in Korea so long as our two governments agree that a U.S. presence is necessary to deter a renewed outbreak of hostilities."[34]

President Clinton maintained a similar policy: preserving existing military deployments and promising to do so as long as the ROK desired. When he visited the South in 1993, he told the Korean National Assembly that "the Korean Peninsula remains a vital U.S. interest."[35] In the aftermath of the June 2000 summit between South Korea's President Kim Dae-jung and the DPRK's Kim Jong-il, Secretary of State Albright emphasized the necessity of maintaining 37,000 troops in the South. Indeed, the Clinton administration actually halted the first Bush administration's planned troop drawdown to 30,000 troops and beefed up U.S. forces in response to North Korea's intransigence on the nuclear issue. Explained the Defense Department in early 1995:

Our security relationship with the Republic of Korea continues to be central to the stability of the Korean Peninsula and Northeast Asia, as it has been for over forty years . . .

The relationship between the United States and the Republic of Korea is more than a treaty commitment, it is a vital component in our national objective of supporting and promoting democracy. Even after the North Korean threat passes, the United States intends to maintain its strong defense alliance with the Republic of Korea, in the interest of regional security.[36]

There was more movement under President George W. Bush, but only in the midst of frustration with the South's relatively pacific approach toward the North over the nuclear issue and pressure to find additional troops to maintain an unexpectedly difficult occupation of Iraq. The administration agreed to give up Yongsan base in Seoul, long an objective of the South Korean government, and arranged to move its forces away from the DMZ, a step not sought by the ROK. Washington has more recently talked of removing upward of 12,000 troops from the peninsula. Barely a year after electing the presidential candidate most critical of the U.S.–ROK alliance, many South Koreans loudly complained that American forces would no longer act as a tripwire, ensuring casualties and hence massive military reinforcement, in the event of another North Korean invasion.[37]

Although moving troops southward could be a sophisticated step to reduce opposition to ultimate disengagement, by making the final step seem less radical, Defense Secretary Rumsfeld proclaimed that America's commitment and capability to deter the North remained unchanged.[38] Deputy Secretary of Defense Wolfowitz promised that the step would actually increase deterrence.[39] In June 2002 Secretary of State Powell claimed that America's mission had not changed despite vastly changing world circumstances: "Our 37,000 military men and women in Korea today have exactly [the] same mission I had when I commanded an infantry battalion 30 years ago facing the DMZ: stop an attack from North Korea at all costs."[40]

Moreover, Washington planned an $11 billion force enhancement program in the South and a shift of air resources to Guam and Okinawa—hardly steps to put more military responsibility on South Korea.[41] Finally, Washington watered down its initial proposal in the face of ROK objections. Reported a Korean magazine, "The fourth-round meeting made significant revisions on several agreements from the previous round that were deemed not to be sustainable in light of the possible security vacuum Korea might suffer as a result of the alignment of front-line U.S. forces," including retaining some Americans near the DMZ.[42] Most important, no American forces were going to be withdrawn: they would simply move 45 miles south of Seoul—out of easy artillery and Scud missile range.[43] The biggest hint of change, but also evidence of its limited nature, came when Secretary Rumsfeld opined during his visit to the ROK in November 2003: "It is time for them to set a goal for becoming somewhat more self-reliant." (Personnel strains caused by the Iraq war, however, are now causing Washington to propose withdrawing one-third of the U.S. forces stationed in the ROK.)[44]

A TIME FOR FULL SELF-RELIANCE

In fact, it is well past time for South Korea to become "somewhat more self-reliant." With large numbers of U.S. troops tied up in a violent occupation of Iraq, fighting resurgent Taliban and al Qaeda elements in Afghanistan, pursuing terrorists elsewhere around the globe, and prepared to handle any number of unexpected international contingencies, why should Washington commit substantial manpower, materiel, and now even more money to Korea? American policymakers remain stuck in the world of a half century ago.

Korea, neglected and exploited by its Japanese colonial overlords, possessed neither economic nor military power when the United States and the Soviet Union moved in. But by 1950 the DPRK had achieved military superiority primarily because of Soviet backing. As historian William Stueck puts it, "The inequality of the contest had much to do with the relative support given the two sides from beyond Korea's boundaries."[45] Washington did less for its client because the United States thought the stakes were less and feared the aggressiveness of its ally, a concern not evident in Moscow. Alas, it took Washington three years of war to redress the imbalance.

The ROK was equally vulnerable at the close of the war in 1953. Both Koreas had been devastated by the fighting and could ill afford to stand alone. No renaissance seemed likely for the South under an authoritarian and unpopular government, led by an aging and unreasonable petty despot. At the same time, hundreds of thousands of Chinese soldiers remained in the North, fully capable of reigniting the conflict. If South Korea was going to be defended, it would be by America.

Although the Chinese troops eventually went home, the DPRK's two major communist allies were next door. And the ROK remained desperately poor, with a per capita GDP estimated to be no more no more than $100, and perhaps under $90, in the early 1960s. The North, though limited by its reliance on Stalinist central planning, initially benefited from the large pool of skilled labor in the northern part of the peninsula, where Japan had concentrated industry, and where there were more plentiful natural resources and hydroelectric power. The ROK had little more global economic contact than did Pyongyang: annual exports, primarily commodities such as animal products and silk, typically totaled a meager $40 million.

But Park Chung-hee, though a military dictator, adopted an export-oriented, market-friendly economic policy. South Korea rapidly turned into one of the world's greatest success stories.[46] From 1962 to 1993 economic growth averaged a staggering 8.5 percent annually. Its economy regularly expanded at double-digit rates in the latter 1980s. As a result, the South became an important regional economic player.[47]

The Asian economic crisis of 1997 notwithstanding, another decade of growth has turned the ROK into a global economic power. Although the country suffered a recession early in 2003, exports jumped an astounding 19.6 percent that year, and the South is expected to enjoy growth of 5 to 6 percent in 2004.[48] With a GDP running $545 billion in 2001, South Korea has the fourth largest economy in Asia, the twelfth largest in the world. Its per capita GDP exceeds that of Russia (its total GDP runs about two-thirds of that of Russia), once the feared ally of its bitter enemy. Better policies should accelerate the South's growth. Seoul unnecessarily prolonged its economic agony after the 1997 crash by resisting many of the liberalizing steps necessary to reduce the expensive and counterproductive privileges enjoyed by entrenched business elites.[49] The country would do better today with further reforms, particularly rationalizing a banking system that continues to provide economic preferences for well-connected business leaders and cutting off subsidies to influential firms.[50]

Pyongyang has been left far behind in the economic contest. The North, which during the 1960s is thought to have had a higher per capita GDP (although a smaller total GDP) than did the ROK, began to fall behind at an accelerating rate during the 1970s. It has since become an economic wreck, whose economy was estimated to have shrunk by half between 1993 and 1996 alone; its subsequent "recovery" is thought to have pushed per capita GDP to about $700, roughly 40 percent of the 1990 level, which suggests a total GDP of about $16 billion.[51] Another GDP estimate runs about $17 billion, although no calculation is easy with such an isolated and antiquated economy.[52]

Food production is down 60 percent over the last 15 years. Much of the country is enveloped in darkness because of electricity shortages much of the time. Life expectancy fell 10 percent during the 1990s; during the same decade hundreds of thousands, and perhaps as many as 2 million, people starved to death. Nearly 6 in 10 North Koreans are thought to be malnourished.[53] Although the DPRK has avoided a repeat of the worst famine of the mid-1990s, it still cannot feed itself and has been reduced to begging for millions of tons of food aid.[54]

Perhaps the best comparison of the two economies comes through purchasing power equivalents rather than exchange rate calculations. Estimates for the South and North respectively in 2002 ran $941.5 billion versus $22.26

billion for GDP; $19,600 versus $1,000 for per capita GDP; and 6.3 percent versus 1 percent real annual growth.[55] Although there seems to have been evidence of limited improvement in the DPRK economy in recent years, continuing famine and grotesque inefficiencies lead to warnings of inevitable collapse.[56]

With the ROK's economic growth has come abundant resources, industrialization, high-technology production, and access to international capital markets. Thus, the longer a war, the greater the South's advantage: as its Ministry of National Defense puts it, "South Korea has a comfortable edge over North Korea in terms of war sustainability."[57]

Economic growth also improves a country's ability to make war materiel. As the South's economy took off, the Pentagon acknowledged that the ROK's aircraft, transportation system, and military-industrial capability were superior to those in the DPRK.[58] Along with the military-industrial capability came development of an indigenous arms industry. A nation that in the 1970s did not even make its own rifles was producing, a decade later, virtually all of its conventional arms, including F–5 fighters, helicopters, rocket launchers, self-propelled howitzers, M48 and T88 tanks, armored personnel carriers, frigates, Hawk and Honest John missiles, and more.[59] Said the ROK's Ministry of National Defense, "South Korea can claim an increasing edge over the North in military science and technology, backed by the rapid growth of its aerospace, automobile, communication and electronic industries."[60] And that was more than a decade ago.

Since then South Korea has begun a serious space program, launching a three-stage liquid-fueled rocket, produced at home, in late 2002; the ROK stated that it hoped to launch a satellite in another two years.[61] Seoul also has unveiled plans for a blue-water navy—one apparently directed at Japan and China more than North Korea.[62] Indeed, in January 2004 the conservative newspaper *Chosun Ilbo* reported that Seoul was developing plans for several nuclear-power submarines to confront "powerful neighbors."[63] Observed one American military analyst: "As the perceived threat from the NKPA [North Korean People's Army] has diminished, the ROK military has looked ahead and attempted to develop military capabilities to reduce its dependence on the United States and to meet future security challenges."[64]

Which leaves only the present, in which the North retains an advantage. According to the International Institute for Strategic Studies, Pyongyang maintains an active-duty force of 1,082,000. It possesses 3,500 main battle tanks; 560 light tanks; 2,500 armored personnel carriers (APCs); 3,500 pieces of towed artillery; 4,400 self-propelled artillery pieces; and 2,500 multiple rocket launchers (MRLs). The South, in contrast, has only 686,000 active-duty soldiers, although its formal reserve is larger than the North's. It also generally lags on equipment, with 1,000 tanks; 1,700 APCs; 3,500 towed artillery pieces; 1,040 self-propelled artillery pieces; and 156 MRLs. The DPRK possesses more naval vessels, although it trails in total tonnage, and more planes, although the South's fleet is more modern.[65]

However, although the North's military is large, it is also decrepit. Not surprisingly, an enfeebled economy is not producing a potent military. In 1997 CIA director George Tenet told the U.S. Senate that "the [North Korean] military has had to endure shortages of food and fuel, increased susceptibility to illness, declining morale, often sporadic training and a lack of new equipment."[66]

The North's latest weapons are often 1990 vintage or older; spare parts and training are nonexistent. Pyongyang's dramatic attempt to put a satellite into orbit in 1998 failed. Reports Defense Intelligence Agency analyst Bruce Bechtol: "The North Korean military is one that is using antiquated 1950s and 1960s vintage weapons while the South Korean military continues to strengthen itself with dynamic new programs such as the building of brand new F–16s. In addition, the South is superior in other key aspects of military readiness, such as command and control and training."[67]

The latter is critically important. The ROK's soldiers are believed to be better trained and led—a significant advantage. Observes *Jane's Intelligence Review:* "The North Koreans may lack the small unit skills necessary to turn military theory into practice."[68] DPRK pilots get far less flight time than their southern counterparts. The North has apparently never run joint-service training exercises—even in the feared special forces. Finally, the North's forces are likely to follow Soviet-style centralized command system, which hinders battlefield initiative, while South Korea's forces are modeled more on the flexible western model.

Moreover, South Korea would be fighting on the defensive in mountainous terrain with limited tank invasion routes. Nearly two decades ago the International Institute for Strategic Studies concluded that "the opposing forces on the Korean peninsula are roughly equivalent. Neither is capable of a successful major offensive against the other without significant foreign assistance."[69] Indeed, in the initial stage of any war, South Korea would have to rely primarily on its own military for ground forces, irrespective of America's defense commitment. It would take the United States three or more weeks to deploy heavy armored and mechanized reinforcements, depending on events elsewhere and available lift capabilities.[70]

Finally, to the extent that the ROK's military lags behind that of its northern antagonist, it is a matter of choice, not necessity—even granted Peter Huessy's "8 year, and perhaps 13 year, procurement and acquisition cycle" for long-range air power and major seapower.[71] Why can Seoul not shorten the process by acquiring U.S. weapons? And why did it not begin to develop new weapons over the last two decades, as economic growth has delivered the necessary resources for increased military investments? Truly shocking is how little the ROK military has grown over the last decade.[72] In fact, not only is the South's effort lower, as a percentage of GDP, than it was before the economic crisis of 1997; it is less than half the peak, back in 1981.[73]

Lack of opportunity does not explain Seoul's failure to augment its forces, if it believes those forces to be inadequate. In 1979 an irritated President Carter asked ROK dictator Park Chung-hee why South Korea, with a much larger economy than the North, did not match the latter's military spending.[74] Park had no good excuse; after all, no special gravitational field prevents Seoul from building a larger force. Rather, an American tripwire discourages it from doing so. Why should Park's government spend more on defense when the money instead could be invested in economic development?

Similarly, why should Roh Moo-hyun's government spend more on defense when the money instead could be invested in economic development? By one estimate, re-creating America's defense capabilities would cost $30 billion, twice South Korea's present annual defense budget.[75] As the South acknowledges in its own defense reports, it *chose* to focus on economic development at the expense of military strength, which it could do secure in America's protection.[76]

Obviously, the ROK can easily outspend—vastly outspend—Pyongyang on defense. Moreover, the North cannot count on any outside factors, such as large-scale Soviet aid and the return of 20,000 battle-hardened Koreans who had served in the Chinese military, which gave it a decided advantage over the ROK in 1950, to fill the gap.[77] Although the United States could sell a full range of weapons to South Korea, financial credit and weapons transfers from China and Russia to the North have largely dried up. Indeed, in the mid-1990s Moscow began shipping arms to Seoul to help pay off its debt and has proposed joint development of high-tech weapons.[78]

Of course, it still would be foolish for Seoul to be complacent. But the ROK should squarely face the problem of complacency. The reasons for allowing the South to free-ride on the United States—the ROK's relative poverty and the DPRK's backing by China and the USSR—have disappeared.

But as long as South Korea can count on American military support, it has no reason not to free-ride, whatever promises it might make to the contrary.

Indeed, President Roh Moo-hyun's apparent conversion from critic of the American military presence to advocate—calling it "precious," for instance—demonstrates the reluctance of even Korean nationalists to accept their nation's responsibility for its own defense.[79] South Koreans (and Americans) have for years prophesied Seoul's imminent achievement of parity against the North. For instance, in 1970, after President Nixon announced his plan to withdraw one U.S. division, South Korea's President Park stated that his nation's forces would be superior to those of the North by 1975.[80] In 1975 Park declared that in just a few more years the ROK would require no American assistance, not even air, naval, or logistical support: "We want the capability to defend ourselves, and that will take four or five years."[81] Similar claims were made throughout the 1980s and 1990s. But the free-riding continues. After all, with America's protection, the Ministry of National Defense admitted that it could concentrate "on its economic and social development" while North Korea emphasized military production.[82]

President Roh Moo-hyun has pledged to increase military spending, returning to the 3.2 percent (up from today's 2.7 percent) of GDP spent before the 1997 economic crisis. His government has proposed a series of qualitative improvements and force restructuring as well as enhanced research and development.[83] The ROK also is deploying 111 U.S.-made missiles with a 300-kilometer range, meaning they can strike most anywhere in North Korea. The program foresees a 42 percent increase in defense investment and reinstates work on AWACS surveillance aircraft, refueling aircraft, and Patriot missiles. Alas, although long overdue, the plan merely moves outlays back to pre-1997 levels. Moreover, the proposal has generated opposition on a variety of grounds, including the argument that the South already could defeat the DPRK and that a collective defense strategy (i.e., continuing to rely on the United States) is a better approach.[84] One magazine article argued that such a budgetary increase "is nearly inconceivable" given "the sluggish economy, and the growing need for more welfare expenditures."[85]

In any case, the ROK's claim to be building a "self-reliant defense" is misleading.[86] President Roh did not aim for genuine self-sufficiency without U.S. support. As he explained: "We should have self-reliance in defending our nation, and a military alliance and multilateral security mechanism should be complementary measures."[87] His government's 2003 defense white paper reported that Washington and Seoul "agreed that the ROK Armed Forces expand its role in defending the Korean Peninsula."[88] Even if Roh wins the necessary funds from a skeptical National Assembly, the free-riding is to continue, just to a somewhat less egregious degree.

Ultimately, the issue comes down to money. Strangely, some South Korean analysts seemed to believe that the ROK was not free-riding if it devoted *anything* toward its own defense. For instance, in the early years of the U.S.–ROK relationship, Chung Jin-young, a professor at Kyung Hee University wrote: "South Korea provided free land for USFK [U.S. Forces in Korea] bases and supported manpower through the Korean Augmentation to the U.S. Army."[89] One is tempted to ask "So what?"—especially since Chung acknowledges that exemption from taxes is counted as support and Seoul contributed no cash toward the American presence until 1989. More incredibly, some South Koreans argue that they were spending too much because, for instance, their nation devotes a larger percentage of its GDP to the military than did Germany and Japan.[90] But the relevant measure is the ROK's contribution compared to both its capability and the magnitude of the threat. Providing some land rent-free while the United States offers its full military faith and credit toward the ROK's defense demonstrates free-riding of the most blatant sort.

Indeed, the problem of free-riding also was evident in the phenomenon noted in chapter 1, of South Koreans insisting on "equality" with the United States even as they resisted contributing toward America's efforts in Iraq. Secretary of Defense Rumsfeld said, "We'd like assistance. We'd like troop assistance, we'd like humanitarian assistance, we'd like financial assistance."[91] However, Seoul's response was reluctant, hesitant, delayed, and miserly.[92] Ill-considered the U.S. war and occupation might be, but the ROK hesitated to spend money and risk lives to aid America even though Washington had for a half century spent money and risked lives to defend South Korea.

Even more blatant was the proposal by the Institute of Foreign Affairs and National Security (IFANS) for continuing the alliance after Korea's reunification. The institute, reported the newspaper *Han Kook Ilbo,* observed: "Any military alliance between a unified Korea and the U.S. . . . would have to be closely restricted to Northeast Asia to stave off the possibility of Korea being involved in global conflicts under U.S. leadership."[93] That is, Washington should continue to defend the ROK; Seoul should do nothing to aid the United States. IFANS scholar Kim Sung-han was forthright in his goal: "If South Korea wants to avoid a situation in which it has to astronomically increase its defense expenditure due to the withdrawal of US forces, it should try to keep the alliance alive—even after the possible future disappearance of the North Korean threat."[94]

Figuring the exact value of America's defense subsidy for the ROK is not easy. The cost of raising and maintaining units stationed in South Korea as well as those destined to reinforce them in event of a conflict—such as the Marine Expeditionary Force on Okinawa—probably runs on the order of $15 to $20 billion annually.[95] Seoul has made various attempts to estimate what it would have to spend to compensate for an American troop withdrawal. In 1989 Defense Minister Lee Sang-hoon estimated that increasing ROK military outlays from 5 to 8 percent of GNP would offset an American withdrawal.[96] In the summer of 1995 analysts at the Korean Institute for Defense Analyses reached much the same result.[97] More recently, as noted earlier, the ROK government figured $30 billion extra spending would be necessary.

That would be a major burden, but hardly unreasonable for a wealthy country threatened by an aggressive and well-armed neighbor. Indeed, no one in the ROK says the country would be helpless without America's presence. Rather, they complain about the added expense. The South simply has refused to do more. That Seoul does not want to up its spending is understandable. But that reluctance is no reason for the United States to maintain troops in the ROK.

In fact, when presented in the past with an obvious need to do more, South Korea has responded. Between 1954 and 1955 the United States withdrew six infantry divisions—China was simultaneously reducing its force presence in the North. Seoul added five infantry divisions. Similar has been South Korea's reaction to later reductions in America's commitment: the Nixon cutbacks, Carter withdrawal program, and conflict with America over human rights all convinced Seoul, observes Asian expert Ralph Clough, "that South Korea must move quickly to become less dependent on the United States for its defense."[98] The Korean government itself admits as much.[99]

Clough writes that President Nixon's withdrawal of the Seventh Division in 1971 came "as a shock to the South Koreans."[100] The result was a dramatic takeoff in South Korean military expenditures and development of indigenous arms production. As one South Korean officer put it, "The disappointing US withdrawal [under Nixon] gave the ROK government and soldiers a chance to realize the importance of self-reliance."[101] Seoul's Five-Year Modernization Plan, supported by U.S. aid, helped trigger a nearly tenfold increase in military spending over 15 years, which soon boosted South Korean defense spending far above that of the North.[102]

Although President Carter's proposal to withdraw U.S. forces was whittled down and eventually abandoned, it, like the Nixon shock, helped push the South toward the "self-reliant" defense that it now claims as a goal. Wrote Makoto Momoi, of Japan's National Defense College:

The Seoul government responded to the withdrawal plan by moving to consolidate the populace behind President Park . . . and by taking steps to accelerate the modernization of the Korean armed forces. Not only was the ROK's Force Improvement Program stepped up, but there was a more rapid development of South Korean defense production capabilities, including substantial improvements in the capabilities for production of sophisticated arms. Equally important, the South Korean people demonstrated an increased willingness to bear sacrifice. Even opposition groups rallied to support the president on this issue. This left the South Koreans feeling stronger and more self-confident than before.[103]

Small-scale force cuts also were made by President George H. W. Bush. In 1993 Seoul's Ministry of National Defense reported that "South Korea has drawn up its own contingency plan, with a view to minimizing the effects of too rapid a reduction of [American] troops, easing military tension on the Korean peninsula, and achieving a more self-reliant defense posture in the long run."[104] Two years later the Ministry noted: "We urgently need to secure a combat capability to replace the reduced U.S. forces as they pursue their reduction and role change. Since assistance from the U.S. has served as the cornerstone of our defense, [the modest Bush troop] reduction has been a major blow."[105]

The Bush II plan to redeploy and (initially) reduce U.S. forces may provide a similar catalyst. For instance, as noted, President Roh suggested pushing ROK defense outlays up from 2.7 percent to 3.2 percent of GDP, the level that existed when South Korea's economy nosedived in 1997.

That is a fine start, but not nearly enough. The objective needs to be full defense devolution. Years ago Henry Rowen, a former president of the RAND Corporation who also served in the Defense Department and the Bureau of the Budget, observed: "Seoul's present military deficiencies exist because of earlier decisions that South Korea would rely on the United States in those areas. So long as a decision has been made to develop ROK capabilities in these areas, it should not be difficult to overcome these weaknesses."[106]

THE COSTS OF FREE-RIDING

South Korean free-riding might be of little concern to America if it was costless. That is, the problem with today's alliance is not that the ROK spends too little; it is that the United States spends too much. Unfortunately, providing

defense guarantees—and maintaining the forces necessary to back them up—
is not cheap.

Most obvious is the financial expense. As noted earlier, it costs upward of
$20 billion annually to maintain the units based in Korea, as well as those des-
tined to intervene in the event of war. The issue is less the expense of basing
the units overseas, since the ROK and Japan, in particular, provide "host nation" support, than the cost of the units themselves, which exist only to back
up the security commitment embodied in the defense treaty. In short, military
spending is the price of America's foreign policy.

Billions in defense subsidies to allied nations (South Korea is merely one
beneficiary, of course) have a dual impact. One is on domestic economic policy, since such outlays further inflate tax collections and government borrow-
ing, diverting resources away from more productive private investment.
Perhaps even more serious is the international impact. American defense subsidies not only impoverish U.S. taxpayers; they simultaneously enrich foreign
nations that are major trade competitors. Allowing South Korea (as well as
Japan and a host of European nations) to concentrate domestic resources on
economic rather than military development puts American enterprises at a dis-
advantage. That cost was modest and probably worth enduring during the
early days of the Cold War; there is no longer any reason to indirectly under-
write large Korean, Japanese, and European businesses as they compete with
U.S. firms.

Also significant are several more intangible costs. Happily, the ROK's
move to democracy has largely eliminated Washington's identification with
military dictators, once a serious problem. For instance, as explained in chapter 1, some Koreans long blamed America for complicity in the 1980 massacre
in the city of Kwangju by South Korean government troops. Many pro-
democracy demonstrators in 1987 believed that the United States could dictate policy to President Chun Doo-hwan and criticized Washington for not
forcing the regime to accept free elections.[107] Nevertheless, the problem has
not entirely disappeared: now many South Koreans fear U.S. manipulation of
elections to promote Washington's interest. As noted earlier, some thought
that America orchestrated the North Korean nuclear crisis to generate hysteria
in the South and thus forestall the election of President Roh. They overestimated Washington's influence and competence, of course, but such beliefs
help poison the relationship between the two nations.

More important is the military risk of U.S. security ties. Although the
American commitment helps deter North Korean aggression, it ensures that
the United States will be involved if hostilities should occur again. Indeed, the

presence of 37,000 American soldiers is to make intervention automatic. Moreover, protecting the South discourages it from enhancing its own military, which reduces deterrence.

Although the risks of war are modest, the consequences would be horrific. The concentration of military power in Korea was unparalleled elsewhere in the world even during the Cold War; roughly 1.5 million troops face each other across a 155-mile border, in contrast to only 2 million soldiers along the entire 4,600-mile Sino-Soviet border when those two nations were involved in serious border skirmishes. Presumably the toll would not match that of the first Korean War, in which America's technological lead was not so great, the South was far less prepared to defend itself, and China intervened on the DPRK's side. However, credible estimates of casualties run 1 to 2 million.[108]

And the possible acquisition by North Korea of atomic weapons increases the potential costs exponentially; should a conflict come, the American troops would become nuclear hostages. The U.S. troop presence also may encourage risk-taking by both Koreas. Pyongyang could see a need to preempt an attempt by the United States at preventive war; a more hawkish South Korean government, feeling secure in America's protection, might challenge the North.[109] (However, Seoul's proximity to the border, and thus increased vulnerability to attack, seemingly counteracts the impact of the latter possibility, at least on the governments of Kim Dae-jung and Roh Moo-hyun.)

There obviously are times when the United States must go to war. But now is not the time, and the Korean peninsula is not the place. As argued in the next chapter, there are no vital American interests at stake warranting such costs and risks. The mere fact that the United States fought in Korea 50 years ago does not mean it should prepare to do so again; the best way to honor the sacrifice of so many soldiers in the last war is to ensure that no Americans will be forced to fight and die in a similar future conflict. This is not to say that Washington has no interests at stake in the peninsula—the cultural, economic, family, and political ties between the United States and the ROK are real—but they do not warrant a security guarantee and troop presence. In any case, Washington no longer needs to provide a military commitment to secure its interests. South Korea is now fully capable of defending itself.

Americans enjoy abundant and wide-ranging ties with South Korea. But the most expensive and dangerous link is the so-called Mutual Defense Treaty, which is mutual in name only. Today the ROK is a military black hole, a peripheral security interest that is not worth defending, and one that in any case is capable of defending itself. Yet, with the acquiescence of American policymakers, Seoul continues to free-ride on the United States. Rather than enhance its own military capabilities, South Korea lobbies Washington to maintain its generous security guarantee. In 1991 Seoul warned against "drastic" U.S. force reductions "until the Republic gains the capability to defend itself on its own."[110] Even then the ROK was capable of doing so. It is decidedly more so today. Unfortunately, it will never have an incentive to defend itself as long as Americans unnecessarily foot South Korea's defense bill. Ironically, as Seoul seemingly has moved closer to its professed goal of a "self-reliant" defense, it only resists more fervently actually creating a self-reliant defense.

The United States and Korea have achieved much together. But links between the two countries are growing increasingly fragile, since the raison d'être for Seoul's military free ride has disappeared. Although officials on neither side of the Pacific are ready to concede the obsolescence of the security structure that they have so laboriously constructed, it is bound to collapse. As the ROK grows richer, Pyongyang reforms or dies, America tires of underwriting a one-sided defense treaty, and South Korea no longer wishes to be treated as a protectorate, there likely will be a nasty divorce. Instead, the two governments should agree to an amicable separation. That means beginning, now, to plan a positive transition emphasizing a relationship of mutuality and equality rather than of dependency and inferiority.

Chapter Five

TIME FOR AN AMICABLE DIVORCE

The United States has defended South Korea for more than 50 years. The alliance with the Republic of Korea—in fact a one-sided security guarantee—has been America's most consistently dangerous commitment since World War II. The nearly 34,000 deaths in the Korean War have been supplemented with more recent occasional acts of war by North Korea: the 1968 seizure of the USS *Pueblo* and the 1976 murder of two U.S. soldiers who were cutting down a tree in the demilitarized zone. Reports of other, unpublicized incidents, including full-fledged firefights between North Korean soldiers entering the South and American forces, abound.[1] The Korea Defense Veterans of America estimate that there have been 1,500 American deaths over the years.[2]

As noted earlier, this costly security commitment has encouraged defense free-riding by the ROK. In the early years, Washington's one-sided guarantee could be justified by South Korea's evident weakness and the Korean peninsula's highly symbolic role in the Cold War. That world has disappeared: no more geopolitical struggle for survival, no more hegemonic communist alliance against the United States, no more impoverished American allies. All that remains is an isolated, desolate North Korea. It poses an ever-diminishing conventional threat to the South, one that the latter is ever more able to counter. As a result, writes Bong Youngshik of Wellesley College: "If one discusses Korean anti-Americanism in the context of the conventional ROK–U.S. military alliance, there exist reasons to doubt the strength of the alliance since it has been in search of a viable foundation to replace its traditional anti-Communist, anti-North Korean entente. In this regard, anti-U.S. sentiment in South Korea may be regarded as benign in the absolute sense yet dangerous in the context of the bilateral military alliance."[3]

WHY WASHINGTON SHOULD WANT A DIVORCE

One would think that the United States, stuck with the cost and risk of defending South Korea, would be most interested in promoting ROK self-sufficiency. Yet for some Americans the Mutual Defense Treaty has become the end rather than the means; a few U.S. analysts seem to regret South Korea's coming-of-age, so to speak, and fear even the perception that the South might become self-sufficient. For instance, at the 1989 U.S.–Korean Security Council conference in Seoul, one audience member asked whether the ROK could take on more responsibility within the current military structure. Yes, a Pentagon representative replied, but "it would call into question the presence of U.S. troops in Korea."[4] In short, if Koreans did more, the American people might wonder why their forces were still needed.

For instance, the 2000 Kim–Kim summit resulted in what Robert Manning of the Council on Foreign Relations called South Korean "giddiness." He worried about the "loose talk about the future of the U.S.–South Korean alliance and the U.S. military presence in Korea."[5]

The Clinton administration was equally concerned. P. J. Crowley, spokesman for the National Security Council, said that "we don't envision any change in the U.S. troop status."[6] Pentagon spokesman Kenneth Bacon explained that the ROK expects American troops to remain "for a long time to come."[7] Opined Secretary of State Madeleine Albright, "our forces, when they are stationed somewhere, provide evidence of America's interest." In Korea, she claimed, they promoted "stability."[8] She quickly dismissed the suggestion from then Senate Foreign Relations committee chairman Jesse Helms that the summit suggested a lessening of tensions that warranted reducing American troop levels. There might be a "new and refreshing spirit of reconciliation," she conceded, "but the continued presence of 37,000 troops" was still needed to promote "stability."[9]

Even now Department of Defense consultant Richard Weitz advocates a continued presence for the purpose of "rapidly halting any North Korean invasion," as if South Korea had no military.[10] Peter Brookes of the Heritage Foundation contends without evidence that "U.S. forces are required in South

Korea to deter future North Korean belligerence."[11] Defense consultant Peter Huessy derided withdrawal as "appeasement" of the North, even though the military deployment no longer serves American interests.[12] A Center for Strategic and International Studies report called for maintenance of the treaty, the continued presence of ground and air forces, and supplementing "the core military ties" with "a broader security agenda."[13] William J. Perry, Ashton B. Carter, and John Shalikashvili—leading Clinton administration figures—wrote of American and South Korean troops standing "shoulder to shoulder to deter North Korean aggression."[14] They did not explain why U.S. shoulders were necessary.

Some American analysts want even more American shoulders along the DMZ. Ralph Cossa, head of the Pacific Forum Center for Strategic and International Studies, has proposed a force buildup.[15] So has the Heritage Foundation.[16] The *Weekly Standard's* William Kristol worried about "shoring up the defense capabilities of South Korea."[17] Indeed, in February 2003 the Bush administration announced that it was supplementing its forces in Asia in response to a request from Admiral Thomas Fargo, Pacific commander of U.S. forces.[18] And as noted earlier, Washington offered the ROK an $11 billion force enhancement program to compensate for the modest troop redeployment.

The only factor that appears to have shaken the confidence of the "Korea alliance forever" crowd is rising South Korean hostility to America's presence. In the wake of President Roh's election, a growing number of American commentators, including some resolute hawks, said that the United States need not stay, and certainly not if it was not wanted.[19] The message has hit home even at the Pentagon. Former deputy assistant defense secretary Kurt Campbell observed: "Generally speaking, it is hard for our senior military people to believe that we are not loved. We are doing God's work, and if people don't appreciate it there is something wrong with them."[20] More broadly, noted Scott Snyder, the Korea representative for the Asia Foundation: "In Washington, within the U.S. government and Congress, there is a distinct, anti-Korean backlash."[21]

At stake is a mixture of pique and common sense. As Nicholas Kristof observed, "We can't want to protect South Koreans more than they want to be protected."[22]

But even if they want to be protected, so what? Another nation's desire for U.S. aid is not an adequate reason to provide it. Washington should do so only to advance American national interests—and fundamental ones, where the threat to go to war is involved. That is especially pertinent since today the alliance is an endless series of costs: unnecessary financial expense; growing anger and hostility from those we are defending; certain involvement in a horrific war should one break out; likelihood of being blamed by many South Koreans and their neighbors for its start, especially if the conflagration spread; and, one of the worst, "the privilege of fruitlessly negotiating with Pyongyang," as former *National Interest* executive editor Adam Garfinkle put it.[23]

What vital U.S. interest supposedly is being served by the alliance? During one of the periodic cycles of crisis during the North Korean nuclear controversy, President Clinton wrote ROK president Kim Young-sam stating that Washington would treat any attack on the South like one on America.[24] This echoed General Douglas MacArthur's promise to Rhee Syngman that "If Korea should ever be attacked by the Communists, I will defend it as I would California."[25] But while the South's security is vital to the ROK, it is rather less important to America. War would be an enormous tragedy, but it would pose no significant threat to the United States. Obviously Kim Jong-il could not strike America unless he contemplated suicide. And, unlike in 1950, a successful North Korean attack—itself highly unlikely given the South's capabilities—would be unconnected to a larger, hegemonic international threat to America. It would be an assault by the DPRK against South Korea, not a communist challenge to the free world.

America's cultural and economic ties with South Korea are valuable, but not critical. For instance, two-way trade in 2003 exceeded $60 billion (it peaked at almost $67 billion in 2000), real money but small change for America's $10 trillion economy.[26] Moreover, notes Stephen W. Bosworth, dean of the Fletcher School at Tufts University, "The relative weights of the United States and South Korea in the increasingly global economic interests of the other are shrinking in relative terms."[27]

The much-proclaimed "leverage" supposedly accompanying military deployments seems either absent or unused: few Koreans appear to buy GM cars out of gratitude to or in response to pressure from Washington. (In fact, lobbying by Washington for trade liberalization has helped push Korean farmers and students together against the United States.)

Real influence might result if Washington threatened to bring home its troops, but it would have to be prepared to follow through, which, of course, would give the lie to the argument that the security commitment serves important American interests. For this reason, William Taylor, then a scholar at the Center for Strategic and International Studies, warned that "a linkage between trade and troop deployment will seriously undermine U.S. interests in the region."[28] And the United States can ill afford to promiscuously issue this most serious of threats; to do so would quickly irritate relations with Seoul.

Thus, preserving the independence of the ROK, a midsize trading partner in a distant region surrounded by competing great powers, does not come up to the standard of an important interest, let alone a vital one. (Obviously, survival is not only important, but vital, for the South Koreans; the fact that it is vital to them does not make it either vital or important to America, however.)

Moreover, even if the security of the South was vital to the United States, Washington's treaty and troops are not necessary to achieve that end. Nearly a decade ago the Department of Defense declared that "our security relationship with the Republic of Korea continues to be central to the stability of the Korean Peninsula and Northeast Asia, as it has been for over forty years."[29] Although America's presence probably was central to the maintenance of peace 50 years ago, it is not so today. After all, the raison d'être for Washington's defense of the ROK, a weak South Korea vulnerable to communist aggression orchestrated by Beijing or Moscow, has disappeared. That America's presence undoubtedly still helps deter the DPRK from military adventurism does not mean that it is necessary to do so.[30] As noted earlier, the South can stand on its own. A recent report from the Center for Strategic and International Studies conceded: "Without U.S. help, South Korea is capable today of defending itself against an invasion from the North."[31] An invasion that would be supported by no other nation, and certainly not by the DPRK's old allies, China and Russia.

Of course, replacing the American tripwire would be expensive for the ROK, since Seoul would have to beef up existing force structure and invest in areas, such as long-range attack and intelligence-imaging capabilities, now dominated by Washington. But as one of the globe's wealthiest nations, South Korea is eminently capable of doing so—and in fact has studied the possibility of doing so.[32]

What if Seoul preferred not to make such investments? Of course, South Korea could underestimate the threat and fail to bolster its forces; it might carelessly put its trust in multilateral remedies.[33] The North could miscalculate and believe that it could win a blitzkrieg campaign even with its antiquated military. The result would be an awful war, whoever won.[34] It is a plausible, but highly unlikely, scenario.

However, it is up to the South Korean people to decide whether they feel sufficiently threatened to warrant spending more on defense and whether they are willing to undertake the burden of doing so. If they unexpectedly decide no, Washington should not waste the funds of U.S. taxpayers and risk the lives of young Americans to bail them out. Seoul itself has argued that "a sovereign state should be able to defend itself independently without relying on foreign assistance."[35] Very true.

The United States cannot be expected to forever protect other nations from their own potential folly. The ROK has matured as a country and should face the consequences of its own decisions. A mistake would be tragic but, unlike during the Cold War, no longer potentially catastrophic for the United States by unsettling the global balance of power. It should not be the American purpose to defend those who believe defense is unnecessary.

Former secretary of defense William Cohen complains that a withdrawal "would have the effect of telling the South Korean people that they're on their own."[36] But that is precisely what Washington should tell the South.

Some argue that perhaps American troops should be withdrawn, only just not now. "Talk of withdrawal could send the wrong signal to both friend and foe alike," worries syndicated columnist Donald Lambro.[37] Former *New York Times* correspondent Richard Halloran says such a step "would be tantamount to surrender," but he does not explain why.[38] This is an old refrain, however, which, as noted earlier, was sung even before President Carter proposed bringing most U.S. soldiers home. For some analysts and policymakers, there will never be a good time to update U.S. policy.

However, even hawkish security analyst Robyn Lim dismisses this argument, arguing: "Some might think that such a policy would play into the hands of Pyongyang's Dear Leader, Kim Jong Il. But keeping U.S. forces in South Korea against the wishes of the government in Seoul would also further Pyongyang's agenda. Moreover, this isn't Saigon in 1975."[39] Richard V. Allen, national security advisor to President Reagan, argued that the South "can plan to assume eventual responsibility for its own front-line defense" and that doing so would "be neither destabilizing nor provocative."[40]

How about larger issues of regional stability? Withdrawal might unsettle neighboring nations, but none needs to rely on the United States to meet its security needs. Indeed, even war on the Korean peninsula would set off no chain of falling dominoes. The DPRK represents the remnant of last century's communist threat, not the advance guard of the future.

A united communist Korea would lack the wherewithal to threaten its closest neighbors, China and Russia. Given the low quality of the North's military and Pyongyang's economic travails, as well as the intensified international isolation that would greet the DPRK as a result of renewed aggression, even the unlikely worst case of a unified communist state would have difficulty developing the military capability to intervene overseas against, say, Japan, which is more than capable of building a powerful defensive force. Pyongyang's possible possession of nuclear weapons would rightly frighten Tokyo, but the latter's development of a countervailing arsenal would, as argued earlier, deter any adventurism.

Obviously, real peace on the peninsula would make it even more difficult to justify the alliance. General Robert Riscassi, the commander of U.S. forces from 1990 to 1993, acknowledged that a formal peace treaty would create pressure for change "almost overnight." He adds: "Clearly there will be a debate. It's inevitable."[41]

Yet some supporters of the U.S. troop presence imagine retaining bases after reunification for reasons unrelated to South Korea's protection. The Clinton administration forthrightly declared: "Even after the North Korean threat passes, the United States intends to maintain its strong defense alliance with the Republic of Korea, in the interest of regional security."[42] More recently Lieutenant Colonel Carl Haselden argued: "The groundwork needs to be laid now for maintaining a continued U.S. presence after unification in order to fulfill our national interests."[43] Heritage Foundation vice president Larry Wortzel said, "Keeping U.S. forces in South Korea as long as they are welcome there is good policy. It's important for Americans and South Koreans to remember that for another 50 years."[44] William Cohen made the same case, to the consternation of many Koreans.[45]

Advocates of a permanent U.S. occupation—not just Americans, but some South Koreans as well—talk grandly of regional stability and preparedness for regional contingencies. "Even in the absence of a military threat from North Korea," writes Kim Sung-han of the Institute on Foreign Affairs and National Security (IFANS), the alliance should be revamped "to focus on promoting stability in Northeast Asia."[46] However, it would be a miraculous coincidence if a commitment forged in the Cold War to deter a ground invasion from a contiguous neighbor would function equally well—or even better—without adjustment to meet completely different future contingencies, despite the collapse of the potential aggressor and disappearance of its hegemonic allies. One cannot help but suspect that the means have become the end for most alliance advocates, to be preserved irrespective of changes in the regional and global security environment.

Still, the view of the U.S. presence in Korea for what Avery Goldstein, director of the Foreign Policy Research Institute's Asia Program, calls "dual-use" purposes is common.[47] Such arguments also are outmoded. In fact, there is nothing for America's soldiers stationed on the peninsula to do other than defend the ROK.

The future course of Chinese–U.S. relations is uncertain, but Beijing is not an inevitable enemy. Moreover, China's defense buildup remains modest and poses no threat to America's survival.[48] Washington's deployments in Korea would provide little use in any case. It is not likely that the ground forces would be used in a conflict with China; no rational administration would initiate a ground invasion of that country. If war comes with Beijing, it most likely will involve the Taiwan issue, requiring use of naval and air forces. Bases on the Korean peninsula might then prove valuable, but South Korea (and Japan, for that matter) is unlikely to allow itself to become the staging ground for battle. To do so would turn itself into China's permanent enemy.

The suggestion that troops in Korea could help contain a resurgent Tokyo is even more fanciful. Some analysts seem stuck in 1945: Wortzel of the Heritage Foundation lauds the fact that America's presence discourages Japan from doing anything to protect regional security.[49] But as argued in more detail in chapter 6, Tokyo should be doing more militarily. Despite disquiet among its neighbors, Japan is not about to embark on another imperialist rampage. Indeed, its involvement in Iraq, though tepid, is nevertheless a positive step, reflecting a greater willingness in Tokyo to take on a more active military role and, equally significant, a greater willingness of nearby states to accept that activity.[50]

That does not mean resistance to an increased Japanese role has disappeared or is about to disappear, but even ROK–Japanese military cooperation is increasing, as it should.[51] A reluctance of East Asian states to undertake the difficult process of working through past conflicts and reconciling with Tokyo is no reason for the United States to defend states capable of defending themselves. A possible glimpse of the future comes from journalist Bill Emmott, who suggests that Japan might be moving toward a more autonomous foreign policy akin to that once implemented by another island nation, Great Britain. If so, writes Emmott, it will indicate "that Japan has truly cast aside its imperialist past, is now willing to take responsibility for regional problems, and is dedicated to peace, democracy, and human rights."[52]

William Cohen worries that a conventional pull-out from South Korea would spark Japan to develop nuclear weapons.[53] This suggests a long, dubious daisy chain of events. Moreover, the end result, as discussed earlier, is still likely to be better than the alternative of American involvement in a regional confrontation involving North Korea, or even worse, the People's Republic of China.

If Washington backs away from defending Japan and the ROK, worries Haselden, "a power vacuum" might ensue, and "the instability between nations with combined strong economies and militaries could lead to an arms race having detrimental effects on regional stability and the global economy."[54] In fact, this was a constant refrain before the collapse of the Soviet Union. Assistant Secretary of State Richard Holbrooke went so far as to contend that the loss of Korea "would be the end of our position in the entire Pacific."[55] Ambassador William Gleysteen Jr. said the alliance contributes "importantly to the regional balance of power."[56] Similarly, Heritage Foundation president Edwin Feulner once called the Mutual Defense Treaty "a linchpin for stability in the entire Northeast Asian region."[57] In 1990 Secretary of Defense Richard Cheney warned that a U.S. withdrawal would be followed by a vacuum. As a result, "There almost surely would be a series of destabilizing regional arms races, an increase in regional tensions, and possibly conflict."[58] In early 1995 the Department of Defense made much the same pitch, promising to maintain the alliance "even after the North Korean threat passes . . . in the interest of regional security."[59]

Yet in 1997, when no one was questioning the U.S. commitment, military analyst Michael Klare reported: "Throughout East Asia, countries are spending more on their military forces, making this the only region in the world where military expenditures have been rising since the end of the Cold War."[60] The regional economic crisis, not the American military commitment, temporarily reversed this process.

In any case, it is difficult to develop a scenario involving real war between real countries, with or without an arms race: no general East Asian conflict seems to be threatening to break out. The region is no longer the focus of global hegemonic competition. All of the major regional powers benefit from peace; none has significant and growing differences with other major powers. Potential sources of discord are mostly within small states—Burma, Cambodia, and the Philippines, in particular. (The only major state with serious internal instability is Indonesia.) The United States might have been the key to regional stability 40, 30, and even 20 years ago. That it was the key 10 years ago is doubtful and that it is the key today is very unlikely.

In the end, the issue again seems to come down to the ROK's preference to free-ride on the United States. For instance, Kim Sung-han of IFANS complains about a "vacuum" in the absence of American troops, which might force the ROK and then Japan to develop nuclear weapons.[61] Perhaps. But even if regional political frictions increased, a stronger ROK and Japan would help contain, not exacerbate, those problems. Both countries would be forces for regional stability, not disruption.

Nor is it clear how unexplained regional "instability," as opposed to widespread conflict, would harm the global economy. Only if the nations throughout East Asia essentially collapsed would there be substantial harm to America and other countries, and, again, it is hard to build a plausible scenario leading to such a result. Moreover, subsidizing the defense of populous and prosperous allies involves a substantial redistribution of wealth from Americans to, in this case, Koreans. Their economy may gain from that process; not so ours, which bears the added military burden.

The end of America's defense commitment to the ROK would not terminate U.S. influence in the region. With the world's largest and most productive economy and dominant culture, a stable constitutional system and attractive entrepreneurial environment, and the globe's most powerful military, America would remain influential. A willingness to station an infantry division that has little practical to do in Northeast Asia is unlikely to augment Washington's authority.

Further, the United States markedly reduces the likelihood of its own involvement in war if it leaves populous and prosperous allies with the responsibility of developing adequate deterrent forces. Should conflict develop between America and China, for instance, it likely would grow out of a dispute between Beijing and a U.S. ally. Yet why should such a conflict warrant American involvement in war? No longer is there a global hegemonic struggle turning local disputes into a cause for global war, and Washington's friends can deploy powerful defensive forces. Wortzel worries about rivalries among China, Japan, Russia, and the two Koreas: "Three of the five nations have nuclear weapons, and, in the case of North Korea, seem willing to use them."[62] Why would Washington want to be in the middle of such rivalries if no vital American interests were at stake? It is precisely the sort of conflict to be sedulously avoided.

Cohen also fears that India would be "potentially motivated to expand its capabilities in reaction to Chinese strategems."[63] This should not bother Washington. To the contrary, it would be a highly positive step for the United States, since New Delhi already poses an important counterweight to Chinese ambitions in Southeast Asia and is likely to become an even more significant player in coming years.[64] The much uglier alternative would be a New Delhi that aligns with China, Russia, and others to counterbalance America's pretensions to global dominance.[65]

Some supporters of America's position in South Korea and elsewhere in Northeast Asia point to the prospect of using forces stationed in Korea to intervene in local conflicts and civil wars. Indeed, a commitment to defend "stability" in East Asia implies a willingness to intervene in a score of local conflicts revolving around border disputes, ethnic divisions, and other parochial squabbles. Again, why would the United States so act when its vital interests were not at stake?

Washington refused to use coercion against Indonesia over East Timor; it is not likely to intervene in intercommunal strife in the Moluccas or independence demands in Irian Jaya. As noted earlier, the greatest threats to regional stability come from within weak states—insurgency and corruption in the Philippines; democratic protests and ethnic conflict in Burma; economic, ethnic, nationalistic, and religious division in Indonesia—and are not susceptible to solution via U.S. military intervention.[66] Rather than preserving units and maintaining them in advanced posts overseas in case something might turn up for them to do, the United States should pare its force structure to match its vital commitments.

Finally, Lieutenant Colonel Haselden writes of such transnational threats as terrorism, piracy, drug trafficking, and infectious diseases.[67] What, one wonders, would troops in Korea do to combat AIDS? Should the air force bomb opium fields in Burma? Why shouldn't South Korea—along with other nations in the region—deploy ships to combat piracy? As for the problem of terrorism, it requires accurate intelligence and local cooperation, not the intervention of thousands of U.S. soldiers.

In sum, without any connection to the larger Cold War and global hegemonic struggle, Korea is relatively unimportant to the United States. Writes Robyn Lim: "America's only vital interest in East Asia is to maintain a balance of power that suits its interests."[68] And that does not require subsidizing the defense of the ROK forever.

A few American policymakers make an entirely different argument: foreign outposts like those in the ROK allow the United States to base soldiers overseas at someone else's expense. But as noted earlier, such security guarantees require Washington to create additional units, a cost that America's allies do not cover. Moreover, friendly states are not likely to long accept a foreign occupation carried out solely to save money for Americans. Richard Halloran admits that "given the emotional anti-Americanism that seems to be raging through South Korea today," simply maintaining the status quo "seems unlikely to satisfy the increasingly nationalistic South Koreans."[69] Even more unlikely would be maintaining the status quo after reunification, or whenever it became obvious to all that Washington was basing troops in Korea for its convenience, not the ROK's defense.

SOUTH KOREA'S INTEREST IN TERMINATING THE ALLIANCE

It should come as no surprise that the majority of South Koreans, who most obviously benefit from their defense free-ride, oppose proposals for America to withdraw its troops and end its security guarantee. After the 2000 summit with North Korean leader Kim Jong-il, which was greeted with such enthusiasm in the ROK, South Korean ambassador Lee Hong-koo said that any withdrawal was "a long way off."[70] President Kim Dae-jung called U.S. forces a stabilizing force.

As an opposition activist, President Roh Moo-hyun criticized the U.S. military presence, but after his divisive election win, he moderated his position. Indeed, he went so far as to say that the alliance was precious.[71] And his government publicly worried about the U.S. plan to redeploy forces *within* the ROK.

Moreover, some leading South Koreans join Americans in advocating a U.S. military presence after reunification; they also reflexively cite the kitchen-sink argument of "stability."[72] In fact, a decade ago the Ministry of National Defense argued: "Over the long term, it would be desirable that an appropriate size of the U.S. forces will be stationed in Korea for the support of the Korean security as well as to carry out the role as the regional balancer."[73]

After the two Kims' summit meeting, the ROK president said he supported retention of the U.S. presence "in order to maintain the balance of power in northeast Asia."[74] At the same time, Hong Choo-hyun, a former ROK ambassador to America, observed: "The South Korean president added it would be better for the [U.S.] forces to be kept in South Korea to prevent Japan and China from engaging in efforts to gain hegemony in the region."[75] Those concerns apparently remain. In 2003 the Institute of Foreign Affairs and National Security advocated turning the alliance between the United States and a united Korea into a regional accord directed against China and Japan.[76] In fact, large numbers of South Koreans see these two nations as potential economic and military rivals.[77]

Yet Roh, at least, seems somewhat uncomfortable with his government's embrace of the status quo. He reportedly ordered the ROK military to prepare for a reduction or withdrawal of U.S. forces.[78]

In fact, there are good reasons for South Koreans and Americans to be dissatisfied with the current relationship. The ROK gains from spending less on its defense than otherwise would be necessary. That is, or at least should be recognized as, an important benefit. (As discussed earlier, some South Koreans naively seem to view the North as not much of a threat. Others unfairly blame the United States for Korea's division. Most, however, seem to have a more realistic view, even if they view America's policies and presence with some mixture of hostility and irritation.)

But the price of turning the ROK's defense over to Washington is turning decisions about the ROK's defense over to Washington. That did not matter so much when war seemed inevitable if the United States was not involved. It also created little danger when, as under President Rhee, Washington was more risk averse than its ally. Today, however, peace is possible apart from the Mutual Defense Treaty. Far more important, the United States—represented by both the Clinton and Bush II administrations—admits to its willingness to take risky actions opposed by the South.

As discussed in chapter 1, Washington has opposed the so-called sunshine policy, criticized cooperative steps between the two Koreas, pushed to cut aid for the North, discussed the possibilities of applying economic sanctions against Pyongyang and interdicting DPRK planes and ships, and even considered taking military action against the North's nuclear facilities. The latter option, seriously considered by President Clinton and apparently still being seriously considered by President Bush, likely would start a full-scale war.[79] A conflict, it should be noted, which would be fought on South Korean territory, likely leading to the destruction of Seoul, the ROK's economic and population heart.

So long as American forces are based in the South, Washington will seek to dominate and control the alliance. And for good reason: the United States has never and should never promise to go to war on someone else's terms. If South Korea wants America's aid, it must accept the conditions under which such assistance is offered. Real equality is simply impossible.

Moreover, Seoul cannot escape being tied to U.S. policy even if it is carried out beyond the South's borders. Imagine the imposition of sanctions, enforcement of a blockade, or military strikes on the North—conducted by American forces located beyond South Korea's borders and acting outside of South Korea's borders over the objections of the ROK. North Korea is unlikely to distinguish the positions of the two members of the "mutual" defense pact and is likely to view the South as an appropriate target of retaliation.

Yet objections from the Blue House might not sway the United States from its chosen course. In early 2004 Senator Richard G. Lugar contended that the United States should "not rule out any options, including—as a last resort—the use of force." Never mind the South Koreans: "North Korea's nuclear program is at odds with American national security."[80]

Even blunter was Senator John McCain, who, as noted earlier, declared: "While they may risk their populations, the United States will do whatever it must to guarantee the security of the American people."[81] Frank Gaffney similarly opined: "The desire of dangerous nations' neighbors to accommodate, rather than confront, them is understandable. But it should not be determinative of U.S. policy. Such pleading today from South Korea and Japan is reminiscent of the Cold War advocacy for detente by leftists in the West German government."[82]

Other dangers also await the South if it continues to tie itself to American defense policy. The most important future international relationship may well be that between the United States and China. Can Beijing peacefully assert itself on the East Asian and global stage, and can the United States accommodate itself with a more influential China? Although conflict is by no means inevitable, it is possible, especially with Taiwan as a flashpoint. The controversy over Taipei's March 2004 referendum, a standard procedure in a democracy, illustrated the tense nature of the three-way dance.[83] Taiwan, believing American backing to be certain, may push toward independence; China, believing American interests dictate noninvolvement, might respond with force; Washington, believing its credibility to be at stake, might intervene.

What if Seoul follows the advice of Kim Sung-han, who advocates maintaining the alliance "after the threat from North Korea disappears in order to head off the regional rivalry between China and Japan and secure safe sea lanes linking Northeast Asia and the Middle East"? Thus, Northeast Asia "would become a provider of regional stability by hosting a U.S. regional force based in Korea."[84] And the ROK, linked to America by alliance and hosting U.S. bases and troops, might be forced to choose between its longtime ally and its permanent neighbors.

In such a circumstance, how much is America's defense subsidy worth? The humiliation of leaving one's destiny in the hands of another state is high enough. But the price could very well be risking South Korea's survival as a prosperous and independent nation.

PAST WITHDRAWALS

A decade ago Korea's Ministry of National Defense acknowledged that "considering the changes in our security environment including the emerging South–North arms control question, reduction of troops will become inevitable."[85] Unfortunately, the Ministry was referring to *South Korean* troop levels. But surely the first cuts should come in U.S. forces, whose presence always has been justified by the exceptional dangers involving the peninsula. Only after the American presence has disappeared should the ROK, which obviously has both the most at stake in and the primary obligation for its own defense, consider downsizing its army. In 1971 Prime Minister Kim Jong-pil responded to the Nixon administration's partial withdrawal: "Now is no time to survive by depending on others—U.S. troops in our country will go home sooner or later, which means that we must defend our country through our own strength."[86] That time is now.

Nevertheless, disengagement would be a dramatic step. Its most important impact would be symbolic. Says Claude Buss of the Hoover Institution: "In the minds of many Korean and American officials, the military role of the U.S. forces is less important than the psychological, political, and diplomatic effects of their presence. As Secretary of Defense James Schlesinger stated in 1974: 'U.S. forces in Korea symbolize America's continued interest in the overall stability of that part of the world.'"[87] Thus, Washington should phase out its presence while aiding the ROK in taking any reasonable steps it believes to be necessary to secure its future.

Despite the tendency to treat the U.S. presence as a given, America has more than a little experience in withdrawing troops from Korea. In April 1948 Washington decided to remove its forces, which had occupied the southern portion of the Korean peninsula since Japan's surrender, by the end of the year (when the Soviet forces had returned home). However, at that time the United States refused to supply the ROK with heavy weapons. The Pentagon doubted both Korea's importance and the longevity of the Rhee regime; it preferred not to waste resources on the South's military. Moreover, Rhee's oft-repeated threat to invade the North made Washington simultaneously reluctant to provide Seoul with potentially offensive weapons and anxious to pull out its forces to avoid entanglement in any invasion of the DPRK.[88] As a result, South Korea was ill-prepared for the northern onslaught of June 25, 1950.[89]

The war brought a return of American soldiers—360,000 at the peak—many more than necessary for even the very cold peace that descended on the peninsula in mid-1953. Thus, a second withdrawal occurred between September 1954 and May 1955. Washington pulled out six divisions, matched by China's withdrawal of 200,000 troops from the North. Two U.S. infantry divisions stayed to help shield Seoul; also remaining were a smattering of artillery, air defense, logistics, service, and other units, for a total of about 60,000 soldiers.

Washington next drew down its forces in the South in 1971. This step reflected U.S. detente with China and what has been variously called the Nixon or the Guam Doctrine, enunciated shortly after Nixon's inauguration in 1969.[90] Explained the president: "We shall look to the nation directly threatened to assume the primary responsibilities for providing the manpower for its defense."[91]

However, Nixon rejected a Defense Department proposal to pull out more troops. His successor, Gerald Ford, planned to withdraw another 15,500 soldiers in 1975, but an adverse vote in the House after the collapse of South Vietnam caused him to reverse course. Then President Jimmy Carter proposed reducing U.S. forces in Korea. For all of the furor surrounding his proposal, it actually was quite limited—"aseptic involvement," in the words of Georgetown University professor Earl Ravenal.[92] Although candidate Carter apparently originally favored withdrawing all U.S. forces, President Carter merely intended to pull out the last infantry division and assorted ground units. He planned to leave some 14,000 air and logistics personnel. Most important, he would have left Washington's treaty promise to go to war unchanged.

The Joint Korean–American communiqué of July 26, 1977, even emphasized the possibility of the return of American forces, if necessary. "Operating here is the incalculable principle of 'compensation,' rather than the principle of strategic requirements," observed Ravenal, and the compensation seemed to become as expensive as the supposed savings for America.[93] Although the administration withdrew one small contingent, it soon postponed the next stage. After U.S. Army estimates of increased DPRK military strength surfaced in 1979, perhaps conveniently timed to undermine withdrawal proponents, Carter dropped the plan.[94] Only 3,670 soldiers had been moved. At the same time, his administration upgraded remaining U.S. forces by adding AWACS aircraft, enhancing naval fleet and air strength, and bolstering ground-based airpower.[95]

Force levels edged upward under Carter's successor, Ronald Reagan. However, the first Bush administration planned, as part of its April 1990 East Asia Strategic Initiative, to implement a modest, three-stage reduction in U.S. forces.[96] The first cut, of 7,000 personnel (5,000 army and 2,000 air force), was completed in 1992. The second phase, which involved restructuring the Second Division and shrinking force levels by 5,000 to 6,000 personnel, was scheduled for 1993 through 1995. However, it was canceled in November 1991 as a result of the North Korean nuclear controversy. Also set aside was the 5- to 10-year review of further cuts intended to leave a minimum force for deterrence purposes.

The second Bush administration is proceeding largely along the same lines. It is rearranging and just modestly reducing the U.S. military presence. At the same time, Washington is offering an $11 billion force enhancement program, promising to increase deterrence, and reaffirming the defense commitment.[97] Again, one should ask: Why bother?

LEARNING FROM THE PAST

Past reductions in U.S. forces offer some useful lessons for the future.

1. Although the United States should structure its withdrawal program to complement South Korean efforts to become genuinely self-reliant, Washington must determine policy based on its own interests and not on South Korea's desires. The ROK may never want America's troops to go home.
2. Washington should completely eliminate its forces in Korea, rather than replay the game of offering expensive "compensations" in an attempt to buy ROK acquiescence for a plan that promises little real change.
3. America should eliminate the Mutual Defense Treaty once the troops are withdrawn, in order to ensure genuine disengagement.
4. The United States should set a short withdrawal time frame, one that could be implemented by one president, preferably within a single term.
5. America must stick with its plan despite the inevitable criticism.

Washington should decide on a rough phase-out period of, say, four years—with the exact timetable subject to negotiation—after which all U.S. forces would be withdrawn from the peninsula and the Mutual Defense Treaty would be canceled. Washington should initiate early consultations with the ROK both to fashion a smooth disengagement process and to enable Seoul to begin its force buildup, adding manpower, purchasing equipment, and enhancing domestic production. Indeed, Seoul should be encouraged to make the formal public announcement, at which time it should publicly challenge Pyongyang to demonstrate the sincerity of its past peace proposals by pulling its troops back from their aggressive posture and engaging in meaningful arms control negotiations.

U.S. infantry units, which the South could replace most easily, should be pulled out quickly. In fact, once the administration moves them, effectively eliminating the tripwire intended to make American military involvement automatic, they will have only a small role in the ROK's defense: South Korean forces would bear the brunt of any assault.

American air and naval units should be withdrawn next and somewhat more slowly. Although some analysts favor continuing to provide air and naval cover after withdrawing the ground units, doing so would not be cheap; it is the *existence* of these formations, as well as those intended for potential reinforcement, not their deployment in Korea, that is expensive. Moreover, there is no reason why Seoul, which currently possesses a technologically superior, if outnumbered, air force and navy, could not quickly develop adequate air and naval support, especially by purchasing U.S. equipment. As Makoto Momoi, a professor at Japan's National Defense College, observed years ago, the primary military contribution of America's forces has been firepower, and Washington can effectively "transfer" much of it to the South.[98]

Washington should give notice that once the forces were withdrawn, it would drop its defense guarantee. This step is critical. In contrast, the Carter administration emphasized that it was making no change in the Mutual Defense Treaty. The administration even sent an aircraft carrier to South Korea after the assassination of President Park to reinforce its commitment to the country's defense. Similarly, William Gleysteen Jr., a former ambassador to the ROK, once suggested cutting U.S. ground forces when the South's army reached parity with that of the North. But he advocated preserving the treaty because "the United States will have to ensure that no misleading signals about unwavering U.S. commitments are conveyed to any player—North, South or beyond the peninsula."[99] Yet why bother removing forces then? Preserving the commitment requires Washington to maintain sufficient military forces to intervene in the event of war, which precludes meaningful cost reduction. The risk of America's involvement in a Korean war would remain largely unchanged. And the problem of America's entanglement in Korean internal affairs would be only ameliorated, not eliminated. Finally, Seoul would remain a de facto protectorate, despite the removal of the most visible symbol of America's dominance.

In the long term, the troops withdrawn from the South should be demobilized. Else, as Peter Huessy argues, the step "would save the U.S. taxpayers nothing."[100] In the short term, until Washington withdraws its forces from Iraq, those units could be used to ease the rotation burden on the army, particularly combat infantry, now facing multiple overseas deployments. The failure to adjust overall force levels was another important flaw in the Carter withdrawal program.

Joining the South's abundant wealth with a willingness to help equip Seoul would avoid the Truman administration's mistake of 1949, when it withdrew America's troops without adequately preparing the Korean army to replace them. Washington's principal reason for leaving the ROK militarily naked was understandable: the Rhee regime's bellicosity, which continued even after the war.[101] Today a South Korean attack seems extremely unlikely;

moreover, Washington should make it clear that such a move would leave Seoul entirely on its own, irrespective of the consequences.

The United States also should forge an agreement, whether formal or informal, with China, Japan, and Russia that all four countries would discourage any aggressive action by either Korea. This would not be a security guarantee, requiring intervention, but a pact barring involvement on behalf of an aggressor. These nations also could work together to help mediate disputes and encourage cooperation between the two Koreas, as well as their participation in larger regional institutions.

Further, the ROK should build stronger regional ties to promote its own security. In particular, Washington should encourage the expansion of ties between South Korea and Japan, which remain tainted by the latter's half century of colonial rule.[102] History should not be forgotten—fear and loathing of Tokyo is one issue that unites many Koreans in both North and South—but it also should not block future cooperation between two prosperous democracies.[103] Relations have warmed some in recent years, in part due to former president Kim Dae-jung's efforts; political scientist Jason U. Manosevitz argues that the two nations' "security relations have reached adolescence."[104] Still, they are far too distant given the shared threat of North Korea in the short term and possibly China in the long term.

But that should change. So far Japan's "political-military 'normalization,'" as John Miller of the Asia-Pacific Center for Security Studies puts it, "has been gradual, hesitant, and contested."[105] As noted earlier, North Korea's periodic threats and fulminations have helped trigger a serious debate in Tokyo over abandoning its quasi-pacifist policy. Japanese officials have taken a hard line toward the DPRK, falling much closer to the United States than to Seoul. Moreover, Tokyo is increasing its defense capabilities.[106] There is no reason why Tokyo could not help fill any security vacuum left by a U.S. pullout, especially since Japan and the ROK share significant interests, including the maintenance of regional peace.

At the same time, Seoul should develop security cooperation with its other neighbors. The ROK government observed a decade ago: "We feel that our strategic concept should change from the existing one aimed at the North to the one that promotes all-azimuth security cooperation with neighboring countries."[107] Ties have improved greatly with both China and Russia, once armorers and allies of the North. Today Pyongyang can trust neither one, even the Chinese.[108]

Broader regional cooperation also is possible. Although an East Asian NATO is not in the offing, organizations like the Association of Southeast

Asian Nations (ASEAN), with its Post Ministerial Conference, Regional Forum, and Free Trade Area; Asia-Pacific Economic Cooperation (APEC); Council on Security Cooperation in the Asia-Pacific; Pacific Economic Cooperation Conference; and East Asian Economic Caucus (EAEC) all offer foundations for serious regional cooperation on issues ranging from economics to security. Perhaps most important, they provide an opportunity for Japan to gradually expand its role within a regional framework. Just as NATO and the European Community helped channel German power and ameliorate regional concern over Berlin's influence, so alliances and associations in East Asia could help promote regional stability in the absence of U.S. military forces.

Nevertheless, while it is important for Washington to work with Seoul to shape the withdrawal and inform other states in the region privately before any plan is announced, it is vital for the United States to emphasize that the decision has been made and to set a deadline, or else the ROK will have an incentive to delay fully augmenting its military as long as possible to maintain America's security guarantee. Moreover, the opponents of disengagement then would seek postponement rather than cancellation, since the former usually turns into the latter, as it did with President Carter's plan. Unfortunately, in the view of many supporters of the ROK defense subsidy, both American and South Korean, the timing will never be right, just as the point when Seoul is to reach military parity with the North always seems to slip a few more years into the future. Therefore, Washington must insist that only the timing and details of the pullout, not the denouement itself, are subject to negotiation.

As mentioned earlier, the United States should encourage the South to use an American phase-out as a bargaining chip with North Korea. Seoul should announce the withdrawal and give the DPRK two choices. One is to engage in serious negotiations over adoption of confidence-building measures and arms reduction. The other is to watch South Korea build up its military to match that of the North. Such an offer could play an important role in attempting to forestall the DPRK's nuclear option through diplomacy.

Although it is impossible to predict how North Korea would respond, this strategy would provide a useful test of Pyongyang's intentions. That would be useful for domestic ROK politics, given the fact, noted earlier, that many South Koreans have an inordinately romantic view of the North: Pyongyang would have to put up or shut up, without being able to use the United States as an excuse for any intransigence. And this strategy might offer the only realistic approach, assuming the North truly fears for its security. After all, Seoul could offer North Korea what it has long demanded, an American pullout joined with the prospect of economic development, while threatening to spend its adversary into the ground. In fact, in 1993 the Seoul government predicted as much:

> From a mid- and long-term perspective, the probability of peaceful coexistence between South and North Korea is predicted to increase. It is very likely that international cross-recognition of the two Koreas will come about as the worldwide conciliatory atmosphere warms after the Cold War era and as the four major regional powers come to increasingly desire stability on the Korean peninsula. When North Korea takes into account the considerable gap between the two Koreas in terms of national power, the predicted loss of their military supremacy and the expected limit of Kim Jong Il's charisma after Kim Il Sung dies, they are predicted inevitably to renounce their strategy of communizing the South by force and to embrace a pragmatic opening and reforming of their society.[109]

That assessment ultimately might turn out to be wildly optimistic, but the thesis should be tested—by Seoul.

It has been evident for years that South Korea is a security free-rider, one that no longer requires American military support. Five decades' worth of American withdrawal plans and proposals have been generally halfhearted, mismanaged, and interrupted. Washington needs to adopt a new approach, based on South Korea's declining security value to America and increasing ability to defend itself. The United States should make a firm decision to pull out all of its troops, while cooperating with Seoul in determining the timing and ordering of the withdrawal. The disengagement decision needs to be final, with demobilization of the troops and cancellation of the Mutual Defense Treaty to follow. The details can and should be negotiated with Seoul, but it is time to free the American people from a commitment that costs far more than it is worth, absorbs valuable military resources, and keeps the Korean people in a dependent relationship that insults their nationhood and puts their destiny in another country's hands.

Chapter Six

FORGING A NEW
U.S. STRATEGY IN EAST ASIA

The North Korean nuclear crisis underscores the gravity of the security burdens and risks the United States continues to bear in Northeast Asia. In a normal international system, the nations that would be most concerned about a possible North Korean nuclear-weapons capability would be Pyongyang's immediate neighbors: South Korea, Japan, China, and Russia. They also logically would take the lead in formulating policies to deal with the crisis.

But thanks to more than a half century of U.S. smothering behavior, there is nothing normal about the situation in Northeast Asia. Japan and South Korea continue to rely heavily on the United States for their defense needs, and, given the ingrained pattern of dependence, they look to Washington to resolve the looming problem posed by North Korea's nuclear ambitions. Even China and Russia expect the United States, as the principal military power in the region, to assume the lead role in that frustrating and probably unrewarding mission.

If it were not for the 37,000 U.S. troops stationed in South Korea and the more than 40,000 stationed in Japan, the United States could afford to view the prospect of a nuclear North Korea with relative detachment. It would be an unpleasant development, to be sure, but except for the possibility of Pyongyang's exporting of nuclear technology to rogue states or terrorist organizations, the existence of such an arsenal would not pose a dire threat to America's security interests. U.S. officials regard troop deployments in East

Asia as crucial military assets that help to stabilize the region and underscore America's power and dominant position. But if Pyongyang cannot be dissuaded from building a nuclear arsenal—and one dare not be optimistic on that score—those troops are no longer assets. They are nuclear hostages.

There is no need to expose American military personnel to such risks. During the early decades of the Cold War, there was a respectable rationale for keeping troops in the region and giving security guarantees to Japan and South Korea. Washington understandably wanted to keep both countries out of the orbit of a rapaciously expansionist Soviet Union or a hostile and volatile China. For many years Japan and South Korea also were too weak to provide for their own defense.

Today's security environment bears no resemblance to that earlier era. The Soviet Union has been replaced by a weak, noncommunist Russia. China's relations with the United States, although tense at times, are dramatically better than they were when America made its security commitments to Northeast Asia. Moreover, China is not even an orthodox communist state any longer, much less the kind of virulently revolutionary state that it was under Mao Zedong. Today China and Russia are both conventional great powers. While such powers may prove difficult to deal with from time to time, they do not pose malignantly expansionist threats to the peace of the region or to America's security.

Equally important, Japan and South Korea are vastly more capable than they were when they became Washington's security dependents. South Korea now has twice the population of North Korea and an economy some 40 times as large. If Seoul spent even a respectable amount on defense, it could easily outpace its decrepit communist neighbor. But it chooses to spend a smaller percentage of its gross domestic product on the military than does the United States—even though North Korea is on its border, not America's. True, political leaders in the ROK are now talking about increases in military spending, but those proposals are still woefully deficient.

Japan's timidity on security matters is even more indefensible. Despite the decade-long recession that has plagued its economy, Japan still has the second largest economy in the world. It also has a population six times larger than North Korea's. It is troubling to see a country with those characteristics—one of the world's great powers—rely on another country to resolve a security issue that so clearly impinges on Japan's vital interests.

Washington should begin to reduce its security risks in Northeast Asia. It is time—indeed, it is well past time—to tell Japan and South Korea that they must provide for their own defense and take responsibility for dealing with security problems in their region. The continuing reliance of those two countries on the United States is not healthy for them—and it certainly is not healthy for America. Japan and South Korea, together with China and Russia, should bear the burden of dealing with a dangerous and unpredictable North Korea.

But the North Korean crisis is merely the latest and most acute reason why the United States should radically alter its security strategy in East Asia. That strategy no longer serves American best interests on an array of issues. Moreover, it is becoming increasingly unsustainable. The United States needs a new approach to the region.

Various scholars have noted that East Asia is the one region in the world where the interests of four major powers—Russia, China, Japan, and the United States—intersect. America's interests in many parts of the world are largely discretionary; those in East Asia are much more intrinsic. Geographically the United States is a Pacific (although not an East Asian) power; economically America has a large and growing stake in East Asia; strategically the region has been and remains relevant to America's security.

That is why it is crucial for the United States to have a wise and sustainable policy toward East Asia. Yet there are warning signals that all is not well with America's current policy and that the need for a new approach is becoming urgent.

Members of the U.S. political elite have an unfortunate habit of branding all proposals for meaningful foreign policy change as harbingers of "isolationism"—a term they almost never define with clarity. But the issue is not one of engagement versus isolationism. Few knowledgeable people would dispute the point that the United States has important strategic and economic interests in East Asia, and even fewer would suggest the adoption of a Fortress America policy or the creation of a hermit republic. Recognizing that America has significant interests in the region, however, is not the end point of an assessment of U.S. policy; it is the starting point. One must then apply a rigorous cost-benefit analysis to U.S. policy. Only if the benefits outweigh the costs and risks—and do so by a decisive margin—does the policy merit support.

All too many analysts focus on the benefits of Washington's East Asia policy (the fostering of regional stability and prosperity, the dampening of incentives for arms races, etc.) while ignoring or minimizing the financial burdens and the risks incurred by being East Asia's policeman.[1] Former assistant secretary of defense Joseph Nye epitomized such myopia when he stated that Washington's security role was akin to providing life-sustaining "oxygen" to the regional environment. Atmospheric oxygen is largely a free good; security commitments are decidedly not.

In addition to determining whether the benefits clearly outweigh the costs and risks, a serious assessment of America's East Asia policy should ask two other questions: First, is the current policy sustainable, not just in the short term (i.e., the next five years or so), but over the long term? Second, even if it is theoretically sustainable, is it the optimal method of advancing America's regional interests, or are there alternative policies that would provide substantially similar benefits at a lower level of cost and risk?

AMERICA'S STRATEGIC AND ECONOMIC INTERESTS IN EAST ASIA

There are three especially important American interests in East Asia. The first is to prevent any single power from dominating the region. The nations of East Asia have a large population, significant military forces, and an impressive (and growing) array of economic and technological capabilities. A regional hegemon able to control those vast assets could pose a serious threat to America's security and economic well-being.

The second important interest is that a reasonable degree of order and stability exist in the region. An East Asia habitually convulsed by armed conflicts would be a difficult and unpleasant neighbor for America. A reasonable degree of order, however, should not be confused with the need to micromanage the region's security affairs to ensure complete order. Some instability is inherent in the international system, and East Asia will not be immune from that reality. As long as problems in the region are not excessively violent and disruptive, America's interests are relatively secure.

The third important interest is economic. East Asia is now the most significant region for U.S. international commerce, having surpassed Western Europe in the 1990s. Ten of America's 24 largest trading partners are located in the region (Japan, third; the People's Republic of China [minus Hong Kong], fourth; the Republic of Korea, seventh; Taiwan, eighth; Singapore, tenth; Malaysia, twelfth; Hong Kong, sixteenth; Thailand, nineteenth; the Philippines, twenty-third; and Australia, twenty-fourth).[2] Many of those same entities also provide important arenas for American investment. Maintaining, indeed strengthening, that array of economic ties constitutes an interest that Washington cannot ignore.

AMERICA AS EAST ASIA'S HEGEMON

Since the end of World War II, the United States has sought to protect and advance all three of its major interests in East Asia. But it has not done so (as some policy experts have alleged) by guaranteeing a stable balance of power in the region. Instead, the United States has done so by arrogating the role of regional hegemon. Preserving that position has now become something bordering on an obsession.

A prominent justification for continuing the large-scale U.S. military presence in the region is to prevent a power vacuum that might be exploited by an expansionist state. That is hardly a new rationale for Washington's policy. Throughout the Cold War, U.S. forces guarded East Asia's security against Soviet (and for a time Soviet/Chinese) threats. The removal of Japan as a significant political and military factor (because of the destruction of Tokyo's military forces in World War II and Washington's insistence on a minimalist Japanese military capability in the postwar era) meant that the United States was the only credible strategic counterweight to the Soviet Union and its communist allies.[3]

Despite the collapse of the Soviet Union, the rationale for a dominant U.S. military role in East Asia remains largely the same. The Pentagon's 1995 security strategy report for the East Asia–Pacific region, for example, contended that forward-deployed U.S. forces ensure a rapid and flexible worldwide "crisis response capability," but it also stated that they are there to "discourage the emergence of a regional hegemon."[4] Although U.S. officials were vague about what rival might aspire to that status, a passage in the report offered an enticing hint about the target of Washington's apprehension. "If the United States does not provide the central, visible, stabilizing force in the Asia and Pacific region," the report cautioned, "it is quite possible that another country might—but not in a way that meets America's fundamental interests."[5] Although it is conceivable that the comment referred to possible Chinese hegemonic ambitions, the reference to a "stabilizing" force points to a different interpretation. Given its territorial claims involving the Spratly, Paracel, and Diaoyu islands (not to mention its claims to Taiwan), China would more likely be a disruptive, "revisionist" power than a stabilizing, conservative power.

There is really only one credible candidate to supplant the United States as regional stabilizer: Japan; and that point is understood by U.S. policymakers. Washington continues, as it has since the end of World War II, to discourage Japan from playing an activist political-military role in East Asia—especially an independent activist role. Even the outcome of the much-touted April 1996 summit between President Clinton and Prime Minister Ryutaro Hashimoto was consistent with that long-standing policy. The joint declaration that emerged from the summit meeting indicated that

U.S. officials had finally accepted the need to modestly increase Japan's involvement in the region's security affairs, but the revised blueprint still conceived of Tokyo as Washington's very junior partner.[6] U.S. caution on the score has diminished only modestly in the years since then. There is no indication that U.S. leaders want Japan to be an ally with a responsibility equal to America's for preserving stability in East Asia—much less that they want Japan to assume the lead role.[7]

That same attitude is reflected in the revisions to the defense guidelines for the U.S.–Japan alliance announced in September 1997 and which remain in effect today.[8] The principal change authorized Japanese logistical support for U.S. military operations in "areas surrounding Japan"—a phrase that was not defined—that are relevant to Japan's own security. Before the 1997 revisions, Japanese officials had argued that Article 9 of Japan's constitution precludes such involvement unless Japan itself is under attack.

Despite the hype on both sides of the Pacific, the reforms fell far short of establishing an equal security partnership between Japan and the United States. In the event of an East Asian conflict that did not involve an attack on Japanese territory, Japan would merely provide nonlethal logistical support for U.S. troops and allow U.S. forces to use facilities in Japan for their operations. There was no suggestion that Japanese Self-Defense Forces would participate in combat missions alongside their U.S. allies. Indeed, the guidelines stressed: "Japan will conduct all its actions within the limitations of its Constitution and in accordance with such basic positions as the maintenance of its exclusively defense-oriented policy."[9]

The bottom line is that American military personnel are still expected to risk their lives to repel any act of aggression that threatens the security of East Asia while Japan merely provides such things as fuel, spare parts, medical supplies, and body bags for American casualties. The revised defense guidelines do little to end Japan's status as a U.S. military dependent; they merely allow Japan to be a slightly more active and helpful dependent.

Washington's policy toward Japan is just the most visible manifestation of a sclerotic overall U.S. East Asian policy. The heart of that policy is to prevent the rise of any political and military rival.[10] In other words, it is a policy to preserve U.S. hegemony. The objective of discouraging other powers from even aspiring to play more active political and military roles was perhaps most candidly expressed in the preliminary draft of the Pentagon's planning guidance document that was leaked to the press in 1992.[11] That document is not the only evidence of a hegemonic policy, however. Statements by various military and civilian officials over the years and the substantive features of Washington's East Asia policy since 1945 point to the same conclusion.

Most recently, the new National Security Strategy (NSS) document that the Bush administration promulgated in September 2002 echoed the sentiments (albeit expressed more elliptically and diplomatically) of the 1992 Pentagon planning guidance document. One provision of the NSS stressed that the United States must build its military power "beyond challenge." Another stated that the United States must "assure our allies and friends," and "dissuade future military competition."[12] The policy outlined clearly envisages America as an undisputed hegemon in East Asia and other regions.

U.S. officials have zealously guarded America's hegemonic prerogatives in an attempt to smother the political-military ambitions of other powers in East Asia. For example, when Japanese prime minister Toshiki Kaifu made a surprise proposal in the summer of 1991 for a "security dialogue"—formal regional meetings on defense issues—between Japan and the members of the Association of Southeast Asian Nations, Washington reacted negatively. In a speech to the annual meeting of ASEAN foreign ministers, Secretary of State James Baker III warned them against adopting new arrangements that would replace "tried and true frameworks" involving the United States. "We have a remarkable degree of stability in this region," Baker said. "We ought to be careful about changing those arrangements and discarding them for something else." Privately, U.S. officials expressed strong opposition to the Japanese proposal because it might weaken the bilateral arrangements between the United States and various nations in East Asia and the Pacific.[13] In other words, Tokyo's modest initiative was seen as a challenge to Washington's political and military primacy.

The Clinton administration was less clumsy in implementing the smothering strategy. It even cautiously encouraged the kind of regional security dialogue that its predecessor so tenaciously opposed. But the administration also emphasized that the United States must be an active participant in such initiatives; there was no sympathy whatever for measures that the East Asian countries might pursue without U.S. input. Moreover, administration officials seized every opportunity to emphasize America's determination to maintain a large military presence in the region and to continue the role of stabilizer.

The comments of Secretary of Defense William Cohen during his April 1997 trip to East Asia epitomized that approach. Noting that Korean reunification might occur at some point in the future, Cohen stressed: "But whether or not that comes about, we will still have to maintain a significant presence in the region. We will still maintain a strong presence in Korea." In case anyone was still unclear about that point, he stated: "We intend to remain in Korea, assuming there is a reunification, into the indefinite future."[14] A year and a half later Cohen again emphasized the need to maintain 100,000 U.S. troops in East Asia indefinitely. "This presence helps us to shape events, to respond to crises, and to prepare for an uncertain future."[15]

The Bush administration has not deviated from the hegemonic strategy in the slightest. Indeed, U.S. officials still seem receptive to maintaining a U.S. troop presence on the Korean peninsula even if North Korea collapses and the peninsula is united under a democratic government. Given Washington's efforts to revitalize security ties with the Philippines and establish new security arrangements (i.e., port access agreements) with Singapore and other Southeast Asian nations, the U.S. security presence in the region appears to be expanding, not diminishing.[16] That approach, in turn, will discourage independent initiative on the part of the East Asian countries, which is the last thing a wise U.S. strategy would seek to achieve.

WHY THE SMOTHERING STRATEGY IS OBSOLETE

Washington's post–World War II smothering strategy has been based on the assumption that if the United States took care of East Asia's security needs, the various countries in the region would forgo the option of building large military establishments and acting as normal great powers (or even midsize powers) have acted throughout history to protect their own interests. The resulting environment of stability would not only reduce the chances of armed conflict but maximize the opportunities for economic growth—something that would benefit the United States as well as East Asia.

That may have been a valid assumption during the first two or three decades after World War II, but several factors have been eroding the foundations of U.S. strategy since that time. Until the late 1970s, the noncommunist East Asian powers (including Japan) did not have economies large enough to fund military establishments capable of supporting independent, self-reliant security policies even if the governments had been so inclined. (At least they could not have done so without endangering their newly vigorous economic growth rates—a price none of them wished to pay.) That factor has changed markedly in the last two and a half decades. Japan is the world's second largest economic power, and the ROK, Taiwan, Indonesia, Malaysia, Singapore, and Thailand have all emerged as serious players in the global economy. Several

East Asian countries now have the economic wherewithal to fund credible national security forces, and although the growth in their military capabilities has thus far been modest, East Asia has become a lucrative arena for arms sales.

There are other subtle but significant indications that the East Asian states are beginning to hedge against the day when the United States might be unwilling or unable to maintain its position as the regional hegemon. Japan's decision following North Korea's missile test in August 1998 to develop a more robust intelligence apparatus instead of continuing to rely on information from U.S. agencies is one example.[17] Tokyo's buildup of plutonium stocks, combined with its development of reprocessing facilities and a sophisticated rocketry program, may also be evidence of a hedging strategy.[18] The willingness of South Korea and other countries to make major arms purchases from non-U.S. suppliers and the development of more extensive domestic armaments industries are other signs.

The growth of economic power has been accompanied by more assertive behavior on territorial matters and other issues of national pride. Such jingoistic spats as those between Japan and South Korea over Toktu island in the mid-1990s and the ongoing three-way quarrel involving Japan, Taiwan, and China over the Senkaku (Diaoyu) islands are only the most visible incidents.

All of this suggests that America's ability to satisfy the security needs of the East Asian states through a smothering strategy is already waning and that the decline is likely to accelerate in the coming years. It was one thing for weak, poor, and insecure countries to accept the protection of a benign distant protector; the price may have involved the swallowing of national pride on occasion, but U.S. hegemony spared the regional powers from spending large sums on their own military establishments and enabled them instead to devote scarce resources to their developing economies. It is quite another matter for societies flush with prosperity to continue accepting such a humiliating dependency. South Korea's growing discontent with U.S. actions that undermine the sunshine policy toward North Korea and that seem to take the ROK for granted is a clear indication of how the political context is changing. Taiwan's decision to go ahead with a popular referendum in March 2004 on policy toward the mainland despite Washington's efforts to discourage it is another example.

There is yet another visible weakness in Washington's smothering strategy. Because it developed during the Cold War, Washington could operate with confidence that its security clients would not have extensive economic ties with America's strategic adversaries. In other words, no tension would exist between the economic interests of those allies and their security relationships with the United States. The situation is now more ambiguous. For example, a chilly relationship (to say nothing of an armed skirmish) between the United States and China would put the other East Asian countries in an extremely difficult position. Many of them have extensive investments in China and maintain lucrative bilateral trade relations with it.

Could Washington count on support from its "friends" and allies in the region for a hard-line policy directed against Beijing, when such support might cost them their multibillion-dollar economic stakes? A positive answer is far from certain. Indeed, given the reaction of the East Asian powers to the brouhaha in the Taiwan Strait in early 1996 and the quarrel between the United States and China over the spy plane incident in April 2001 (discussed below), U.S. policymakers have reason to worry about the prospect of such support. A Japanese scholar's explanation for his country's unwillingness to publicly endorse the U.S. deployment of the Seventh Fleet to waters near Taiwan in 1996 was most revealing. He did not cite the danger that a military collision between the United States and China might lead to Chinese attacks on Japanese territory because of the U.S. bases there. Rather, he emphasized concerns that an endorsement of U.S. policy might jeopardize Japanese investments in China.[19]

A final reason for the increasing inviability of the smothering strategy is that the United States now encounters a power whose security needs and policy objectives Washington is not in a position to satisfy. That power is China. The reemergence of Japan as a great power (at least economically) has posed problems for the smothering strategy. But Japan's security interests and those of the United States are at least reasonably compatible, and Japan is a status quo power. Tokyo has been the principal beneficiary of the existing political and economic system in East Asia. (Indeed, Japan has achieved by peaceful economic penetration and subtle political influence many of the objectives that it unsuccessfully pursued by force in the 1930s and 1940s when it sought to create the Greater East Asia Co-Prosperity Sphere.) The Japanese have no incentive to disrupt the current arrangement, nor have they shown any desire to do so.

The situation with respect to China is different in crucial ways. Although Beijing's expanding economic ties with its East Asian neighbors (and with the United States) are an important incentive for status quo behavior, other factors produce incentives for aggressive revisionism.[20] Most important, China is still nursing grievances about the territorial amputations that occurred during its period of weakness in the nineteenth century. That is why the return of Hong Kong in the summer of 1997 acquired an importance that transcended the territory's (admittedly substantial) economic value. It was a powerful symbol of China's restored national pride. The return of Macao in 1999 was another stage in that process. But it is not at all certain that the process will be complete in the view of China's leaders and population until Taiwan is regained, the land taken by the Russian empire is recovered, and Beijing's claims in the South China and East China seas are vindicated.

Some experts argue that China does not harbor expansionist ambitions.[21] That is possible, but the existence of such an extensive array of unresolved matters points to a less sanguine conclusion. So too does the history of international relations. Rising great powers, especially those with territorial grievances and claims, typically pursue assertive, and often abrasive, policies. One need only recall the behavior of the United States during the nineteenth century or Wilhelmine Germany during the late nineteenth and early twentieth centuries.

That fact poses an enormous dilemma for the United States. It is difficult to see how Washington can appease China on any of the outstanding issues without causing massive dislocations to the other components of U.S. policy in East Asia. An attempt to appease China would rapidly undermine the smothering strategy, since the other East Asian powers would conclude that the United States was unwilling to protect—or was incapable of protecting—their vital interests. Yet an attempt to thwart Chinese ambitions would entail its own dangers. As China's economic and military power grows, Beijing will likely see a resistant America as an intolerable impediment to the achievement of legitimate Chinese goals.[22] Again, history suggests that a rising great power sooner or later tries to become the dominant player in its region. (All of this assumes, of course, that China can overcome its internal problems—especially its corrupt and rigid political system—and establish itself as a great power over the long term.[23]) Such a power does not generally get on well with the incumbent regional hegemon.[24] The structure of the international system tends to produce bitter, and often violent, rivalries in such situations.

That is not to say that China poses a dire military challenge to the United States today. Despite growing efforts at modernization, its military is still no match for America's. The United States enjoys overwhelming conventional military superiority, and the vast U.S. nuclear arsenal dwarfs China's modest deterrent. Those factors are likely to inhibit any inclination China might have to challenge U.S. hegemony in East Asia in the near term, and it may be as much as a generation before China's military can compete with that of the United States.[25] Nevertheless, the political and strategic rivalry is likely to grow, creating tensions in the U.S.–China relationship.

Moreover, there is always the possibility of a miscalculation by a power that is objectively weaker than the incumbent hegemon—especially if an emotional issue like the status of Taiwan is a catalyst. Washington should not be complacent with its current advantages and assume that they will last forever. Instead, it should begin to adjust its policies to deal with the day when China may become a serious challenger.

For all of these reasons, the smothering strategy that the United States has pursued since the end of World War II appears to be unsustainable. Indeed, even attempting to preserve it may pose serious dangers to America.

THE DOWNSIDE TO POLICING EAST ASIA

America's dominant position in East Asia has contributed to the region's stability, but the policy also entails mounting costs and risks. The financial burden alone is substantial. Yet there is scant evidence that Washington's security commitments give the United States significant leverage in securing access to important East Asian markets. The difficulties encountered in attempting to open the Japanese market have been discussed at length in the American news media, but the problem is not confined to Japan. Even South Korea, a much smaller client heavily dependent on its alliance with the United States and on the U.S. troop presence, has been surprisingly recalcitrant and exclusionary. The office of the U.S. Trade Representative has been critical of South Korean practices. An April 2003 report noted, "The combination of relatively high tariffs and value-added taxes continues to render a variety of [U.S.] products uncompetitive in Korea . . . Korea maintains standards and conformity assessment procedures" that "appear to have a disproportionate impact on imports." Moreover, "U.S. exporters cite Korea's non-transparent and burdensome labeling requirements as barriers to entry."[26] The evidence is, at the very least, ambiguous on whether Washington's security policy in East Asia is effectively promoting its economic interests.[27]

The tensions between China and Taiwan in late 1995 and early 1996, and again in the lead-up to Taiwan's presidential election in the spring of 2000, illustrated that the policy has a disturbing drawback in terms of risk. And President Bush has increased America's risk exposure. He startled people on both sides of the Pacific in April 2001 when he seemingly ended Washington's longstanding policy of "strategic ambiguity" regarding Taiwan. Previously, U.S. leaders had indicated that the United States would regard the use of force by the People's Republic against Taiwan as a serious breach of the peace and might—depending on the circumstances—intervene militarily. That posture did little more than reiterate the vague provisions of the Taiwan Relations Act of 1979.[28]

In a series of television interviews on April 25, Bush appeared to discard all nuances and caveats. When asked by ABC News reporter Charles Gibson if the United States had an obligation to defend Taiwan, the president replied, "Yes, we do, and the Chinese must understand that." Would the United States respond "with the full force of the American military?" Gibson pressed. "Whatever it took to help Taiwan defend herself," Bush replied.[29]

Although the president and his advisors scrambled to provide various "clarifying" comments in the following hours and days, their efforts did little to allay the suspicions of an angry China. And Bush likely spoke the undiplomatic truth. In all probability the United States would try to come to Taiwan's aid militarily in the event of an attack by China. Such are the obligations of East Asia's hegemon.

Not only could the United States find itself entangled in a perilous military confrontation with China over Taiwan, it might have to wage the ensuing struggle virtually alone. Taiwan would undoubtedly contribute to its own defense, but the reaction in various East Asian capitals to Beijing's menacing behavior toward Taiwan in both 1996 and 2000 indicated that assistance from Washington's other "friends" would be problematic, at best.

Indeed, virtually all East Asian governments made a concerted effort to distance their policies from that of the United States when the Clinton administration dispatched two aircraft carriers to the western Pacific to demonstrate concern about the rising tensions in the Taiwan Strait in 1996. South Korea and the Philippines both stressed that their "mutual" defense treaties with the United States did not cover contingencies in the strait. Malaysia, Indonesia, Thailand, and Australia contented themselves with the banal response of urging restraint on all sides, conspicuously declining to endorse Washington's moves. Indeed, they echoed Beijing's position that Taiwan is merely a renegade province. Even Japan, the principal U.S. ally in the region, merely expressed "understanding" of the naval deployment.[30]

Indeed the lack of allied support is not confined to the Taiwan issue. It also was evident in April 2001 when a Chinese jet collided with a U.S. spy plane that was conducting surveillance from international airspace. The collision forced the U.S. plane to land on China's Hainan Island, where authorities held the crew for nearly two weeks, until Washington conveyed a carefully worded expression of regret for the incident, and kept the plane. During this period of acute tension, what was the response of America's East Asian allies?

Vocal support for the U.S. position was notably absent. Even Washington's treaty allies in the region—Japan, South Korea, Thailand, Australia, New Zealand, and the Philippines—declined to say that a U.S. apology to Beijing was unwarranted. Only Singapore's elder statesman Lee Kuan Yew unequivocally supported the U.S. position.

Japan's tepid, ambiguous stance epitomized the reaction of America's so-called friends and allies. Kauzuhiko Koshikawa, a spokesman for Prime Minister Yoshiro Mori, stated: "We strongly hope this case will be settled in an appropriate and acceptable manner."[31] Beijing could take as much comfort as Washington from such a comment.

Such responses underscore an important point: China's neighbors have no incentive to antagonize that rising power by backing the United States in disputes that do not seem vital to—or even relevant to—their interests. We can expect such discreet neutrality in most, if not all, future confrontations between the United States and the People's Republic. Beijing has fostered the tendency toward neutrality through astute diplomacy that has lessened its abrasive image among its neighbors in the region while quietly underscoring its economic importance to the economies of those nations.[32]

That lack of support suggests that Washington's encouragement of dependency on the part of the noncommunist East Asian countries has created a most unhealthy situation. Those nations seek the best of both worlds: they want the United States to protect them from Chinese aggression or intimidation, if that problem should become acute, but they do not want to incur Beijing's wrath (or even jeopardize their commerce with China) by allying themselves with a hard-line U.S. policy. That may be a good, albeit cynical, strategy for them, but it puts the United States in a precarious position. If China does make a bid for regional hegemony at some point, there is literally no power other than the United States positioned to block that bid. That is a blueprint for a U.S.–Chinese confrontation in which China's neighbors conveniently remain on the sidelines.

Instead of creating a situation in which the only alternative to a dangerous power vacuum is America's continuing willingness to be point man in every East Asian crisis, the United States should move toward fostering a reasonably stable balance of power in East Asia. A new policy with that aim would view Japan as the primary strategic counterweight to an increasingly assertive China—a role that the United States will otherwise be pressured to fill by default.[33]

Japan is the most crucial component of an East Asian balance of power, but it is not the only relevant factor. A vigorous South Korea can play an important role, and a united democratic Korea (which is certainly a possibility within a generation) would be an even more important player. Such midsize powers as Vietnam and Indonesia also must be taken into consideration—especially since both of them have historical suspicions about China's ambitions. Even peripheral powers such as Australia, Malaysia, Singapore, and the Philippines are part of the overall balance of power. Individually their roles may be modest, but if they work cooperatively—through ASEAN or some other organization—their impact on the stability of the region could be substantial.

America has important strategic and economic interests in East Asia and cannot be indifferent to the region's fate. But the current strategy, based on the United States' being the regional military hegemon, is proving increasingly difficult to sustain. (The growing friction between American military personnel and the Japanese and South Korean civilian populations is only the most visible symptom of trouble.[34]) More important, it is neither a necessary nor an optimal method of securing America's interests. The costs and risks of Washington's smothering strategy are beginning to far outweigh the benefits.

Most disquieting are the risks the United States continues to incur because of its role as the guarantor of East Asia's security and stability—risks that normally would be borne primarily by Japan and other regional powers. Japan's long-standing reluctance to play even a supporting military role in regional crises is especially disturbing. Whatever the relevance of Korea, Taiwan, or the Spratlys to the economic and security interests of the United States, their importance to Japan is far greater.

It is highly unusual for a major power to choose to remain passive in the face of significant security problems in its own region. But Japanese leaders know that they do not have to incur the costs and risks of playing a more active role to protect their country's interests. The United States has obligingly agreed to incur them. Americans have every reason to ask, however, whether U.S. military personnel should be put in harm's way to deal with problems that are—or at least ought to be—much more important to Japan than they are to the United States. The prospect of American troops dying in an East Asian war, while the Japanese (and other nominal allies) merely provide moral and financial support (if that), is not very appealing. Yet that is the possibility that U.S. security policy in East Asia has created.[35]

TOWARD A SUSTAINABLE STRATEGY

Several steps need to be taken to establish a more sustainable policy. First, the United States should inform Japan and South Korea that it intends to withdraw its forces from both countries within the next few years and that, upon completion of the withdrawals, it will terminate the "mutual" security treaties. At that point, both Japan and South Korea will be expected to provide for their own defense. Washington should implement its withdrawal strategy without rancor or a desire to punish the allies for policy differences. The *Wall Street Journal* editorial suggesting that the United States condition its continuing troop presence in South Korea on Seoul's willingness to support hard-line policies toward North Korea is an example of precisely how *not* to proceed.[36]

But it is important to change the incentive structure. At present South Korea and Japan have few incentives to assume the costs and risks of providing fully for their own defense when they know that the United States is willing to bear that burden on their behalf. In both countries, assuming a larger military role would require overcoming entrenched domestic constituencies that prefer the status quo. The security treaties with the United States and the U.S. troop presence allow the diversion of financial resources to domestic priorities. And relying on the United States for security avoids painful debates about what kind of policy those countries need to pursue. The U.S. security blanket is entirely too comfortable for Washington's clients. Without a decisive move by the United States to take away that security blanket by a certain date, changes in the security posture of South Korea and Japan will be very slow to occur.

Second, the United States should encourage the various nations of East Asia to take greater responsibility for the security and stability of their region. In limited and at times hesitant ways that process is taking place even without U.S. encouragement. ASEAN has begun to address security issues, most notably taking an interest in the disorders in Indonesia that threatened to spiral out of control in the late 1990s and that continue to pose a problem. Australia assumed a leadership role in helping to resolve the East Timor crisis. It was revealing that Canberra became more proactive after the United States declined to send peacekeeping troops or otherwise become deeply involved in that situation.[37] According to the conventional wisdom that U.S. leadership is imperative lest allies and client states despair and fail to deal with regional security problems, Australia's actions suggest just the opposite. When countries in a region facing a security problem cannot offload that problem onto the United States, they take action to contain a crisis and defend their own interests.

More recently, Australia has developed a more defined and robust regional strategy. In a June 2003 speech, Foreign Minister Alexander Downer stated that Australia would not necessarily turn to the United Nations before acting in crises that could affect its security. Instead, Canberra was prepared to join—and sometimes even lead—coalitions of the willing to address urgent regional challenges. Downer spoke as Australia prepared to send 2,000 police officers and supporting military personnel to the Solomon Islands, which had experienced such an epidemic of violence and corruption that it verged on being a failed state. Earlier, Prime Minister John Howard had told Australian lawmakers that having failed states in its neighborhood threatened Australia's interests, because such states could become havens for criminals and political extremists.[38] Perhaps most revealing, the Australian government plans to double its defense spending over the next three years with the intent of becoming a much more serious military player.[39]

Third, Washington should indicate to Tokyo that it no longer objects to Japan's assuming a more active political and military posture in East Asia. Quite the contrary, U.S. officials ought to adopt the position that, as the principal indigenous great power, Japan will be expected to help stabilize East Asia, contribute to the resolution of disputes, and contain disruptive or expansionist threats that might emerge. Washington also should use its diplomatic influence to encourage political and security cooperation between Japan and its neighbors, but U.S. policymakers must not let East Asian apprehension about a more assertive Japan dictate American policy and keep the United States in its role as regional policeman.

It is reasonable to explore with Tokyo avenues of cooperation in those areas where there is a sufficient convergence of interests. That cooperation should not, however, take the form of a new alliance. Proposals to reform and strengthen the alliance are unwise.[40] They will perpetuate Japan's unhealthy dependence on the United States even as they arouse China's suspicions of a U.S.–Japanese attempt to contain the People's Republic. An ongoing security dialogue and occasional joint military exercises would be more appropriate than a formal alliance for East Asia's security needs in the twenty-first century.

Elaborate, formal treaty commitments are a bad idea in general. They are excessively rigid and can lock the United States into commitments that may make sense under one set of conditions but become ill-advised or even counterproductive when conditions change. Beyond that general objection, a U.S.–Japanese alliance would be likely to create special problems in the future. Such an alliance would provide tangible evidence to those in the People's Republic who contend that Washington is intent on adopting a containment policy directed against China.[41] The United States should retain the ability to work with Japan and other powers if Beijing's ambitions threaten to lead to Chinese dominance of the region, but Washington must be wary of creating a self-fulfilling prophecy. An informal security relationship with Japan would preserve the flexibility to block China's hegemony, if that danger emerges, without needlessly antagonizing Beijing.

America still can have a potent power projection capability with a reduced military presence based in Guam and other U.S. territories in the central and west-central Pacific. There is no need to have large numbers of forward-deployed forces, much less units to serve as automatic tripwires if even a minor conflict erupts. Press reports in the spring of 2003 indicated that discussions were under way to redeploy U.S. troops in East Asia. In August 2004 Bush confirmed a global redeployment. That would mean a drawdown of U.S. forces in Japan and South Korea.

It would be a worthwhile step. However, if the initial reports are accurate, the administration apparently would redeploy many of those troops to Singapore, Australia, and Malaysia for the purpose of counterterrorism efforts in Southeast Asia.[42] It is not at all clear how stationing forces in those countries would be useful in the war against al Qaeda, since with the possible exception of the Philippines, there is no prospect of U.S. combat troops being used in antiterrorism operations. The "war" against al Qaeda and its allies is much more a matter of law enforcement cooperation with friendly regimes in the region than it is an area for conventional military measures. The antiterrorism rationale seems little more than another excuse to keep large numbers of U.S. troops in East Asia.

The United States should be the balancer of last resort, not the intervener of first resort, in East Asia's security equation. The most crucial step in adopting that strategy is to transfer primary security responsibilities to Japan, the region's leading conservative, status quo power. The key question is whether Japan would take up that responsibility if the United States phased out its security protection and thereby changed the incentive structure.

One cannot be certain about the outcome, but as mentioned previously, there are, at long last, subtle signs that Japan is beginning to take security issues more seriously. Japan's political elite reacted sharply to North Korea's missile launch in August 1998 and proceeded to develop an independent intelligence-gathering and evaluation capability, including spy satellites. And as the current nuclear crisis has heated up, Prime Minister Koizumi stresses the need for more rapid progress on developing a ballistic missile defense for his country.[43] The defense minister, Shigeru Ishiba, went considerably further than talking about ballistic missile defenses. He warned that Japan might launch a preemptive strike against North Korea if there was solid evidence of an impending missile attack. "It is too late if [a missile] flies toward Japan," he emphasized.[44]

There have been other subtle changes in Japan's security posture. Following the September 11 attacks on the World Trade Center and the Pentagon, the Diet passed legislation authorizing the Maritime Self Defense Forces (SDF) to send vessels to the Indian Ocean to support the U.S. antiterrorism campaign in Afghanistan.[45] True, the ships were tasked merely to provide refueling and supplies for U.S. forces, not to pursue any combat missions, but it signified that the SDF were willing to conduct operations farther away from the home islands than ever before. That trend continued a month later when the Diet passed legislation approving the prime minister's decision to send 1,000 peacekeeping personnel to Iraq.[46] (It is revealing, though, that implementation of that measure was put on hold because the security environment in Iraq was deemed too dangerous. Although Japanese political leaders gradually are becoming more flexible about troop deployments, they remain reluctant actually to put their military forces in harm's way.[47])

More relevant to issues in East Asia, the Diet approved three laws in June 2003 redefining the rules under which Japan can respond to a security threat. The new laws give the government far greater latitude in deploying the Self Defense Forces when a security threat emerges, instead of having to wait for an overt hostile act from an adversary. Notably, this legislation, which would have been extraordinarily controversial even a few years ago, passed the Diet by an overwhelming vote, with only the Japanese Communist Party and the Japanese Social Democratic Party in opposition.[48]

And Tokyo is beginning to back up such legal changes with tangible efforts to expand the capabilities of its military. For example, Japan is acquiring a midair refueling capability to lengthen the reach of its small but potent air force.[49] Such a capability would be essential if Japanese planes needed to retaliate for a North Korean attack. Even more startling, Japan has decided to build its first aircraft carriers since World War II.[50] The first two ships planned will be relatively small, displacing some 16,000 tons when fully loaded and carrying about 18 STOV (short-takeoff, vertical-landing aircraft) or a slightly larger number of attack helicopters. The carriers are tiny compared to the latest U.S. carrier launched in July 2003, the *Ronald Reagan*, which displaces 90,000 tons and can carry 80 aircraft, but it is a start. When the new carriers are launched in 2008 and 2009, they will give Japan a modest force-projection capability in the western Pacific for the first time in more than six decades. Although such changes are hardly sufficient to enable Japan to replace the United States as the principal power guaranteeing East Asia's security and stability, they are an important beginning.

Moreover, there are indications that more substantive changes may be on the way. Elements of the governing Liberal Democratic Party (as well as the opposition Democratic Party) now speak openly of the need to modify Article 9 so that Japan can be more proactive in the security realm. Indeed, some prominent Japanese consider Article 9 wholly obsolete and talk of abolishing it. Washington should quietly encourage such developments. There is even some evidence that Japan is hedging on the nuclear issue, as officials have suggested in off-the-record statements that Japan might reconsider its nonnuclear status if other countries (i.e., North Korea) acquired a nuclear-weapons capability. Although the Japanese government has officially reaffirmed its commitment to its nonnuclear principles,[51] the frequency of such "unofficial" comments indicates that the policy is not etched in granite.

BENEFITS OF A NEW U.S. STRATEGY

There are numerous benefits to such a shift from U.S. hegemony to a regional balance of power. The first is financial, since a "minimalist" policy would cut the $35 billion to $40 billion annual cost of U.S. security commitments roughly in half. By compelling Washington's security clients to internalize the full cost of their own defense, the United States would achieve a multibillion-dollar savings for American taxpayers.

The second benefit would be to reduce America's risk exposure in the event of an armed conflict in East Asia. As the self-appointed regional stabilizer, the United States is currently on the front lines. Although Washington's hegemonic policy may reduce the overall likelihood of a conflict in Korea, the Taiwan Strait, the South China Sea, or elsewhere, it also virtually guarantees that the United States will be caught up in any conflict that does erupt. The existence of treaty obligations, the deployment of tripwire forces, and the pressure of hegemonic responsibilities all combine to eliminate the element of choice. At the very least, U.S. policymakers should want to restore America's ability to choose whether to intervene or not.

Moreover, America's role as hegemonic protector may inadvertently encourage irresponsible behavior on the part of security clients. Manila is more likely to press its dubious claims to the Spratly Islands in the teeth of Chinese and Vietnamese opposition if Filipino leaders are confident that Washington (as a treaty ally) is in their corner. Similarly, pro-independence forces in Taiwan may press their agenda dangerously far, provoking a crisis with Beijing, if they believe that the United States is serious about guaranteeing Taiwan's security. ROK leaders can indulge in bizarre and foolish defense schemes (i.e., wanting submarines to guard against a Japanese military "threat") as long as the United States takes ultimate responsibility for protecting their country from the real threat: North Korea. In a more normal regional system, South Korea could not indulge in such emotional luxuries as Japan bashing over historical grievances. Astute ROK leaders would soon realize that a strong, democratic, status quo–oriented Japan would be a useful ally that could strengthen South Korea's security.

Finally, a lower-profile security policy promises to be more sustainable in the coming decades. America's preponderant position in East Asia arose because of the convergence of unusual circumstances. Japan's total defeat in World War II, China's continuing weakness and political turmoil, the death throes of decrepit European colonial empires (and the initial economic weakness of the independent successor states) created a vast power vacuum that the United States successfully filled. America's hegemonic status was not without cost; the Korean and Vietnam wars provide ample testimony to that truth. But America had no credible challengers and its role as East Asia's pacifier has yielded important benefits.

Whatever the value of that policy in the past, however, conditions have changed radically over the past two decades or so. The United States will find it increasingly difficult to preserve its hegemonic status in a region with not one but two rising great powers. Moreover, the explosive economic growth of the East Asian region as a whole inexorably narrows the advantage that has undergirded America's strategy of preponderance. The United States has been rightly described as the world's sole superpower, and it is indisputably the single strongest nation, both economically and militarily. Nevertheless, the United States now has less than 5 percent of the world's population and accounts for barely 20 percent of global economic output. And both percentages are slowly declining. In two decades America will likely have only 3.5 percent of the world's population and account for no more than 15 or 16 percent of global economic output. By that time China may well be on the verge of having the world's largest economy and Japan may be a strong third in that race. Is it really credible that the United States can continue to dominate a region thousands of miles from its homeland—a region that has an enormous edge in population and is rapidly acquiring the economic clout to match?

Instead of vainly trying to sustain an ebbing hegemony, the United States should restructure its policy to protect its important interests in a new East

Asia characterized by multiple power centers. America can play a meaningful role in East Asia's affairs indefinitely—if it husbands its strengths and does not attempt to overreach. It will assuredly be more difficult to be merely one major power among several rather than the regional hegemon, but the benefits of relinquishing the burdens of hegemony significantly outweigh the liabilities.

NOTES

CHAPTER 1

1. Quoted in David R. Sands, "Defection of Roh Ally Rocks Voting Day," *Washington Times,* December 19, 2002, p. A17; and Ralph A. Cossa, "Trials, Tribulations, Threats, and Tirades," *Comparative Connections* (4th quarter, 2002), www.csis.org.
2. Quoted in Doug Struck, "Alliance Falls Apart on Eve of South Korean Elections," *Washington Post,* December 19, 2002, p. A20.
3. Quoted in Peter S. Goodman, "S. Korean Seeks Mediation Role to End Standoff," *Washington Post,* January 4, 2003, p. A10.
4. Callum MacDonald, *Korea: The War Before Vietnam* (New York: Free Press, 1986), pp. 13–14.
5. See, e.g., Hakjoon Kim, "The U.S.-Korea Alliance: Past, Present and Future," *International Journal of Korean Studies,* 7, no. 1 (Spring/Summer 2003): 2.
6. America's ambivalence is discussed in Edward Olsen, "South Korea Under Military Rule: Friendly Fascism?" in *Friendly Tyrants: An American Dilemma,* eds. Daniel Pipes and Adam Garfinkle, pp. 336–37. (New York: St. Martin's Press, 1991).
7. Hakjoon Kim, "U.S.-Korea Alliance," pp. 6–10.
8. These and other instances are discussed in Manwoo Lee, "Anti-Americanism and South Korea's Changing Perception of America," *Alliance Under Tension: The Evolution of South Korean-U.S. Relations,* ed. Manwoo Lee, et al., pp. 7–27, 221–23 (Boulder, CO: Westview Press, 1988), and Kim Kyong-dong "Korean Perceptions of America," in *Korea Briefing, 1993: Festival of Korea,* ed. Donald Clark, pp. 172–74. (Boulder, CO: Westview Press, 1993).
9. Manwoo Lee, "Double Patronage Toward South Korea: Security vs. Democracy and Human Relations," in *Alliance Under Tension,* eds. Lee et al. pp. 43–44.
10. "Banner Battle Rouses Crowd at Seoul Rally," *Washington Post,* July 19, 1987, p. A18.
11. Selig Harrison, "Dateline South Korea: A Divided Seoul," *Foreign Policy,* no. 67 (Summer 1987): 157. Also quoted in Kim Jin-wung, "Recent Anti-Americanism in South Korea: The Causes," *Asian Survey* 29, no. 8 (August 1989): 755.
12. Nicholas Kristof, "In Kwangju, Rage and New Cynicism," *New York Times,* July 6, 1987, p. 6.
13. Linda Lewis, "The 'Kwangju Incident' Observed: An Anthropological Perspective on Civil Uprisings," in *The Kwangju Uprising: Shadows Over the Regime in South Korea,* ed. Donald Clark, p. 23. (Boulder, CO: Westview Press, 1988).
14. Sanford Ungar, "South Korea: Old Ally, New Competitor," *Atlantic* (December 1983): 23.

15. Edward Olsen, "South Korea Under Military Rule: Friendly Fascism?" in *Friendly Tyrants: An American Dilemma,* eds. Pipes and Garfinkle, p. 340.

16. Hakjoon Kim, "U.S.-Korea Alliance," pp. 13–15.

17. For instance, see accounts of anti-American student demonstrations in Seoul, Kwangju, and elsewhere reported in Foreign Broadcast Information Service (FBIS), *Daily Report: East Asia,* September 27, 1995, pp. 54–55.

18. James Matray, "Korea's Quest for Disarmament and Reunification," in *Korea and the Cold War: Division, Destruction, and Disarmament,* eds. Kim Chull Baum and James Matray, p. 237. (Claremont, CA: Regina Books, 1993). More generally, see Kim Jin-wung, "Recent Anti-Americanism," pp. 749–63.

19. See, e.g., Kristof, "Subway Brawl Inflames Issue of G.I.'s in Korea," *New York Times,* August 24, 1995, p. A3. This is not the first time that crimes committed by American servicemen created pressure for revising the SOFA. Kim Jin-wung, "Recent Anti-Americanism," pp. 756–58.

20. For example, see Jim Lea, "High DOD Aide Assails ROK Press," *Pacific Stars & Stripes,* September 8, 1995, p. 1.

21. Quoted in Kristof, "Subway Brawl Inflames Issue." See also Kevin Sullivan and Mary Jordan, "S. Korea Wants to Be Grown-Up Ally," *Washington Post,* October 19, 1995, pp. A31, A33.

22. Jack Anderson and Michael Binstein, "Korean Press Distorts 'Crime' by GIs," *Washington Post,* August 31, 1995, p. B23.

23. Quoted in Kristof, "Subway Brawl."

24. Manwoo Lee, "Anti-Americanism and South Korea's Changing Perception of America," in *Alliance Under Tension,* eds. Lee et al., p. 26.

25. Kim Kyong-dong, "Korean Perceptions," p. 177.

26. Kim Jin-wung, "Can the U.S. and South Korea Forge a More Equal Alliance?" *Korea Monitor* 1, no. 5 (December 2003): 41.

27. Rowan Scarborough, "American Citizens in S. Korea Warned," *Washington Times,* July 6, 2000, p. A1.

28. See, e.g., John Burton, "Fears Grow Over Widening Rift Between Seoul and U.S.," *Financial Times,* January 13, 2003, p. 4; Peter S. Goodman and Joohee Cho, "Anti-U.S. Sentiment Deepens in S. Korea," *Washington Post,* January 9, 2003, pp. A1, A18; Robert Marquand, "Anti-US Voices Surge in Streets of a Major Asian Ally," *Christian Science Monitor,* December 16, 2002, pp. 1, 7; and Doug Struck, "Resentment Toward U.S. Troops Is Boiling Over in South Korea," *Washington Post,* December 9, 2002, p. A17.

29. Quoted in Goodman and Cho, "Anti-U.S. Sentiment," p. A18.

30. Aidan Foster-Carter, "Spleen Versus Sense in Seoul," *Far Eastern Economic Review,* December 19, 2002, p. 25. See also Hakjoon Kim, "U.S.-Korea Alliance," pp. 28–29.

31. Kim Jin-wung, "'Little Brother' Grows Up and Talks Back," *Korea Monitor* (October 2003): 21.

32. Stephen Bradner, "The ROK-U.S. Alliance: Military and Non-Military Issues," paper presented to Korean Association of International Studies conference, Seoul, September 25, 2003, pp. 14–17.

33. Howard W. French, "Clouds Slowly Lift in South Korea," *New York Times,* February 3, 2003, p. A8.

34. James Brooke, "When American Villains Thwart Lovesick Koreans," *New York Times,* October 12, 2003, p. WK12. Some South Koreans also criticized the recent James Bond movie in which a North Korean was the villain. Charles Scanlon, "U.S. Faces Korean

Dilemma," BBC News, January 8, 2003, http://news.bbc.co.uk/1/hi/world/asia-pacific/2634911.stm.

35. Hakjoon Kim, "U.S.-Korea Alliance,"p. 28.

36. Bong Youngshik, "Anti-Americanism and the U.S.-Korea Military Alliance," in *Confrontation and Innovation on the Korean Peninsula,* ed. James M. Lister et al., p. 23. (Washington, DC: Korea Economic Institute, 2003).

37. See, e.g., Sangmee Bak, "Suddenly, Three's a Crowd in South Korea," *Washington Post,* January 26, 2003, pp. B1, B4; and James Brooke, "South Koreans Divided on North Korean Atom Threat," *New York Times,* December 29, 2002, p. 14.

38. Quoted in Doug Struck, "N. Korea's Neighbors Unmoved by Threats," *Washington Post,* February 11, 2003, p. A13.

39. Nicholas Eberstadt, "Our Other Korea Problem," *National Interest* no. 68 (Fall 2002): 112–13.

40. Nicholas Eberstadt, "Seoul on Ice," *Wall Street Journal,* December 18, 2002, p. A18; and Eberstadt, "Our Other Korea Problem," p. 112. The new white paper announces that "North Korea does not seem to have given up its strategy to communize the South as evidenced by its lukewarm response to ROK's offers to discuss military confidence building measures." *Participatory Government Defense Policy 2003* (Seoul: Ministry of National Defense, 2003), p. 26.

41. Quoted in Hakjoon Kim, "U.S.-Korea Alliance," p. 30.

42. Quoted in Peter Ford, "Is America the 'Good Guy'? Many Now Say, 'No,'" *Christian Science Monitor,* September 11, 2002, www.csmonitor.com.

43. Bong Youngshik, "Anti-Americanism and the U.S.-Korea Military Alliance," p. 23.

44. Hakjoon Kim, "U.S.-Korea Alliance," p. 30.

45. Bong Youngshik, "Anti-Americanism and the U.S.-Korea Military Alliance," p. 23.

46. Nicholas Kralev, "U.S. Sees Bias in S. Korea Textbooks," *Washington Times,* September 29, 2003, pp. A1, A14.

47. Kim Jin-wung, "'Little Brother' Grows Up and Talks Back," pp. 23–24.

48. See, e.g., Goodman and Cho, "Anti-U.S. Sentiment," p. A18; Andrew Ward, "Roh's Poll Win a 'Generational Earthquake,'" *Financial Times,* December 23, 2002, p. 4; and Kim Jin-wung, "'Little Brother' Grows Up and Talks Back," p. 19.

49. Gi-wook Shin, "A New Wave of Anti-Americanism in South Korea," *San Diego Union-Tribune,* December 27, 2002, p. B7.

50. Kim Jin-wung, "'Little Brother' Grows Up and Talks Back," p. 20.

51. Bong Youngshik, "Anti-Americanism and the U.S.-Korea Military Alliance," p. 21.

52. Quoted in Ford, "Is America the 'Good Guy'?"

53. Quoted in Doug Struck, "Korean Vets, Wary of North, Are Voices of Past," *Washington Post,* January 25, 2003, p. A18.

54. Kim Jin-wung, "'Little Brother' Grows Up and Talks Back," p. 17.

55. Norman D. Levin and Yong-Sup Han, *The Shape of Korea's Future: South Korean Attitudes Toward Unification and Long-Term Security Issues* (Santa Monica, CA: RAND Corporation, 1999), pp. 26–28.

56. Quoted in Norimitsu Onishi, "S. Korea Marks War Anniversary with Divided Emotions," *San Diego Union-Tribune,* July 27, 2003, p. A24.

57. Quoted in Ford, "Is America the 'Good Guy'?"

58. Quoted in Jay Solomon, "For U.S. Forces in Korea, Change Appears Inevitable," *Wall Street Journal,* December 19, 2002, p. A13.

59. Levin and Young-Sup Han, *The Shape of Korea's Future,* pp. 17–19.

60. Hakjoon Kim, "U.S.-Korea Alliance," p. 37.

61. See, e.g., Aidan Foster-Carter, "Nuclear Shadow Over Sunshine," *Comparative Connections* (4th Quarter 2002), www.csis.org/pacfor/cc/0204Qnk_sk.html.

62. Kim Jinwung, "'Little Brother' Grows Up and Talks Back," p. 22.

63. See, e.g., Howard R. French and Don Kirk, "American Policies and Presence Are Under Fire in South Korea, Straining an Alliance," *New York Times,* December 8, 2002, p. 10.

64. See, e.g., Sang-hun Choe, "After Acquittals, Anti-U.S. Feelings Boil Over in Korea," *Washington Times,* December 8, 2002, p. A9; Barbara Demick, "Anti-Americanism Sweeps South Korea," *Los Angeles Times,* November 27, 2002, p. A3; and Patrick Goodenough, "Acquittal of U.S. Soldier Prompts Fury in South Korea," Cybercast News Service, November 21, 2002, http://www.cnsnews.com.

65. See, e.g., James Brooke, "G.I.'s in South Korea Encounter Increased Hostility," *New York Times,* January 8, 2003, p. A10; Patrick Goodenough, "Anti-US Feeling Could Spark Anti-Korean Boycott, Businesses Warn," Cybercast News Service, December 16, 2002, http://www.cnsnews.com; Patrick Goodenough, "Chilly Winter Looms for American Troops in Korea," Cybercast News Service, December 9, 2002, http://www.cnsnews.com; and "Seoul Restaurants Bar U.S. Diners," BBC News, November 28, 2002, www.bbc.co.uk.

66. Don Kirk, "Korean Mob Briefly Detains U.S. Soldier After Subway Fight," *New York Times,* September 16, 2002, p. A7; and Patrick Goodenough, "U.S. Soldiers Attacked in South Korea, Prompting U.S. Protest," Cybercast News Service, September 18, 2002, http://www.cnsnews.com.

67. Hae Won Choi, "Long a U.S. Ally, South Koreans Sour on America," *Wall Street Journal,* December 24, 2002, p. A8.

68. See, e.g., Patrick Goodenough, "Korean Presidential Candidates Exploit Anti-U.S. Feeling," Cybercast News Service, December 9, 2002, http://www.cnsnews.com; Jong-heon Lee, "U.S. Considers Changes to Treaty with Seoul," *Washington Times,* December 11, 2002, p. A13; Patrick Goodenough, "Korean Protests: U.S. May Amend Forces Agreement," Cybercast News Service, December 11, 2002, http://www.cnsnews.com; and "Candidates Clash," *Korea Now,* December 14, 2002, p. 6. Washington now allows some offenses by off-duty U.S. personnel to be tried in civilian Korean courts. The first case, involving a hit-and-run/drunk driving case, went to trial in January 2004. Don Greenlees, "Alliance on Trial," *Far Eastern Economic Review,* January 29, 2004, pp. 18–19.

69. Quoted in Peter M. Beck, "Korea's Next President," *Korea Insight* (Korea Economic Institute) 5, no. 1 (January 2003): 1; and Paul Shin, "Pro-Govt. Candidate Wins in South Korea," Associated Press, December 19, 2002, www.aol.com. Roh also charged previous ROK leaders of "groveling" before the United States. Quoted in Christopher Torchia, "S. Korea New Chief Vows to Work with U.S.," Associated Press, December 19, 2002.

70. Quoted in Hakjoon Kim, "U.S.-Korea Alliance," p. 29.

71. Kim Tae-hyo, "A Challenge During Transition: Korean Perception of ROK-U.S. Relations," paper presented to Korean Association of International Studies conference, Seoul, September 25, 2003, p. 12.

72. Kim Sung-han, "Challenges and Visions of the ROK-U.S. Alliance: A Korean Perspective," paper presented to Korean Association of International Studies conference, Seoul, September 25, 2003, pp. 31–32.

73. Kim Jin-wung, "Can the U.S. and South Korea Forge a More Equal Alliance?" p. 46.

74. Lee Nae-young and Jeong Han-wool, "Anti-Americanism and the ROK-U.S. Alliance," *East Asian Review* 15, no. 4 (Winter 2003): pp. 26–27.

75. "Strengthening the U.S.-ROK Alliance: A Blueprint for the 21st Century," Center for Strategic and International Studies, 2003, www.csis.org, p. 3.

76. Seongho Sheen, "Grudging Partner: South Korea's Response to U.S. Security Policies," in *Asia-Pacific Responses to U.S. Security Policies,* ed. Satu P. Limaye, p. 10–7. (Honolulu: Asia-Pacific Center for Security Studies, March 2003).

77. Gregory F. Treverton, Eric V. Larson, and Spencer H. Kim, "Bridging the Open Water in the U.S.-South Korea Military Alliance," in *Confrontation and Innovation on the Korean Peninsula,* eds. Lister et al., p. 32.

78. David Frum and Richard Perle, *An End to Evil: How to Win the War on Terror* (New York: Random House, 2003), p. 99.

79. See, e.g., Doug Bandow, "Mutually Assured Frustration," *American Spectator* January 9, 2004, www.spectator.org/dsp_article.asp?art_id=5999. Moreover, according to the forecasting firm Stratfor, Seoul decided to contribute forces primarily "in preparation for the coming draw-down of U.S. forces on the Korean peninsula and to establish itself as a stronger player on the global stage in its own right." "Iraq Deployment: Bellwether for South Korea's Future?" Stratfor, January 12, 2004, www.stratfor.info/Story.neo?storyId=226915.

80. Chung Jin-young, "Cost Sharing for USFK in Transition: Whither the ROK-U.S. Alliance?" in *Recalibrating the U.S.-Republic of Korea Alliance,* ed. Donald W. Boose, Jr. et al., p. 45. (Carlisle, PA: U.S. Army War College, May 2003).

81. Ibid., p. 46.

82. Kim Jin-wung, "Can the U.S. and South Korea Forge a More Equal Alliance?" pp. 43–46.

83. Seongho Sheen, "Grudging Partner," p. 10–6.

84. See, e.g., "South Korea: Growing Anti-American Sentiment Targets SOFA Talks," December 5, 2000, Stratfor, www.stratfor.biz. It is also an issue in Japan. See, e.g., "Japanese Lawmaker: Tokyo, Seoul Should Share SOFA Changes," Stratfor, January 8, 2003, www.stratfor.biz.

85. "Protestors' Voices Heard," *Korea Now,* December 14, 2002, pp. 8–9.

86. "South Korea: U.S. Soldier to be Tried in Road Death," *New York Times,* January 9, 2004, p. A5.

87. David Scofield, "The Mortician's Tale: Time for US to Leave Korea," *Asia Times Online,* January 28, 2004, http://atimes.com/Korea/FA28Dg02.html.

88. "Korean Mob Briefly Detains U.S. Soldier After Subway Fight," *New York Times,* September 16, 2002, p. A7; and Patrick Goodenough, "U.S. Soldiers Attacked in South Korea, Prompting U.S. Protest." Cybercast News Service, September 18, 2002, http://www.cnsnews.com/ViewForeignBureaus.asp?Page=\ForeignBureaus\archive\200209\FOR20020918c.html.

89. As columnist Joseph Harsh put it 17 years ago, "The U.S. has the right of any imperial power to intervene in the internal domestic affairs of one of its protégés and clients." Joseph Harsh, "South Korea: A Classic Imperial Problem," *Christian Science Monitor,* June 23, 1987, p. 16.

90. Seongho Sheen, "Grudging Partner," p. 10–5.

91. David Wall, "Euphoria Fading Fast in South Korea," *Japan Times,* July 7, 2000, p. 16.

92. Hakjoon Kim, "U.S.-Korea Alliance," pp. 13–15.

93. The latter alone is resulting in unprecedented contact between workers from South and North. Shim Jae Hoon, "Nuclear Test," *Far Eastern Economic Review,* September 4, 1997, p. 16.

94. In fact, the North accounted for $190 million of the trade, principally gold and other minerals. Seoul shipped $60 million worth of petrochemicals and textiles. "Korea: Bilateral Trade Up," *Far Eastern Economic Review,* February 5, 1998, p. 57.

95. J. C. Yang, "Global Groups Beat Path to Pyongyang," *Nikkei Weekly,* February 2, 1998, p. 21.

96. Robert Manning, "Toward What New Ends?" *Washington Times,* July 2, 2000, p. B3.

97. "An Opinion Poll on the Inter-Korean Summit," *Korea Update* 11, no. 4, (June 25, 2000): p. 4.

98. *Korea Now,* June 17, 2000, front cover.

99. Ibid., pp. 4–13.

100. Quoted in Calvin Sims, "A Cease-Fire Takes Hold in Korean Propaganda War," *New York Times,* June 17, 2000, p. A3.

101. For a description of the reaction of South Koreans, see Doug Struck, "S. Koreans See North in New Light," *Washington Post,* June 16, 2000, pp. A1, A25. Kim even claimed to have previously traveled to China and Indonesia, to the surprise of North Korea watchers. Less rapturous were some South Korean veterans, who criticized their government for downgrading the fiftieth-anniversary celebrations.

102. See, e.g., Paul Eckert, "China 'Rejoices' in Korean Summit, Urges Them On," Reuters, June 15, 2000.

103. See, e.g., Jonathan Watts, "How North Korea Is Embracing Capitalism by Any Other Name," *Guardian,* December 3, 2003, www.guardian.co.uk/korea/article/0,2763, 1098533,00.html; Anthony Faiola, "A Crack in the Door in N. Korea," *Washington Post,* November 24, 2003, pp. A1, A12; Nguyen Nhat Lam, "N. Korea Exports Fast-Food Restaurants," *Washington Times,* October 12, 2003, p. A9; Anthony Faiola, "N. Korea Shifts Toward Capitalism," *Washington Post,* September 14, 2003, p. A20; Marcus Noland, "Economy's Ills Shape N Korean Crisis," BBC News, April 22, 2003, http:// news.bbc.co.uk/1/hi/world/asia-pacific/2965875.stm; Frank Ching, "North Korea's Other Face," *Far Eastern Economic Review,* June 15, 2000, p. 36; Michael Schuman, Jane Lee, and Neil King, "Two Koreas Still Face a Tortuous Road," *Wall Street Journal,* June 16, 2000, pp. A10, A12; David Kang, "We Should Not Fear the North Koreans," *Los Angeles Times,* June 13, 2000, p. A17; and John Burton, "Historic Korean Summit May Thaw Last Frontier of the Cold War," *Financial Times,* June 13, 2000, p. 8.

104. See, e.g., Eliot Syunghyun Jung, Youngsoo Kim, and Takayuki Kobayashi, "North Korea's Special Economic Zones: Obstacles and Opportunities," in *Confrontation and Innovation on the Korean Peninsula,* eds. Lister et al., pp. 43–59.

105. See, e.g., Jay Solomon and Charles Hutzler, "North Korea Flirts with Capitalism—As Best It Can," *Wall Street Journal,* " October 3, 2002, pp. A1, A7; Doug Struck, "A Taste of Capitalism in N. Korea," *Washington Post,* September 13, 2002, pp. A1, A34; "North Korea Takes Tentative Steps Towards Reform," *Economic Intelligence,* Asia Intelligence Ltd., September 2002, www.asiaint.com; Chong Bong-uk, "Unprecedented Market-Oriented Measures," *Vantage Point* 25, no. 12 (December 2002): 9–13; Hong Ihk-pyo, "A Shift Toward Capitalism? Recent Economic Reforms in North Korea," *East Asian Review* 14, no. 4 (Winter 2002): 93–106; Kwak Seung-ji, "Sinuiju Special Administrative Region," *Vantage Point* 25, no. 10 (October 2002): 2–10; and "'Modeling China,'" *Korea Now,* September 21, 2002, p. 18.

106. Doug Struck, "On Pyongyang's Streets, Sound of Change," *Washington Post,* September 21, 2002, pp. A1, A16.

107. John W. Lewis, "Hope on N. Korea," *Washington Post,* January 27, 2004, p. A17; Christopher Marquis, "American Group Says North Koreans Are Eager to Deal with West," *New York Times,* January 21, 2004, p. A8; and Glenn Kessler, "N. Korea Progressing, U.S. Visitor Says," *Washington Post,* January 16, 2004, p. A14.

108. Sungwoo Kim, "North Korea's Unofficial Market Economy and Its Implications," *International Journal of Korean Studies* 7, no. 1 (Spring/Summer 2003): 147.

109. Kwan Weng Kim, "Sinuiju Sputters Even Before Take-Off," *Straits Times,* October 12, 2002, http://straitstimes.asia1.com.sg; Sebastian Moffett, "A Snapshot of Pyongyang's Methods," *Wall Street Journal,* November 8, 2002, pp. A8, A9; "'Wait and See,'" *Korea Now,* December 14, 2002, p. 24; and Foster-Carter, "Nuclear Shadow Over Sunshine."

110. See, e.g., Samuel Len, "Despite Thaw, Western Businesses Wary of North Korea," *International Herald Tribune,* July 7, 2000, p. 16; Mark Schuman and Jane Lee, "Pact May Open Business Channel, but Firms Face Obstacles," *Asian Wall Street Journal* (Weekly Edition), June 19–25, 2000, p. 11; and Mark Magnier, "Seoul Sees Long-term Potential in N. Korea," *Los Angeles Times,* June 10, 2000, p. A1.

111. And those zones have been affected by the North's poverty and interference from China. See, e.g., Joseph Kahn, "China Seizes Entrepreneur Named to Run North Korea Enclave," *New York Times,* October 4, 2002, p. A10.

112. See, e.g., James Brooke, "Looming Trade Penalties Could Sever a North Korean Link to Japan," *New York Times,* January 16, 2003, p. A12.

113. Quoted in Andrew Ward, "European Business Chamber Opens in N Korea," *Financial Times,* January 14, 2004, p. 4.

114. See, e.g., John Pomfret, "Reforms Turn Disastrous for North Koreans," *Washington Post,* January 27, 2003, p. A16.

115. Dominique Dwor Frecaut, "Korean Reunification: One Country, Two Systems?" in *Confrontation and Innovation on the Korean Peninsula,* eds. James M. Lister et al., p. 61.

116. See, e.g., Gordon Fairclough, "North Korea's Plans for Its Economy Are Enigmatic," *Wall Street Journal,* November 24, 2003, p. A12; "Progress at a Snail's Pace," *Economist,* October 11, 2003, pp. 43–44; Kate McGeown, "On Holiday in North Korea," BBC News, September 17, 2003, http://news.bbc.co.uk/1/hi/world/asia-pacific/3113352.stm; Len, "Despite Thaw, Western Businesses Wary of North Korea"; Schuman and Lee, "Pact May Open Business Channel"; and Magnier, "Seoul Sees Long-term Potential in N. Korea."

117. Tom Carter and David Sands, "North Koreans Facing Starvation," *Washington Times,* January 20, 2004, p. A15.

118. Marcus Noland, "Trainspotting in North Korea," *Far Eastern Economic Review,* October 24, 2002, p. 29. A detailed analysis of the DPRK economy is provided by Kim, "North Korea's Unofficial Market Economy and Its Implications," 147–64. Noland offers a detailed look at the DPRK's economic reforms. Marcus Noland, *Korea After Kim Jong-il* (Washington, DC: Institute for International Economics, January 2004), pp. 46–57.

119. Yang Moon-soo, "Macroeconomic Policy in the Early Stages of Marketization in North Korea," *East Asian Review* 15, no. 4 (Winter 2003): 92.

120. See, e.g., Park Hyeong-jung, "A Stepwise Scenario for Rebuilding the North Korean Economy, *Eastern Asian Review* 15, no. 4 (Winter 2003): 95–118.

121. Noland, *Korea After Kim Jong-il,* p. 43.

122. "What Thaw in North Korea?" *Far Eastern Economic Review,* June 29, 2000, p. 6.

123. Quoted in Christopher Torchia, "U.S. Envoy: New Unity May Be Swift," *Washington Times,* June 27, 2000, p. A14.

124. Quoted in Schuman, Lee, and King, "Two Koreas," p. A10.

125. Quoted in Sonni Efron, "Korean Summit Opens with Hope, Handshake,"* Los Angeles Times,* June 11, 2000, p. A6.

126. Jonathan D. Pollack, "The United States, North Korea, and the End of the Agreed Framework," *Naval War College Review* 41, no. 3 (Summer 2003): 24.

127. Ibid., p. 25.

128. For a review of Bush administration policies toward the DPRK, see ibid., pp. 24–26.

129. Ibid., p. 27.

130. Ibid., p. 28.

131. Barbara Demick, "U.S. Accused of Blocking 'Sunshine Policy,'" *Los Angeles Times*, January 15, 2003, p. A4.

132. "Seoul Fears Impending Crisis on Korean Peninsula," Stratfor, March 29, 2002, www.stratfor.biz.

133. See, e.g., Sebastian Moffett et al., "North Korea Opens Door to New Ties with Japan, World," *Wall Street Journal*, September 18, 2002, pp. A1, A16; "Inter-Korea Breakthrough," *Korea Update* 13, no. 7 (August 2002): 1–3; "Bipolar Diplomacy Disorder," *New York Times*, September 22, 2002, p. WK3; Doug Struck, "Asian Games Offer Venue for Bridging Two Koreas," *Washington Post*, September 30, 2002, p. A16; Howard R. French, "North Korean Fans Draw Crowds of Their Own," *New York Times*, October 2, 2002, p. A8; Joseph A. B. Winder, "North Korea Takes Steps to Break Out of Its Shell," *Korea Insight* 4, no. 10 (October 2002): 21–22; "The Koreas United, for a Day," *Economist*, October 5, 2002, p. 39; "P'Yang Continues to Get Aid," *Korea Now*, November 2, 2002, p. 13; and James Brooke, "On Ice, 2 Koreas Cross Sticks, Not Swords," *New York Times*, February 4, 2003, p. C17.

134. "North Korea Makes Rapid Progress on Cyber Front," Asia Intelligence Ltd., September 2001, www.asiaint.com.

135. Doug Struck, "N. Korea's Closed Society Keeps Trade Routes Open," *Washington Post*, February 3, 2003, p. A18.

136. Foster-Carter, "Nuclear Shadow Over Sunshine."

137. One analysis of the power structure is provided by "Inside North Korea's Ruling Elite," AsiaInt, January 2003, www.asiaint.com.

138. Don Gregg, "Kim Jong Il: The Truth Behind the Caricature," *Newsweek*, February 3, 2003, p. 13.

139. Doug Struck, "Japan and North Korea Spar Over Kidnap Victims' Return," *Washington Post*, November 16, 2002, p. A14; "Pyongyang Talks Shelved for Now," *Asahi Shimbun*, November 26, 2002, www.asahi.com; "N Korea Says No Talks Unless Abductees Come Back," *Japan Today*, November 29, 2002, www.japantoday.com. Yet a day after Kim Jong-il made his dramatic admission, Japanese officials were reported to have said that "the main obstacles toward normalization have been removed. The talks are simply to work out the details of full normalization, a legal requirement before the economic assistance can start." Quoted in Doug Struck, "N. Korea Admits It Abducted Japanese," *Washington Post*, September 18, 2002, p. A18.

140. James Brooke, "North Korea Eases Stormy Ties with Japan," *New York Times*, January 19, 2004, p. 2.

141. Pollack, "End of the Agreed Framework," pp. 35–38. U.S. intelligence analysts began suspecting the North Koreans of cheating in 2001, but took some time to conclude that the North was pursuing a uranium enrichment program. Ibid., p. 13.

142. See, e.g., ibid., p. 29.

143. The administration's argument for why Iraq was a greater problem than North Korea was not particularly persuasive. See, e.g., ibid., pp. 38–39. That rationale looked particularly thin when it became evident that Baghdad possessed no weapons of mass destruction.

144. See, e.g., Jeff Shesol, "The 'Axis of Evil' Guy," *New York Times*, Book Review section, January 26, 2003, p. 8; Hendrik Hertzberg, "Axis Praxis," *The New Yorker*, January 13, 2003, pp. 27–29.

145. Democratic presidential candidates were soon making this argument. Joseph I. Lieberman, "Crisis of Our Own Creation," *Washington Post*, January 8, 2003, p. A19. For one

description of the administration's uncertain reaction, see Richard Wolffe, "Iraq or North Korea: Who is the Bigger Threat?" *Newsweek*, January 13, 2003, pp. 21–23.

146. Walter Clemens, "Peace in Korea? Lessons from Cold War Detente," in *Confrontation and Innovation on the Korean Peninsula*, ed Lister et al., p. 15.

147. See, e.g., Robert Marquand, "How S. Korea's View of the North Flipped," *Christian Science Monitor*, January 22, 2003, www.csmonitor.com; and Hae Won Choi, "Seoul's Textbook Detente," *Wall Street Journal*, January 14, 2003, p. A10.

148. Quoted in John Larkin, "New Leader, New Crisis," *Far Eastern Economic Review*, January 9, 2003, p. 14.

149. Quoted in French, "South Korea's President-Elect Rejects Use of Force," p. A25.

150. Nicholas D. Kristof, "Cookies and Kimchi," *New York Times*, January 17, 2003, p. A25.

151. Not only was he an opposition lawyer who opposed military rule, but his father-in-law was a leftist who was jailed after the Korean War for allegedly killing right-wing opponents. "Seoul Faces a Summer of Political Maneuvering," Asia Intelligence Ltd., May 2002, www.asiaint.com.

152. Quoted in Sands, "Defection of Roh Ally Rocks Voting Day."

153. For an analysis of the election, see Peter M. Beck, "Korea's Next President," *Korea Insight* 5, no. 1 (January 2003): 1. See also Patrick Goodenough, "Korean Presidential Candidates Exploit Anti-US Feeling," Cybercast News Service, December 9, 2002, http://www.cnsnews.com.

154. See, e.g., Reihan Salam, "Real Sunshine," *National Review Online*, December 19, 2002, www.nationalreview.com.

155. See, e.g., Hakjoon Kim, "U.S.-Korea Alliance," pp. 15–19.

156. Ibid., pp. 19–28.

157. Larkin, "New Leader, New Crisis," 2003, p. 13.

158. Quoted in Hakjoon Kim, "U.S.-Korea Alliance," p. 31.

159. Quoted in Joel Mowbray, "Doing Nothing," *National Review Online*, February 12, 2003, www.nationalreview.com.

160. Edward A. Olsen, "A Korean Solution to the United States' Korean Problems," *Journal of East Asian Affairs* 17, no. 2 (Fall/Winter 2003): 225.

161. See, e.g., James Brooke, "Once Again, North Korea Unsettles South Korea's Politics," *New York Times*, December 12, 2002, p. A18. One probably has to go back to the late 1980s, during the waning days of the Chun Doo-hwan dictatorship, to find similarly intense, but more limited, popular outbursts against the United States and complaints about perceived American meddling in Korean affairs. See, e.g., Doug Bandow, "Korea: The Case for Disengagement," Cato Institute Policy Analysis, no. 96, December 8, 1987, pp. 6–9, 12–13.

162. Treverton, Larson, and Kim, "Bridging the Open Water," p. 32.

163. Quoted in French, "South Korea's President-Elect Rejects Use of Force Against North Korea," *New York Times*, January 17, 2003, p. A11.

164. Sheen, "Grudging Partner," p. 10–3.

165. He apparently also threatened military action if the North Koreans reopened the Yongbyon reactor. Dana Milbank, "U.S. Open to Informal Talks with N. Korea," *Washington Post*, December 30, 2002, p. A4.

166. Quoted in Struck, "Alliance Falls Apart on Eve of South Korean Elections." In contrast, many U.S. officials in defense circles did know it. See, e.g., George Gedda, "Bush Not Set to Pick Fight with N. Korea," Associated Press, December 18, 2002, www.aol.com.

167. Quoted in Struck, "S. Korean Envoy to Go North for Talks," *Washington Post*, January 25, 2003, p. A18.

168. See, e.g., Struck, "S. Korea's Next Leader: The Indispensable Man?" *Washington Post,* December 21, 2002, p. A16; and Robert Marquand, "U.S. Bides Times on N. Korean Crisis," *Christian Science Monitor,* January 3, 2003, p. 7.

169. For instance, Secretary of State Colin Powell stated in January 2004 that "President Bush, along with the other leaders, is looking for a diplomatic solution, and he has made that clear." Quoted in "U.S. Wants Diplomatic Solution to North Korea—Powell," Reuters, January 11, 2004, http://aolsvc.news.aol.com/news/article.adp?id=20040111053709990001.

170. See, e.g., Doug Bandow, "Defusing the Korean Bomb," Cato Institute Foreign Policy Briefing, no. 14, December 16, 1991, pp. 5–6; and Doug Bandow, "North Korea and the Risks of Coercive Nonproliferation," Cato Institute Foreign Policy Briefing, no. 24, May 4, 1993, pp. 4–6.

171. See, e.g., John McCain, "Rogue State Rollback," *Weekly Standard,* January 20, 2003 ; Mona Charen, "Ticking Time Bomb," *Washington Times,* January 16, 2003, p. A16; Heritage Institution analyst Baker Spring quoted in Brian Mitchell, "N. Korea Gets What It Wants from Nuclear Arms—Clout," *Investor's Business Daily,"* October 28, 2002, p. A17; and "Gen. Singlaub: Plan for Strikes Against North Korea," December 26, 2002, www.newsmax.com.

172. Charles Krauthammer, "Korea Follies," *Washington Post,* January 17, 2003, p. A23. Columnist Paul Greenberg also said Iraq first. "There will be time to neuter Kim Jong Il's ambitions, diplomatically or more abruptly." Paul Greenberg, "One War at a Time," October 25, 2002, www.townhall.com. See also "Pyongyang's Nuclear Blackmail," *Wall Street Journal,* October 18, 2002, p. A10. Richard Perle, chairman of the Pentagon Defense Policy Board, emphasizes that military action remains an option. Ju Yong-jung, "US Hawk Warns Not to Rule Out Military Option," *Digital Chosun Ilbo,* December 18, 2002, http://english.chosun.com. Similar in thought but operating on a longer time frame is West Point professor Barry McCaffrey. Barry R. McCaffrey, "North Korea's Global Threat," *Wall Street Journal,* December 12, 2002, p. A18.

173. Quoted in Doug Struck, "S. Korean Says U.S. Considered Attack on North," *Washington Post,* January 19, 2003, p. A18; and Christopher Torchia, "Officials Said to Have Pondered North Korea Attack Last Month," *Washington Times,* January 19, 2003, p. A7.

174. Phil Reeves, "South Korean Leader Claims US Hardliners Discussed Attacking North," *Independent,* January 20, 2003, http://news.independent.co.uk; and Jae-suk Yoo, "South Korea: U.S. Didn't Debate Attack," Associated Press, January 19, 2003, www.aol.com.

175. Quoted in James Dao, "Bush Urges Chinese President to Press North Korea on Arms," *New York Times,* February 8, 2003, p. A9.

176. Ju Yong-jung, "US Hawk Warns Not to Rule Out Military Option."

177. Quoted in John J. Tkacik Jr., "China Must Pressure Pyongyang," Heritage Foundation Press Room Commentary, December 31, 2002, www.heritage.org.

178. Quoted in "North Korean Move Prompts U.S. Warnings," *Wall Street Journal,* February 8, 2003, p. A14. Secretary of State Powell essentially said the same thing the day before while testifying before the Senate Foreign Relations Committee, but added that "we have no intention of attacking North Korea as a nation." Quoted in James Dao, "Bush Administration Defends Its Approach on North Korea," *New York Times,* February 7, 2003, p. A3.

179. McCain, "Rogue State Rollback." *Washington Post* columnist Fred Hiatt makes a similar argument, complaining that "South Korea's proximity to North Korea's army, in fact, may cloud its vision of the danger of a nuclear arsenal." Fred Hiatt, "Seoul May Not Know Best," *Washington Post,* January 6, 2003, p. A15.

180. Frank Gaffney, "North Korea Scorecard," *Washington Times,* January 14, 2003, p. A15.

181. Stephen J. Morris, "Averting the Unthinkable," *National Interest,* no. 74 (Winter 2003–04): 107.

182. Frum and Perle, *An End to Evil,* pp. 99–100.

183. Quoted in David R. Sands, "S. Korea Opposes Attack on North," *Washington Times,* February 14, 2003, p. A1.

184. Quoted in Nam Jeong-ho and Kang Min-Seok, "Roh Says 'Yes' to Cash Aid to North; Lee Says 'No,'" *Joong Ang Daily,* December 4, 2002, http://joongangdaily.joins.com.

185. Quoted in Sang-Hun Choe, "S. Korea Appeals for Calm in Nuke Crisis," Associated Press, February 8, 2003, www.aol.com.

186. Howard R. French, "Reversals in U.S. South Korean Links, and Some Jagged Fault Lines," *New York Times,* February 11, 2003, p. A13.

187. *Participatory Government Defense Policy 2003* (Seoul: Ministry of National Defense, 2003), p. 84.

188. Quoted in French, "South Korea's President-Elect Rejects Use." It was, said one press report, "a hastily arranged ceremonial visit" intended "to blunt a wave of anti-American sentiment and shore up the alliance as a nuclear crisis intensifies on the Korean Peninsula." Peter S. Goodman, "South Korea's President-Elect Visits U.S. Forces," *Washington Post,* January 16, 2003, p. A16.

189. Quoted in Patrick Goodenough, "U.S.-South Korean Alliance 'Precious,' President-Elect Says," Cybercast News Service, January 15, 2003, http://www.cnsnews.com. See also Howard R. French, "Aides Declare U.S. 'Willing to Talk' in Korea Dispute," *New York Times,* January 14, 2003, p. A12. South Korean envoy Yoo Jay-kun made much the same pitch when visiting the United States in late January. Christian Bourge, "Seoul Envoy Sees Ties to U.S. Vital in Nuclear Crisis," *Washington Times,* January 24, 2003, p. A17.

190. See, e.g., Hakjoon Kim, "U.S. Korea Alliance," pp. 31–34; Young Whan Kihl, "Nuclear Issues in U.S.-Korea Relations: An Uncertain Security Future," *International Journal of Korean Studies* 7, no. 1 (Spring/Summer 2003), p. 83.

191. Quoted in Patrick Goodenough, "S. Korean Lawmakers to Discuss U.S. Troop Reduction Concerns," Cybercast News Service, January 2, 2003, http://www.cnsnews.com.

192. "South Korea: Roh's Independence Push Speaks to Military Necessities," Stratfor, January 13, 2003, www.stratfor.biz.

193. Quoted in Howard French, "Shifting Loyalties: Seoul Looks to New Alliances," *New York Times,* January 26, 2003, p. 15.

194. Christopher Cooper, "U.S. Plan Puts Korea on Edge," *Wall Street Journal,* October 21, 2003, p. A4.

195. Frum and Perle, *An End to Evil,* pp. 103–4. They hope the United States will not actually have to use those plans, if China acts to remove Kim Jong-il.

196. Obviously, such circumstances often are murky, and in this case may have involved personal criticism of President Roh by ministry officials. But the shake-up appeared more to reflect policy than personality. See, e.g., Andrew Ward, "Roh Shakes Up South Korean Ministry After U.S. Policy Dispute," *Financial Times,* January 21, 2004, p. 4; Jaewoo Choo, "Seoul's New Envoy May Not Please U.S.," *Asia Times Online,* January 21, 2004, Korea/FA21Dg 03.html; "Time Running Out in North Korean Crisis," *Financial Times,* January 20, 2004, p. 14; "New S. Korean Foreign Minister Says No Policy Shift," Reuters, January 17, 2004, http://aolsvc.news.aol.com; "President 'Dumps' Pro-US Minister," *The Guardian,* January 16, 2004, www.guardian.co.uk/korea/article/0,2763, 1124505,00.html; and "S Korea Foreign Minister Resigns," BBC News, January 15, 2004, http://news.bbc.co.uk/2/low/asia-pacific/3398203.stm.

197. Lee and Jeong, "Anti-Americanism and the ROK-U.S. Alliance," p. 24.

198. Ibid., p. 26.

199. Ibid., pp. 27–28. Much ink has been spilled of late, especially on the Korean side, about anti-Americanism. Even ROK government publications tend to worry about the phenomenon, acknowledge changing assessments of America and North Korea, and recognize the divergence in generational attitudes towards the United States. See, e.g., Balbina Hwang and Caroline Cooper, *U.S.-Korea Relations: Opinion Leaders Seminar* (Washington, DC: Korea Economic Institute, 2003).

200. Morris, "Averting the Unthinkable," p. 104.

201. Ibid., p. 105.

202. Lee and Jeong, "Anti-Americanism and the ROK-U.S. Alliance," p. 51.

203. Ibid., p. 46.

204. Quoted in Charles Pekow, "Explaining the Alliance: The U.S. Counters Anti-Americanism with a Public Relations Push," *Korea Monitor* (October 2003): 30.

205. Quoted in Solomon, "Change Appears Inevitable," p. A13.

206. Levin and Han, p. 11.

207. Quoted in Gavan McCormack, "North Korea: Coming in from the Cold?" Japan Policy Research Institute Working Paper, no. 91 (January 2003): 6.

208. Quoted in David R. Sands, "S. Korean Official Says 'Fear' Motivates North," *Washington Times,* February 4, 2003, p. A1.

209. Quoted in Howard French, "South Korea's President-Elect Rejects Use of Force Against North Korea," *New York Times,* January 17, 2003, p. A11.

210. Quoted in Sands, "'Fear' Motivates North," p. A1.

211. Quoted in Moon Ihlwan and Ian Bremner, "The Other Korea Crisis," *Business Week Online,* January 20, 2003, www.businessweek.com/magazine/content/03_03/b3816020. html.

212. Quoted in Peter R. Goodman, "Treaty Pullout May Signal Desire for Arms—or a Deal," *Washington Post,* January 11, 2003, p. A16.

213. The summit payment resulted in the prosecution of several Hundai employees and ROK government officials. Andrew Ward, "Korean Summit Scandal Dims 'Sunshine' Policy," *Financial Times,* December 29, 2003, p. 4.

214. "Koreas Open Arena in Pyongyang," *Korea News,* October 18, 2003, p. 10.

215. See, e.g., Sharon Behn, "Pyongyang's Nuke Stance Scares Off Aid from South," *Washington Times,* October 21, 2003, p. A14. The Roh government has, at times, been downright obsequious in dealing with the North, apologizing for anti-DPRK protestors, for instance. Patrick Goodenough, "South Korea Tries to Appease North Ahead of Nuclear Talks," Cybercast News Service, August 25, 2003, www.cnsnews.com.

216. Quoted in Norimitsu Onishi, "Seoul Has Big Plans for North Korea (Nightmares, Too)," *New York Times,* December 17, 2003, p. A4.

217. Seo Hyun-jin, "Roller Coaster Ride with N. Korea," *Korea News,* October 18, 2003, p. 11.

218. See, e.g., Nicholas Eberstadt, "Atomic Shakedown," American Enterprise Institute, January 12, 2004, www.aei.org/include/news_print.asp?newsID=19709.

219. See, e.g., Selig Harrison, "N. Korean 'Good Guys' Require U.S. Assistance," *USA Today,* January 7, 2004, p. 13A.

220. See Jack Pritchard, "What I Saw in North Korea," *New York Times,* January 21, 2004, p. A29.

221. See, e.g., Victor D. Cha, "Isolation, Not Engagement," *New York Times,* December 29, 2002, p. WK–9.

222. Jay Solomon and Christopher Cooper, "North Korea Is Vulnerable as U.S. Vows Economic Pressure," *Wall Street Journal*, December 30, 2002, pp. A1, A4.

223. See, e.g., James Brooke, "U.S. Plan for Trade Penalties for North Korea Worries South Korean Investors," *New York Times*, December 30, 2002, p. A7.

224. Olsen, "South Korea Under Military Rule," p. 236.

225. Quoted in Jay Solomon, "Pyongyang Warns of 'Total War' If U.S. Attacks," *Wall Street Journal*, February 7, 2003, p. A9.

226. Howard R. French, "Reversals in U.S.-South Korea Links, and Some Jagged Fault Lines."

227. Doug Struck, "In the South, One Korea Is Distant Goal," *Washington Post*, June 17, 2000, p. A14. Marcus Noland of the Institute for International Economics figured that an investment of at least $700 billion would be necessary to prevent a mass migration south. Helle Bering, "The Twain Shall Meet," *Washington Times*, June 21, 2000, p. A21.

228. Moon and Bremner, "The Other Korea Crisis."

229. Ibid.

230. Quoted in Sang-Hun Choe, "North Korea Silent on U.S. Offer of Talks," Associated Press, January 8, 2003, www.aol.com.

231. For the rare mention of this prospect, see David Ignatius, "Of Two Minds on North Korea," *Washington Post*, January 7, 2003, p. A17.

232. Irene M. Kunuii, "Why Japan Just Might Build Nukes," *Business Week*, January 20, 2003, p. 52. A similar attitude was evident a decade ago, when South Koreans similarly foresaw inheriting any DPRK bomb and a more serious book contended that a united Korea would need nuclear weapons to withstand pressure from China and Japan. James Fallows, "The Panic Gap: Reactions to North Korea's Bomb," *The National Interest* (Winter 1994/95): 42–43.

233. Kim Sung-han, "Challenges and Visions," p. 31.

234. Morris, "Averting the Unthinkable," p. 106.

235. Quoted in Pekow, "Explaining the Alliance," p. 28.

236. Quoted in Doug Struck, "Anti-U.S. Mood Lifts South Koreans," *Washington Post*, December 20, 2002, p. A46.

237. Quoted in Richard Halloran, "Troops to Shift from S. Korea," *Washington Times*, November 24, 2003, p. A19.

238. Quoted in "Sorry, No Time for a Honeymoon," *Economist*, January 4, 2003, p. 31.

239. Quoted in Howard R. French, "Bush and New Korean Leader to Take Up Thorny Issues," *New York Times*, December 21, 2002, p. A8.

240. Eberstadt, "Our Other Korea Problem," 111.

CHAPTER 2

1. On the origins of the DPRK's nuclear program, see Ministry of National Defense, *Defense White Paper: 1994–1995* (Seoul: Republic of Korea, 1995), p. 67; and Don Oberdorfer, *The Two Koreas: A Contemporary History*, rev. and updated (New York: Basic Books, 2001), pp. 251–55.

2. For a discussion of the South's efforts to develop nuclear weapons in the 1970s, see Selig S. Harrison, *Korean Endgame: A Strategy for Reunification and U.S. Disengagement* (Princeton, NJ: Princeton University Press, 2002), pp. 246–50.

3. Mohamed ElBaradei, "No Nuclear Blackmail," *Wall Street Journal*, May 22, 2003, p. A14.

4.   Doug Bandow, *Tripwire: Korea and U.S. Foreign Policy in a Changed World* (Washington, DC: Cato Institute, 1996), p. 105.

5.   Quoted in David Rosenbaum, "U.S. to Pull A-Bombs from South Korea," *New York Times,* October 20, 1991, p. A3.

6.   Quoted in Don Oberdorfer, "North Korean A-Arms Danger Is Downgraded," *Washington Post,* November 1, 1992, p. A34.

7.   For discussions of the North Korean nuclear crisis during the administration of George H. W. Bush and the reaction of the United States and other parties, see Michael J. Mazarr, "North Korea's Nuclear Program: The World Responds, 1989–1992," in *Korea and World Affairs* 16, no. 2 (Summer 1992): 294–318; Leon V. Sigal, *Disarming Strangers: Nuclear Diplomacy with North Korea* (Princeton, NJ: Princeton University Press, 1998), pp. 17–47; and Oberdorfer, *The Two Koreas,* pp. 255–70.

8.   Nancy E. Soderberg, "Escaping North Korea's Nuclear Trap," *New York Times,* February 12, 2003, p. A35.

9.   Pyongyang went to great lengths to camouflage the two waste depositories in an unsuccessful attempt to fool the IAEA. For a discussion of the episode, see Nayan Chanda, "Bomb and Bombast," *Far Eastern Economic Review,* February 10, 1994, pp. 16–17.

10. Harrison, *Korean Endgame,* p. 203.

11. Quoted in Warren Strobel, "North Korea Risks Sanctions, Christopher Warns," *Washington Times,* March 26, 1993, p. A7.

12. Quoted in Nicholas Kristof, "China Opposes UN over North Korea," *New York Times,* March 24, 1993, p. A6.

13. Paul Greenberg, "Unhappy Precedent," *Washington Times,* March 19, 1993, p. F3.

14. [Frank Gaffney], "What to Do about North Korea's Nuclear Threat: Execute the 'Osirak' Remedy," Center for Security Policy Decision Brief 93-D20, March 19, 1993, p. 3. Emphasis in original.

15. Larry DiRita, "Clinton's Naivete on North Korea Could be Deadly," *Wall Street Journal,* August 23, 1993, p. A8.

16. Statement by Senator John McCain on United States policy and the crisis in Korea, May 24, 1993, p. 7. Copy in authors' possession.

17. Quoted in Robert D. Novak, "Aborted Ultimatum," *Washington Post,* December 16, 1993, p. A25.

18. Bill Gertz, "U.S. and Allies Discuss Sanctions on North Korea," *Washington Times,* June 6, 1994, p. A4.

19. Bill Gertz, "Dole, Mitchell Support Sanctions on North Korea," *Washington Times,* May 16, 1994, p. A1.

20. Quoted in Bill Gertz, "Shalikashvili Tells Fears on Korea," *Washington Times,* March 16, 1994, p. A6.

21. Quoted in Gertz, "U.S. and Allies Discuss Sanctions."

22. Quoted in Rowan Scarborough, "Air Strike Rejected in Taming N. Korea," *Washington Times,* April 4, 1994, p. A4. See also R. Jeffrey Smith, "Perry Sharply Warns North Korea," *Washington Post,* March 31, 1994, p. A1.

23. Quoted in David Usborne, "Pentagon Talks War to N. Korea," *Independent,* April 1, 1994, p. 13.

24. Ashton B. Carter and William J. Perry, " Back to the Brink," *Washington Post,* October 20, 2002, p. B1. For a discussion of the growing tensions in the first half of 1994, see Oberdorfer, *The Two Koreas,* pp. 297–326.

25. Quoted in Patrick Goodenough, "Clinton: We Drew Up Plans to Destroy N. Korean Nuclear Reactor," Cybercast News Service, December 16, 2002, http://www.cnsnews.com.

26. Selig Harrison describes his trip in "The North Korean Nuclear Crisis: From Stalemate to Breakthrough," *Arms Control Today* (November 1994): 18–21. For detailed discussions of Carter's role, see Young Whan Kihl, "Confrontation or Compromise on the Korean Peninsula: The North Korean Nuclear Issue," *Korean Journal of Defense Analysis* 6, no. 2 (Winter 1994): 112–18; Harrison, *Korea Endgame*, pp. 216–20; Sigal, *Disarming Strangers*, pp. 155–62; and Oberdorfer, *The Two Koreas*, pp. 326–36.

27. For a detailed account of the events leading up to the 1994 Framework Agreement, see Sigal, *Disarming Strangers*, pp. 131–92.

28. There is actually some question about how "proliferation-resistant" light-water reactors actually are. Defense analysts Albert Wohlstetter and Gregory S. Jones pointed out that although light-water reactors do produce less plutonium per thermal watt, "these two light water reactors would produce more plutonium in total than the three natural uranium reactors they are supposed to replace." Albert Wohlstetter and Gregory S. Jones, "'Breakthrough' in North Korea?" *Wall Street Journal,* November 4, 1994, p. A12.

29. U.S. Department of State, "Agreed Framework between the United States of America and the Democratic People's Republic of Korea," October 21, 1994; U.S. Department of State, "Agreement on the Establishment of the Korean Peninsula Energy Development Organization," October 21, 1994; and U.S. Department of State, "U.S.-DPRK Framework Agreement Time Line for Implementation (Briefed to Foreign Embassies on October 24, 1994), October 21, 1994.

30. Charles Krauthammer, "Romancing the Thugs," *Time,* November 7, 1994, p. 90.

31. Angelo M. Codevilla, "The Senate Needs to Avert Creeping Catastrophe in the Pacific," *Washington Times,* October 26, 1994, p. A17.

32. Frank Gaffney, "Whistling Past Gallucci Gulch," *Washington Times,* October 24, 1994, p. A20.

33. Paul Greenberg, "Trusting a Tyrant," *Washington Times,* October 24, 1994, p. A20.

34. Quoted in William Safire, "Clinton's Concessions," *New York Times,* October 24, 1994, p. A17.

35. Letter to William Jefferson Clinton, October 19, 1994. Copy in authors' possession.

36. Quoted in Bandow, *Tripwire,* p. 113.

37. See, e.g., the comments of Senators Craig Thomas (R-Wy.) and Hank Brown (R-Col.) during Senate hearings on the Framework Agreement. U.S. Senate, Committee on Foreign Relations, *North Korea Nuclear Agreement: Hearings before the Committee on Foreign Relations,* 104th Cong., 1st sess., January 24–25, 1995, pp. 41, 46.

38. Daryl M. Plunk, "Five Ways to Fix Our Korea Policy," *Washington Times,* April 15, 1996, p. A21.

39. James R. Lilley, "Underwriting a Dictatorship," *Washington Post,* July 19, 1996, p. A27.

40. Victor Galinsky, "Nuclear Blackmail: The 1994 U.S-Democratic People's Republic of Korea Agreed Framework on North Korea's Nuclear Program," Hoover Institution Essays in Public Policy, 1997.

41. Bill Gertz, "Hwang Says N. Korea Has Atomic Weapons," *Washington Times,* June 5, 1997, p. A12.

42. Thomas W. Lippman, "Senate Panel Joins House in Cutting Funds for Nuclear Accord," *Washington Post,* June 20, 1996, p. A23; Thomas W. Lippman, "Funding Issue Imperils N. Korea Pact, Christopher Says," *Washington Post,* June 21, 1996, p. A24; and Chiharu Kaminura, "S. Korean Envoy Says Cuts Will Upset North," *Washington Times,* October 14, 1998, p. A14.

43. See, e.g., Thomas W. Lippman, "N. Korea-U.S. Nuclear Pact Threatened," *Washington Post,* July 6, 1998, p. A1.

44. Martin Gross, "Iran's Nuclear Menace," *Washington Times,* June 19, 2003, p. A21. The point of Gross's article was that the United States should not make the same mistake of restraint with regard to Iran.

45. Steven Mufson, "Bush and North Korea: Where's the Big Stick?" *Washington Post,* December 29, 2002, p. B1.

46. For an assessment of the U.S.-DPRK relationship in the mid- and late 1990s, see Mark P. Berry, "An Assessment of United States-DPRK Relations: Lessons for the Future," in *Two Koreas in Transition: Implications for U.S. Policy,* ed. Ilpyong J. Kim, pp. 95–130 (Rockville, MD: In Depth Books, 1998).

47. Steven Lee Myers, "North Korea Agrees to Join 4-Party Talks," *New York Times,* July 1, 1997, p. A11.

48. Willis Witter, "Koreas Embark on Nuclear Project," *Washington Times,* August 18, 1997, p. A1; and Sang-Hun Choe, "N. Korea Getting Nuclear Reactors," Associated Press, December 15, 1999.

49. Barton Gellman, "U.S., Allies Struggling to Fulfill N. Korea Pact," *Washington Post,* May 2, 1998, p. A15; and Steven Erlanger, "U.S. Squeezes Allies to Help North Koreans on Fuel Costs," *New York Times,* May 2, 1998, p. A7.

50. Harrison, *Korean Endgame,* pp. 259–60.

51. Quoted in Ben Barber, "Critics Altered Clinton's Position," *Washington Times,* January 27, 1999, p. A11.

52. "U.S. 'Considering' Lifting Sanctions on DPRK," *Seoul Chungang Ilbo,* January 9, 1996, Foreign Broadcast Information Service (FBIS)—East Asia, January 11, 1996, p. 44; Michael Schuman, "U.S. May Ease North Korea Embargo; Pyongyang Is to Return MIA Remains," *Wall Street Journal,* May 10, 1996, p. A6.

53. Bill Gertz, "U.S. Will Pull Sanctions if Pyongyang Halts Missile Program," *Washington Times,* June 5, 1996, p. A20.

54. For a discussion of the food aid issue and its connection to other issues, see Scott Snyder, "Deterrence, Diplomacy, and Crisis Management: Choices in U.S. Policy Toward the Korean Peninsula," *Korean Journal of National Unification* 6 (1997): 209–33.

55. Carol Giacomo, "U.S. May Open Trade with N. Korea If It Cuts Regional Tensions," *Washington Times,* March 12, 1998, p. A9.

56. David W. Jones, "N. Korean Official in U.S. Calls for Closer Ties, Food Aid," *Washington Times,* April 28, 1996, p. A7.

57. Quoted in "N. Korea Says U.S. Fails on Nuclear Reactor Deal," *Washington Times,* May 8, 1998, p. A19. See also Kevin Sullivan, "N. Korea Threatens Revival of Its Nuclear Program," *Washington Post,* May 15, 1998, p. A33.

58. Quoted in John Burton, "N. Korea in Threat to Nuclear Freeze," *Financial Times,* January 13, 1999, p. 4.

59. Bill Gertz, "N. Korea Building Missiles that Could Hit American Forces," *Washington Times,"* October 22, 1997, p. A1.

60. Sheryl WuDunn, "North Korea Fires Missile Over Japanese Territory," *New York Times,* September 1, 1998, p. A6.

61. Steven Lee Myers, "U.S. Calls North Korean Rocket a Failed Satellite," *New York Times,* September 15, 1998, p. A6.

62. Quoted in Robert S. Greenberger, "North Koreans Launch Missile, Stirring Call to Halt U.S. Funds," *Wall Street Journal,* September 1, 1998, p. A14.

63. Quoted in Dana Priest and Sandra Sugawara, "North Korea Missile Test Threatens Nuclear Pact," *Washington Post,* September 1, 1998, p. A15.

64. Dana Priest and Thomas W. Lippman, "N. Korea Expanding Missile Programs," *Washington Post,* November 20, 1998, p. A1.

65. Bill Gertz, "N. Korea Continues to Develop Missiles," *Washington Times,* October 28, 1999, p. A1.

66. Quoted in Barbara Opall-Rome, "Congress Attacks North Korea Deal," *Defense News,* May 31, 1999, p. 3.

67. Bill Tarrant, "U.S. Warns N. Korea Against Further Missile Tests," Reuters, March 31, 1999.

68. William Drozdiak, "N. Korean Pledge Eases Fears of Missile Test," *Washington Post,* September 13, 1999, p. A1.

69. David E. Sanger, "Trade Sanctions on North Korea Are Eased by U.S.," *New York Times,* September 18, 1999, p. A1.

70. "North Korea's Strategy," editorial, *Washington Post,* September 14, 1999, p. A28.

71. [Frank Gaffney], "Clinton as the Anti-Reagan: Appeasement of North Korea Would 'End the Cold War' by Capitulation, Not Roll-Back," Center for Security Policy Decision Brief, no. 99-D 103, September 16, 1999. See also Neil King Jr., "Clinton's Decision to Ease Sanctions on North Korea Sparks Policy Debate," *Wall Street Journal,* September 20, 1999, p. A30; and David R. Sands, "Clinton Softens Korea Embargo; GOP Protests," *Washington Times,* September 18, 1999, p. A1.

72. John R. Bolton, "U.S. Must Stand Up to North Korea," *Los Angeles Times,* September 22, 1999, p. A15.

73. Quoted in Philip Shenon, "North Korea Said to Block Inspection of Nuclear Sites," *New York Times,* July 15, 1998, p. A10.

74. Dana Priest, "Activity Suggests N. Koreans Building Secret Nuclear Site," *Washington Post,* August 18, 1998, p. A1; and David E. Sanger, "North Korea Site an A-Bomb Plant, U.S. Agencies Say," *New York Times,* August 17, 1998, p. A1.

75. Quoted in Dana Priest, "U.S. Warns N. Korea on Suspect Facility," *Washington Post,* August 26, 1998, p. A16.

76. See, e.g., Richard Fisher, "Missile Blackmail from North Korea," *Washington Times,* September 9, 1998, p. A15.

77. Benjamin Gilman, "Reality Required for North Korea Policy," *Washington Times,* October 21, 1998, p. A15.

78. Quoted in David Briscoe, "Republicans Attack N. Korea Policy," Associated Press, October 13, 1999.

79. "North Korea Puts a Price on U.S. Inspections," *Washington Times,* November 12, 1998, p. A11.

80. Quoted in Eduardo Lachica, "U.S. Says Move by North Korea Could Hurt Pact," *Wall Street Journal,* November 12, 1998, p. A26.

81. "Energy Deal with North Korea Firm Despite Nuke Question, Albright Says," *Washington Times,* November 14, 1998, p. A6.

82. James Kitfield, "The Next Korean Conflict," *National Journal,* December 5, 1998, pp. 2876–78.

83. Selig S. Harrison, "The Korean Showdown that Shouldn't Happen," *Washington Post,* November 22, 1998, p. B1.

84. Quoted in Betsy Pisik, "Deal Permits U.S. to See N. Korea Site for Price," *Washington Times,* March 17, 1999, p. A1.

85. Bill Gertz, "North Korean Site Yields Only a System of Empty Tunnels," *Washington Times,* May 28, 1999, p. A1.

86. "North Korea's Creative Thinkers," editorial, *Washington Times,* June 10, 1999, p. A20. The editorial page of the *Wall Street Journal* had predicted as much in March when the inspection deal was first announced. "North Korea's Black Hole," editorial, *Wall Street Journal,* March 22, 1999, p. A22.

87. North Korea Advisory Group, *Report to the Speaker, U.S. House of Representatives,* November 1999, http://www.house.gov/international_relations/nkag/report.h.

88. Quoted in Thomas E. Ricks, "U.S. Policy on North Korea Faces Criticism by GOP Task Force," *Wall Street Journal,* November 4, 1999, p. A4.

89. Neil King Jr., "U.S. May Take North Korea Off Terror List," *Wall Street Journal,* May 1, 2000, p. A24.

90. Neil King Jr., "U.S. Relaxes Broad Sanctions on North Korea," *Wall Street Journal,* June 20, 2000, p. A18.

91. "N. Korea Stops Work on Inspected Nuclear Site—U.S.," Reuters, May 30, 2000.

92. Kyong-hwa Seok, "Pyongyang Vows to Discontinue Long-Range Missile Tests," *Washington Times,* June 22, 2000, p. A15.

93. See, e.g., Edward A. Olsen, "U.S. Security Policy and the Two Koreas," *World Affairs* 162, no. 4 (Spring 2000): 150–57.

94. Gus Constantine, "Kim Creates Furor with Call to Lift N. Korea Sanctions," *Washington Times,* June 3, 1998, p. A15; and Betsy Pisik, "Kim Proposes an Approach to North Korea," *Washington Times,* June 9, 1998, p. A15.

95. "S. Korea Kim Vows to End Cold War with N. Korea," Reuters, September 18, 1999.

96. Howard W. French, "Koreas Reach Accord Seeking Reconciliation After 50 Years," *New York Times,* June 15, 2000, p. A1.

97. Barbara Demick, "Charge Bolstered that N. Korea Was Bribed into Summit," *Los Angeles Times,* January 31, 2003, p. A3.

98. Steven Mufson, "Albright, N. Korea's Kim Meet for Historic Talks," *Washington Post,* October 24, 2000, p. A1; and Robin Wright, "Albright, N. Korean Leader Hold Upbeat Talks," *Los Angeles Times,* October 24, 2000, p. A1. For Albright's account of the visit, see Madeleine K. Albright with Bill Woodward, *Madame Secretary: A Memoir* (New York: Random House, 2003), pp. 459–68.

99. Albright with Wooodward, *Madame Secretary,* p. 459.

100. David E. Sanger, "Bush Tells Seoul Talks with North Won't Resume Now," *New York Times,* March 8, 2001, p. A1.

101. Authors' conversation with Bill Taylor, June 4, 2003.

102. See Ben Barber, "Hyde Hits N. Korea Over Deal on Nukes," *Washington Times,* March 14, 2001, p. A1; and Henry Sokolski and Victor Galinsky, "Bush Is Right to Get Tough with North Korea," *Wall Street Journal,* February 11, 2002, p. A22.

103. See, e.g., the warning expressed by North Korean foreign minister Paik Nam Soon to Selig Harrison in May 2001. Harrison, *Korean Endgame,* p. 264.

104. Text of the State of the Union Address available at http://www.whitehouse.gov/news/releases/2002/0120020129–11.html.

105. David E. Sanger, "In North Korea and Pakistan, Deep Roots of Nuclear Barter," *New York Times,* November 22, 2002, p. A1. Some press reports alleged that Russia provided assistance as well, although Russian officials heatedly denied the allegations. See Carla Anne Robbins and Zahid Hassain, "North Korea Had Russian Parts Suppliers," *Wall Street Journal,* October 21, 2002, p. A3.

106. See James T. Laney and Jason T. Shaplen, "How to Deal with North Korea," *Foreign Affairs* 82, no. 2 (March-April 2003): 19; and Henry Sokolski, "Contending with a Nu-

clear-Armed North Korea," *Joint Force Quarterly* 32 (Autumn 2002): 36–37. Georgetown University professor Victor D. Cha and Dartmouth College professor David C. Kang reach a similar conclusion. See Victor D. Cha and David C. Kang, "The Korea Crisis," *Foreign Policy* 137 (May-June 2003): 26.

107. Sonni Efron, "N. Koreans Disclose Secret Arms Program," *Los Angeles Times,* October 17, 2002, p. A1.

108. Howard W. French, "North Korean Radio Asserts Country Has Nuclear Arms," *New York Times,* November 18, 2002, p. A10; Howard W. French, "North Korea Clarifies Statement on A-Bomb," *New York Times,* November 19, 2002, p. A16; Doug Struck, "N. Korea Quiets Buzz on Nuclear Assertion," November 19, 2002, p. A22; and "N. Korea Mixes Signals on Nukes," *Washington Times,* November 19, 2002, p. A14.

109. Quoted in Peter Slevin and Glenn Kessler, "Bush Plans Diplomacy on N. Korea's Arms Effort," *Washington Post,* October 18, 2002, p. A1.

110. James Dao, "Bush Administration Halts Payments to Send Oil to North Korea," *New York Times,* November 14, 2002, p. A7.

111. Doug Struck, "North Korea Says It Will Renew Work at Reactors," *Washington Post,* December 13, 2002, p. A1.

112. Doug Struck, "N. Korea Hints at Missile Test," *Washington Post,* November 6, 2002, p. A3; and Barbara Demick and Paul Richter, "N. Korea May Test Missiles," *Los Angeles Times,* January 12, 2003, p. A1.

113. Peter S. Goodman, "N. Korea Moves to Activate Complex," *Washington Post,* December 27, 2002, p. A1.

114. For the text of the DPRK's announcement of withdrawal from the NPT, see "Statement on Pullout," *New York Times,* January 11, 2003, p. A7.

115. Howard W. French, "North Korea Restarts Plant with Ability to Fuel Arms," *New York Times,* February 6, 2003, p. A19.

116. David E. Sanger, "U.S. Suspects North Korea Moved Ahead on Weapons," *New York Times,* April 8, 2003, online edition.

117. Daniel Cooney, "U.S. Satellite Photos Hint of Nuclear Activity," *Washington Times,* May 9, 2003, p. A15.

118. Quoted in Sang-Hun Choe, "North Korea Nullifies No-Nuke Accord," Associated Press, May 12, 2003.

119. Juliet Eilperin, "Democrats Fault White House Efforts on North Korea," *Washington Post,* March 6, 2003, p. A13; and Sonni Efron and Barbara Demick, "Democrats Say Focus Should Be on N. Korea," *Los Angeles Times,* March 6, 2003, p. A3.

120. Charles Hutzler and Jay Solomon, "Allies Press U.S. to Ease Position on North Korea," *Wall Street Journal,* January 6, 2003, p. A10.

121. Glenn Kessler, "U.S. Backs Direct Talks with N. Korea," *Washington Post,* January 8, 2003, p. A1; and Nicholas Kralev, "U.S. Says 'Talks' with N. Korea Won't Be 'Negotiations,'" *Washington Times,* January 8, 2003, p. A1.

122. Quoted in Glenn Kessler, "Security Assurances Possible for N. Korea," *Washington Post,* January 9, 2003, p. A1.

123. Peter S. Goodman, "U.S. May Offer Aid to N. Korea In Deal on Arms," *Washington Post,* January 13, 2003, p. A12.

124. Doug Struck, "U.S. Signals It Won't Seek Sanctions Against N. Korea," *Washington Post,* January 23, 2003, p. A17.

125. Nicholas Kralev, "U.S. Presses Security Council on N. Korea Nukes," *Washington Times,* January 22, 2003, p. A1.

126. "Paper: U.S., N. Korea Held Talks in Feb.," Associated Press, March 9, 2003.

127. Ellen Sorokin, "Richardson Says Pyongyang Preparing for 'Negotiation,'" *Washington Times,* January 13, 2003, p. A1.

128. Quoted in Doug Struck, "North Korea Drops Its Demand for One-on-One Talks with U.S.," *Washington Post,* April 13, 2003, p. A22. See also James Brooke, "North Korea Shifts Stance on Discussing Nuclear Arms," *New York Times,* April 13, 2003, p. A4.

129. Mike Allen, "Bush: Iraq War Drove N. Korea to Concede," *Washington Post,* April 14, 2003, p. A11.

130. Karen DeYoung and Doug Struck, "Beijing's Help Led to Talks," *Washington Post,* April 17, 2003, p. A1.

131. Doug Struck and Glenn Kessler, "Clashing Agendas Threaten Start of North Korea Talks," *Washington Post,* April 20, 2003, p. A12.

132. Glenn Kessler, "N. Korea Says It Has Nuclear Arms," *Washington Post,* April 25, 2003, p. A1.

133. John Pomfret and Glenn Kessler, "China Puts North Korea Talks in Brighter Light," *Washington Post,* April 29, 2003, p. A20.

134. David E. Sanger, "CIA Said to Find Nuclear Advances by North Koreans," *New York Times,* July 1, 2003, p. A1.

135. Mark Riley and Tom Allard, "Pre-Nuclear Blasts in North Korea," *Sydney Morning Herald,* July 10, 2003, smh.com; and Patrick Goodenough, "South Korea Says the North Is Advancing Nuke Program," Cybercast News Service, July 10, 2003, http://www.cnsnews.com.

136. David E. Sanger, "North Korea Says It Has Made Fuel for Atom Bombs," *New York Times,* July 15, 2003, p. A1.

137. Thom Shanker with David E. Sanger, "North Korea Hides New Nuclear Site, Evidence Suggests," *New York Times,* July 20, 2003, p. A1.

138. Quoted in "U.S. Building a Coalition of the Willing to Halt N Korean Arms Trade," Agence France-Presse, July 8, 2003. Also see Patrick Goodenough, "Nations Will Train to Intercept Ships from Rogue States," Cybercast News Service, July 11, 2003, http://cnsnews.com.

139. Bruce B. Auster and Kevin Whitelaw, "Upping the Ante for Kim Jong Il: Pentagon Plan 5030, A New Blueprint for Facing Down North Korea," U.S. News.com, July 21, 2003.

140. James Kynge and Andrew Ward, "U.S. Set for 'Bilateral' Talks with N. Korea," *Financial Times,* August 27, 2003, p. 1.

141. Peter Slevin, "U.S. to Urge N. Korea Nuclear Disarmament Commitment," *Washington Post,* August 24, 2003, p. A23.

142. David R. Sands, "Reactor Project Ends for N. Korea," *Washington Times,* August 27, 2003, p. A1.

143. Christopher Marquis, "Top U.S. Expert on North Korea Steps Down," *New York Times,* August 26, 2003, p. A1.

144. Sam Howe Verhover, "N. Korea Says It's Ready to Test a Nuclear Weapon," *Los Angeles Times,* August 29, 2003, p. A1; and Sharon Behn, "U.S. Rejects Nuclear Blackmail at Six-Way Talks," *Washington Times,* August 30, 2003, p. A7.

145. Quoted in Joseph Kahn, "Chinese Aid Says U.S. Is Obstacle in Korean Talks," *New York Times,* September 2, 2003, p. A3.

146. David R. Sands, "Allies to Help U.S. Nip Weapons," *Washington Times,* September 10, 2003, p. A15; and Paul Richter and Sonni Efron, "U.S. and Allies Set to Search Vessels," *Los Angeles Times,* September 10, 2003, p. A3.

147. Anthony Faiola, "N. Korea Claims Nuclear Advance," *Washington Post,* October 3, 2003, p. A1.

148. David E. Sanger, "Intelligence Puzzle: North Korean Bombs," *New York Times,* October 14, 2003, p. A7.

149. See Mike Allen and Anthony Faiola, "Bush Floats Idea of North Korean Deal," *Washington Post,* October 18, 2003, p. A14; and David E. Sanger, "Bush Proposes North Korea Security Plan to China," *New York Times,* November 20, 2003, p. A1.

150. Martin Nesirky and Kim Kyoung-wha, "North Korea Says U.S. Security Offer Laughable," Reuters, October 21, 2003.

151. Barbara Demick, "N. Korea Rethinks U.S. Offer," *Los Angeles Times,* October 26, 2003, p. A1; and Andrew Ward and Guy Dinmore, "North Korea Agrees to Fresh Talks on Nuclear Programme," *Financial Times,* October 31, 2003, p. 6.

152. Glenn Kessler, "N. Korea Displays 'Nuclear Deterrent,'" *Washington Post,* January 11, 2004, p. A1; David E. Sanger, "Visitors See North Korean Nuclear Capacity," *New York Times,* January 11, 2004, p. A9; and Glenn Kessler, "N. Korean Evidence Called Uncertain," *Washington Post,* January 22, 2004, p. A1.

153. Jack Pritchard, "What I Saw in North Korea," *New York Times,* January 21, 2004, p. A29. The *Washington Post* reports that U.S. intelligence agencies now believe that North Korea possesses at least eight nuclear weapons. Glenn Kessler, "N. Korea Nuclear Estimate to Rise," *Washington Post,* April 28, 2004, p. A1.

154. Harrison, *Korean Endgame,* pp. 226–30.

155. Andrew Browne, "N. Korea Conceals Nuclear Material," *Washington Times,* May 28, 1997, p. A9.

156. Quoted in Tom Carter, "Regime Would Make Nukes If Pact Collapses," *Washington Times,* October 13, 1999, p. A12. See also William J. Perry, "Korea: Why We Can't Stand Still," *Washington Post,* October 17, 1999, p. B9.

157. In the years following the conclusion of the framework agreement, there was widespread expectation throughout the American foreign policy community that the North Korea system would collapse. See, e.g., Mary Jordan, "Speculation Grows on Demise of N. Korea," *Washington Post,* April 6, 1996, p. A11; George Melloan, "If North Korea Folds, What Comes Next?" *Wall Street Journal,* June 3, 1996, p. A15; Jim Hoagland, "Rush Toward Reunification," *Washington Post,* April 10, 1997, p. A25.

158. R. Jeffrey Smith, "Dim Prospects Seen for N. Korean Regime," *Washington Post,* August 10, 1996, p. A24.

159. Thomas E. Ricks and Steve Glain, "U.S. Gears Up for North Korean Collapse," *Wall Street Journal,* June 26, 1997, p. A14. Some liberal scholars argued that the United States should adjust its policies to minimize the likelihood of a collapse, aiming instead at a gradual transformation of the North Korean system as a prelude to the reunification of the two Koreas. See Selig S. Harrison, "Promoting a Soft Landing in Korea," *Foreign Policy,* no. 106 (Spring 1997): 2–22. For a wide-ranging discussion of North Korea's prospects for either reform or collapse, see Kongdan Oh and Ralph Hassig, "North Korea Between Collapse and Reform," *Asian Survey* 39, no. 2 (March-April 1999): 287–309.

160. For a detailed discussion of the famine in North Korea during the late 1990s, see Marcus Noland, *Avoiding the Apocalypse: The Future of the Two Koreas* (Washington, DC: Institute for International Economics, 2000), pp. 171–94.

161. Quoted in Guy Dinmore and Andrew Ward, "Hawks at Home See No Scope for a Deal with the 'Axle of Evil,'" *Financial Times,* August 28, 2003, p. 6.

162.   See, e.g., Nicholas Eberstadt, "The Most Dangerous Country," *National Interest,* no. 57 (Fall 1999): 46–54.

163.   Samuel R. Berger and Robert L. Gallucci, "Shut Down North Korea's Nuclear Wal-Mart," *Wall Street Journal,* May 14, 2003, p. A14.

164.   Michael O'Hanlon and Mike Mochizuki, *Crisis on the Korean Peninsula: How to Deal with a Nuclear North Korea* (New York: McGraw-Hill, 2003), p. 35.

165.   Anthony Lake and Robert Gallucci, "Negotiating with Nuclear North Korea," *Washington Post,* November 6, 2002, p. A21.

CHAPTER 3

1.   Quoted in Barbara Demick, "N. Korea: Nuclear Weapons Cut Costs," *Los Angeles Times,* June 10, 2003.

2.   International Institute for Strategic Studies, *The Military Balance, 2002–2003* (London: Oxford University Press, 2002), pp. 153, 334.

3.   Quoted in Bob Woodward, *Bush at War* (New York: Simon and Schuster, 2002), p. 340.

4.   Although that may be the perception driving embryonic nuclear-weapons states, the evidence is ambiguous about whether the possession of a small nuclear arsenal actually would deter a country with a much larger arsenal. See Lyle J. Goldstein, "Do Nascent WMD Arsenals Deter? The Sino-Soviet Crisis of 1969," *Political Science Quarterly* 118, no. 1 (Winter 2003): 53–79.

5.   "Lawmakers Told of Plan to Expand Nuke Program," *Washington Times,* June 3, 2003, p. A14.

6.   Karen Elliott House, "The Lesson of North Korea," *Wall Street Journal,* January 3, 2003, p. A10.

7.   Steve Chapman, "Unhappy Choices," *Washington Times,* October 22, 2002, p. A17.

8.   The DPRK does have a long record of using bluff and bluster when conducting negotiations on almost any issue . See Scott Snyder, *Negotiating on the Edge: North Korean Negotiating Behavior* (Washington, DC: U.S. Institute of Peace, 1999).

9.   Nancy Soderberg, "Escaping North Korea's Nuclear Trap," *New York Times,* February 12, 2003, p. A35.

10.   Examples in addition to those mentioned in the text include Alan D. Romberg and Michael D. Swaine, "The North Korean Nuclear Crisis: A Strategy for Negotiations," *Arms Control Today,* May 2003, http://www.armscontrol.org/act/; William S. Cohen, "Huffing and Puffing Won't Do," *Washington Post,* January 7, 2003, p. A17; Steven R. Weisman and Erik Eckholm, "Mediator [Bill Richardson] Urges Direct Dialogue in Korea Crisis," *New York Times,* January 12, 2003, p. A1; Philip H. Gordon, "Deal with North Korea," *Washington Times,* January 15, 2003, p. A17; and James Goodby and Kenneth Weisbrode, "Time for Jaw-Jaw with North Korea," *Financial Times,* March 6, 2003, p. 12.

11.   Jimmy Carter, "Back to the Framework," *Washington Post,* January 14, 2003, p. A19.

12.   Joseph I. Lieberman, "Crisis of Our Own Creation," *Washington Post,* January 8, 2003, p. A19.

13.   Brent Scowcroft and Daniel Poneman, "Korea Can't Wait," *Washington Post,* February 16, 2003, p. B7.

14.   Quoted in David R. Sands, "Lugar to Pursue N. Korea Nuke Deal," *Washington Times,* November 19, 2002, p. A1. Also see Peter Slevin, "Biden, Lugar Assail North Korea Policy," *Washington Post,* February 5, 2003, p. A9.

15. Quoted in Helen Fessenden and Carolyn Skorneck, "Lugar Challenges Bush on Hard-Line Korea Stance," *CQ Today*, March 6, 2003, http://www.cq.com.

16. Quoted in Jay Solomon, "Lawmakers Back From Pyongyang Report on Threat," *Wall Street Journal*, June 3, 2003, p. A13.

17. Curt Weldon, "A Korea Peace Initiative," Foreign Policy Research Institute E Note, June 26, 2003, www.fpri.org.

18. The Center for International Policy and the Center for East Asian Studies, University of Chicago, *Turning Point in Korea: New Dangers and New Opportunities for the United States*, Report of the Task Force on U.S. Korea Policy, Selig S. Harrison, chairman, February 2003.

19. Ibid., p. 6.

20. Ibid., p. 8.

21. Ibid., pp. 19–21.

22. Quoted in Mark Magnier, "U.S. Works to Pressure North Korea Over Arms," *Los Angeles Times*, October 20, 2002, p. A5.

23. Quoted in Paul Eckert, "U.S., Allies Push to Stop N. Korea Nuclear Move," Reuters, December 23, 2002.

24. Glenn Kessler, "Bush Says He'd Consider Aid to N. Korea for Disarmament," *Washington Post*, January 15, 2003, p. A1.

25. Carla Anne Robbins and David S. Cloud, "Powell Urges Tougher North Korea Nuclear Pact," *Wall Street Journal*, January 14, 2003, p. A3.

26. Quoted in Audrey McAvoy, "U.S. Studies N. Korea Sanctions," Associated Press, November 8, 2002. Scholar Victor Cha has coined the term "hawk engagement" to describe this type of carrot-and-stick approach to the North Korean problem. See Victor D. Cha and David C. Kang, *Nuclear North Korea: A Debate on Engagement Strategies* (New York: Columbia University Press, 2003), pp. 70–100.

27. Don Kirk, "Korea Leader Backs Plan to Block Oil to the North," *New York Times*, November 16, 2002, p. A9; and "Key U.S. Allies Cut Off Oil Aid to North Korea," Associated Press, November 15, 2002.

28. "No More Carrots for North Korea," editorial, *Wall Street Journal*, November 19, 2002, p. A24.

29. Quoted in Nicholas Kralev, "U.S. Rejects Direct Talks with N. Korea on Nukes," *Washington Times*, June 19, 2003, p. A1.

30. Quoted in Glenn Kessler, "N. Korea's Nuclear Ambitions Are Urgent Issue, Powell Says," *Washington Post*, June 19, 2003, p. A23.

31. Colum Lynch, "U.S. Seeks Rebuke of N. Korea on Arms," *Washington Post*, June 19, 2003, p. A23.

32. Sonni Efron, Henry Chu, and Mark Magnier, "U.S. Begins Diplomatic Offensive on North Korea," *Los Angeles Times*, October 19, 2002, p. A1; and Magnier, "U.S. Works to Pressure North Korea Over Arms."

33. Quoted in Arshad Mohammed, "Powell Sets Off to Seek Asian Allies Over N. Korea," Reuters, February 21, 2003.

34. Quoted in Amy Goldstein, "Two Leaders Warn North Korea," *Washington Post*, May 24, 2003, p. A9.

35. Quoted in Nicholas Kralev, "U.S. Dismisses War Concerns," *Washington Times*, December 17, 2002, p. A11.

36. Michiyo Nakamoto and Andrew Ward, "Roh and Koizumi Differ Over Stance on North Korea," *Financial Times*, June 9, 2003, p. 3.

37. James Brooke, "South Opposes Pressuring North Korea, Which Hints It Will Scrap Nuclear Pact," *New York Times*, January 1, 2003, p. A9; Chaitanya Kalbag, "S. Korea Hopeful for

Nuke Talks," *Washington Times,* May 28, 2003, p. A15; and Doug Struck, "Bush's N. Korea Efforts Stymied," *Washington Post,* June 1, 2003, p. A22.

38. Quoted in David S. Cloud, "U.S. Says Korean Nuclear Threat Won't Spur Concessions or Fight," *Wall Street Journal,* January 8, 2003, p. A1.

39. James A. Baker III, "U.S. Needs to Put a Stop to N. Korea's Blackmail," *Los Angeles Times,* January 12, 2003, p. M5.

40. Glenn Kessler, "Plan for N. Korea Will Mix Diplomacy and Pressure," *Washington Post,* May 7, 2003, p. A1.

41. Quoted in ibid.

42. James Dao, "Powell, in Asia, Is Dealt a Setback on North Korea," *New York Times,* February 25, 2003, p. A12.

43. "China, N. Korea Officials Pledge to Boost Ties," Reuters, February 22, 2003.

44. See David M. Lampton, "China: Fed Up with North Korea?" *Washington Post,* June 4, 2003, p. A27; and Glenn Kessler and John Pomfret, "North Korea's Threats a Dilemma for China," *Washington Post,* April 26, 2003, p. A1.

45. Victor D. Cha and David C. Kang, "The Korea Crisis," *Foreign Policy* 137 (May–June 2003): 23.

46. Elizabeth Rosenthal, "China Asserts It Has Worked to End Nuclear Crisis," *New York Times,* February 13, 2003, p. A15.

47. See, e.g., Jay Solomon and Charles Hutzler, "China's Hu Urges Bush to Engage North Koreans," *Wall Street Journal,* March 20, 2003, p. A16; and John Pomfret, "China Urges N. Korea Dialogue," *Washington Post,* April 4, 2003, p. A16.

48. William C. Triplett II, "Road to Pyongyang Through Beijing?" *Washington Times,* February 21, 2003, p. A20. Similarly, Professor Haesook Chae argues that Beijing is pursuing an elaborate strategy to get a deal between the United States and North Korea whereby U.S. troops would be withdrawn from South Korea. See Haesook Chae, "China's Little Korea Secret," *Los Angeles Times,* February 25, 2003, p. A13.

49. For an informative discussion of the hierarchy of Chinese interests and objectives on the Korean peninsula, see David Shambaugh, "China and the Korean Peninsula: Playing for the Long Term," *Washington Quarterly* 26, no. 2 (Spring 2003): 43–56.

50. James T. Laney and Jason T. Shaplen, "How to Deal with North Korea," *Foreign Affairs* 82, no. 2 (March–April 2003): 27.

51. See Martin Sieff, "Crisis in Korea: Why China Won't Help," United Press International, January 3, 2003; and Philip P. Pan, "China Treads Carefully Around North Korea," *Washington Post,* January 10, 2003, p. A14.

52. Nicholas D. Kristof, "'The Greatest of Great Men,'" *New York Times,* January 7, 2003, p. A23.

53. Quoted in Peter Wonacott, "Korea Tensions Put Beijing in a Tight Spot," *Wall Street Journal,* January 3, 2003, p. A6.

54. Jay Solomon, Murray Hiebert, and Charles Hulzer, "Some Speak of Pyongyang Blockade," *Wall Street Journal,* May 5, 2003, p. A13.

55. David Frum and Richard Perle, *An End to Evil: How to Win the War on Terror* (New York: Random House, 2003), p. 103.

56. Andrew Ward, "U.S. May Seek to Put Naval Blockade on North Korea," *Financial Times,* June 10, 2003, p. 3.

57. Nicholas Kralev, "U.S. Asks Aid Barring Arms from Rogue States," *Washington Times,* June 5, 2003, p. A15.

58. Steven R. Weisman, "Plan to Block North Korean Nuclear Shipments Gains Support," *New York Times,* June 18, 2003, p. A5; and Nicholas Kralev, "U.S. Seeks Asian Aid for Ship Searches," *Washington Times,* June 18, 2003, p. A1.

59. Quoted in Kralev, "U.S. Seeks Asian Aid for Ship Searches." See also Doug Struck, "N. Korea Vows to Fight Any Blockade," *Washington Post,* June 18, 2003, p. A21; and Barbara Demick and Robin Wright, "N. Korea Makes Explicit Threat," *Los Angeles Times,* June 18, 2003, p. A3.

60. Paul Richter and Sonni Efron, "U.S. and Allies Set to Search Vessels," *Los Angeles Times,* September 10, 2003, p. A3.

61. See, e.g., Nicholas Eberstadt, "A Turn of the Screw," American Enterprise Institute, *On the Issues* (March 2003), pp. 1–2.

62. Quoted in Elaine Lies, "Sanctions Impact on N Korea Would be Slight—UNICEF," Reuters, June 6, 2003.

63. "U.S. to Maintain N. Korean Food Aid," *Washington Times,* January 2, 2003, p. A1.

64. Steven R. Weisman, "U.S. in No Rush Over North Korea's Food Aid," *New York Times,* January 6, 2003, p. A11; Doug Struck, "U.S. Criticized for Halting N. Korea Aid," *Washington Post,* January 19, 2003, p. A18; and Jay Solomon and Carla Anne Robbins, "Amid Nuclear Standoff, Food Aid Shrinks for Hungry North Korea," *Wall Street Journal,* May 15, 2003, p. A1.

65. Doug Struck, "Aid Used as Lever with Pyongyang," *Washington Post,* December 5, 2002, p. A18. See also Sonni Efron, "Food Donations Are at Stake in North Korea," *Los Angeles Times,* January 2, 2003, p. A1.

66. Quoted in David E. Sanger and Julia Preston, "U.S. Assails Move by North Koreans to Reject Treaty," *New York Times,* January 11, 2003, p. A1. See also Ellen Sorkin, "Richardson Says Pyongyang Preparing for 'Negotiation,'" *Washington Times,* January 13, 2003, p. A1.

67. Selig S. Harrison, "Bargain with North Korea," *USA Today,* October 22, 2002, p. 11A.

68. Leon V. Sigal, "A Bombshell That's Actually an Olive Branch," *Los Angeles Times,* October 18, 2002, p. A13.

69. Quoted in Michael R. Gordon with Felicity Barringer, "North Korea Wants Arms, and More Aid from U.S., Chief of C.I.A. Suggests," *New York Times,* February 13, 2003, p. A15. Emphasis added.

70. Robert Madsen, "Pyongyang Needs Nuclear Bargaining Power," *Financial Times,* February 11, 2003, p. 15.

71. A few experts accept that possibility and urge the United States to learn to live with the new reality. See, e.g., Bennet Ramberg, "Accept Nuclear Reality on the Korean Peninsula," *Los Angeles Times,* January 16, 2003, p. A11. That is very much a minority view, however.

72. General John Singlaub and Admiral Thomas Moorer, "Korean Monster," *Newsmax* magazine (March 2003): 1, 14–17.

73. Roger D. Carstens, "Attack North Korea Now," *Washington Times,* October 28, 2002, p. A21.

74. Jim Wolf, "U.S. Can't Rule Out N. Korea Strike, Perle Says," Reuters, June 11, 2003.

75. Carolyn Skornek, "Lugar Won't Rule Out Use of Force to Eliminate North Korea's Nuclear Threat," *Congressional Quarterly Today,* January 21, 2004, p. 1.

76. "No More Carrots for North Korea."

77. Jed Babbin, "Time, Terror and Arms Control," *The American Prowler,* October 22, 2002, www.spectator.org/article.asp?art_id=2002_10_21_23_16_27.

78. Ralph A. Cossa, "NBR's Japan Forum (POL) Koizumi's Korean Crisis: Scowcroft–Poneman Article," Japan–U.S. Discussion Forum, November 17, 2002, japanforum@lists.nbr.org.

79. See, e.g., William Kristol and Gary Schmitt, "Lessons of a Nuclear North Korea," *Weekly Standard,* October 28, 2002, p. 8; James Hackett, "Not One Cent for Tribute," *Washington*

Times, February 12, 2003, p. A16; and Stephen J. Morris, "Averting the Unthinkable," *National Interest* (Winter 2003–04): 99–107.

80. John McCain, "Rogue State Rollback," *Weekly Standard,* January 20, 2003, pp. 12–13.

81. Dennis Ross, "Don't Rule Out Force," *Washington Post,* January 10, 2003, p. A21.

82. Charles Krauthammer, "Korea Follies," *Washington Post,* January 17, 2003, p. A23.

83. For a detailed discussion of why a preemptive military strike would be an unwise option, see Doug Bandow, "Wrong War, Wrong Place, Wrong Time: Why Military Action Should Not Be Used to Resolve the North Korean Nuclear Crisis," Cato Institute Foreign Policy Briefing, no. 76, May 12, 2003.

84. The fear that North Korea does have at least a small number of nuclear weapons appears to have been a major reason why the Bush administration has proceeded cautiously in this crisis, in marked contrast to its conduct toward Iraq. See Glenn Kessler, "No Support for Strikes Against North Korea," *Washington Post,* January 2, 2003, p. A10.

85. Michael Sheridan, "Koreans May Have Five Nuclear Missiles," *Times* (London), October 27, 2002, http://www.timesonline.co.uk/. See also Bill Gertz, "N. Korea Can Build Nukes Right Now," *Washington Times,* November 22, 2002, p. A1. North Korea's own statements on this issue have sent conflicting messages. See Howard W. French, "North Korean Radio Asserts Country Has Nuclear Arms," *New York Times,* November 18, 2002, p. A10; and Howard W. French, "North Korea Clarifies Statement on A-Bomb," *New York Times,* November 19, 2002, p. A16.

86. Kanako Takahara, "U.S. Has Warned Japan Over Pyongyang Warhead Threat," *Japan Times,* June 21, 2003, http://www.japantimes.co.jp/; David E. Sanger, "CIA Said to Find Nuclear Advances By North Koreans," *New York Times,* July 1, 2003, p. A1; and Glenn Kessler, "N. Korea Nuclear Estimate to Rise," *Washington Post,* April 28, 2004, p. A1.

87. David E. Sanger, "Intelligence Puzzle: North Korean Bombs," *New York Times,* October 14, 2003, p. A7.

88. Barbara Slavin and John Diamond, "N. Korean Nuclear Efforts Look Less Threatening," *USA Today,* November 6, 2003, p. 18A.

89. Joshua Muravchik, "Facing Up to North Korea," *Commentary* (March 2003): 37.

90. "In Search of a North Korea Policy," editorial, *Washington Times,* May 6, 2003, p. A28.

91. Frum and Perle, *An End to Evil,* p. 104.

92. "Stopping North Korea," editorial, *Defense News,* May 26, 2003, p. 28.

93. Quoted in Nicholas D. Kristof, "Tunneling toward Disaster," *New York Times,* January 21, 2003, p. A23.

94. Seymour M. Hersh, "The Cold Test," *New Yorker,* January 27, 2003, pp. 42–47.

95. Samuel R. Berger and Robert L. Gallucci, "Shut Down North Korea's Nuclear Wal-Mart," *Wall Street Journal,* May 14, 2003, p. A14.

96. Paul Richter and Richard Simon, "U.S. Seeks Peaceful N. Korea Solution," *Los Angeles Times,* October 18, 2002, p. A1.

97. Michael Dobbs, "For Wary White House, a Conflict, Not a Crisis," *Washington Post,* December 29, 2002, p. A1.

98. Quoted in Mike Allen, "Bush Sees Resolution on N. Korea," *Washington Post,* January 1, 2003, p. A1.

99. Quoted in James Dao, "Bush Urges Chinese President to Press North Korea on Arms," *New York Times,* February 8, 2003, p. A9.

100. Joseph Curl, "U.S. Keeps Pre-Emption Doctrine 'Open,'" *Washington Times,* May 13, 2003, p. A–1.

101. White House, Office of the Press Secretary, *The National Security Strategy of the United States of America,* September 17, 2002, p. 14. Emphasis added.

102. White House, Office of the Press Secretary, *National Strategy to Combat Weapons of Mass Destruction,* December 2002, p. 1.

103. Quoted in John Larkin and Murray Hiebert, "Talks Needed to Avert Attack," *Far Eastern Economic Review,* December 26, 2002–January 2, 2003, p. 17.

104. Nicholas D. Kristof, "Secret, Scary Plans," *New York Times,* February 28, 2003, p. A29.

105. Quoted in Hersh, "The Cold Test," p. 47.

106. Quoted in Doug Struck, "S. Korean Says U.S. Considered Attack on North," *Washington Post,* January 19, 2003, p. A18.

107. Howard W. French, "G.I.'s Will Gradually Leave Korea DMZ to Cut War Risk," *New York Times,* June 6, 2003, p. A1; and Doug Struck, "U.S. Troops Will Leave Korean DMZ," *Washington Post,* June 6, 2003, p. A1.

108. Sonni Efron, "Wolfowitz Tries to Reassure S. Koreans," *Los Angeles Times,* June 3, 2003, p. A3.

109. James Brooke, "DMZ Twist: U.S. Retreat Unsettles North Korea," *New York Times,* June 16, 2003, p. A8.

110. See Frum and Perle, *An End to Evil,* p. 103.

111. Charles Krauthammer, "The Japan Card," *Washington Post,* January 3, 2003, p. A19.

112. For discussions of this issue from various perspectives, see Benjamin L. Self and Jeffrey W. Thompson, eds., *Japan's Nuclear Option: Security, Politics, and Policy in the 21st Century* (Washington, DC: Henry L. Stimson Center, 2003).

113. Bill Gertz, "N. Korea Missile Threat Increases," *Washington Times,* November 1, 2002, p. A1.

114. For a discussion of the complex South Korean and Japanese attitudes toward nuclear weapons, see Harrison, *Korean Endgame,* pp. 231–56; and Hiroshi Hiyama, "Tokyo Seen Unlikely to Build Nukes," *Washington Times,* January 17, 2003, p. A19.

115. This is a point noted by Senator John McCain. In response to a question on the CBS program Face the Nation, McCain stated: "One of the options we have is, of course, to remove our objections to Japan developing nuclear weapons, since they are now directly threatened by North Korea. I'm sure the Chinese would not like to see that happen." http://www.cbsnews.com/stories/2003/01/06.

116. Krauthammer, "The Japan Card."

117. Robert Kagan and William Kristol, "North Korea Goes South," *Weekly Standard,* January 20, 2003, p. 9.

118. Stephen Fidler, "North Korea Could Become 'Plutonium Supermarket,'" *Financial Times,* January 11–12, 2003, p. 3.

119. The North has developed a sophisticated sales network for marketing its military wares. Bertil Lintner and Steve Stecklow, "Paper Trail Exposes Missile Merchants," *Far Eastern Economic Review,* February 13, 2003, pp. 12–15.

120. Doug Struck, "Heroin Trail Leads to North Korea," *Washington Post,* May 12, 2003, p. A1; Austin Bay, "Deadly Mix of Heroin and Nukes," *Washington Times,* May 15, 2003, p. A16; David R. Sands, "U.S. Fears Heroin Paying for Nukes," *Washington Times,* May 21, 2003, p. A12; James Dao, "North Korea Is Said to Export Drugs to Get Foreign Currency," *New York Times,* May 21, 2003, p. A16; Anna Fifeld and Andrew Ward, "Australia Seizes More N Korean Heroin," *Financial Times,* May 28, 2003, p. 6; David Ibson, "Pyongyang's Spy Ship Reveals a Dark Secret," *Financial Times,* May 28, 2003, p. 6; and Andrew Ward, "North Korea Suspected Source of Illegal Drugs Seized in South," *Financial Times,* June 5, 2003, p. 4.

121. Quoted in Marc Lerner, "N. Korea Weapons a 'Nuclear Nightmare,'" *Washington Times,* January 17, 2003, p. A1.

122. Quoted in James Dao, "U.S. Official Says North Korea Could Sell Bomb Material," *New York Times,* February 5, 2003, p. A12.

123. Joshua Kurlantzick, "Traffic Patterns," *New Republic,* March 24, 2003, pp. 12–13.

124. Susan Shirk, "A New North Korea?" *Washington Post,* October 22, 2002, p. A27.

125. Quoted in Barbara Demick, "Communist State Pushes Free Enterprise," *Los Angeles Times,* June 19, 2003, p. A3.

126. David C. Kang, "The Avoidable Crisis in North Korea," *Orbis* 47, no. 3 (Summer 2003): 501.

127. James Brooke, "Quietly, North Korea Opens Markets," *New York Times,* November 19, 2003, p. W1.

128. For a detailed case for multilateral negotiations, see Doug Bandow, "All the Players at the Table: A Multilateral Solution to the North Korean Nuclear Crisis," Cato Institute Policy Analysis, no. 478, June 26, 2003.

CHAPTER 4

1. Quoted in Georgie Anne Geyer, "South Korea Grateful for U.S. Help," *San Diego Union-Tribune,* July 23, 1995.

2. Peter Huessy, "A Final Word on Korea," *In the National Interest,* September 3, 2003, www.inthenationalinterest.com/Articles/Vol2Issues34/Vol2Issue34HuessyPFV.html.

3. Christopher Langton, ed., *The Military Balance: 2003–2004* (London: International Institute for Strategic Studies, 2003), pp. 160–61.

4. For a discussion of America's earliest contacts with Asia and the Open Door policy, see A. Whitney Griswold, *The Far Eastern Policy of the United States* (New York: Harcourt, Brace and Co., 1938), and Ernest May and James Thomson, eds., *American-East Asian Relations: A Survey* (Cambridge, MA: Harvard University Press, 1972).

5. Richard O'Connor, *Pacific Destiny: An Informal History of the U.S. in the Far East* (Boston: Little, Brown and Co., 1969), p. 150. Two years later a former interpreter at the U.S. consulate in Shanghai joined a similar expedition. Pyong-Choon Hahm, "The Korean Perception of the United States," in *Korea and the United States: A Century of Cooperation,* eds. Youngnok Koo and Dae-Sook Suh, p. 25. (Honolulu: University of Hawaii Press, 1984).

6. Hahm, "Korean Perception of the United States," p. 26.

7. Ibid., p. 39.

8. Ibid., pp. 32–34; John Chay, "The American Image of Korea to 1945," in *Korea and the United States: A Century of Cooperation,* eds. Koo and Suh, pp. 64–70.

9. As army historian James Schnabel notes, "the 38th Parallel cut more than 75 streams and 12 rivers, intersected many high ridges at variant angles, severed 181 small cart roads, 104 country roads, 15 provincial all-weather roads, 8 better-class highways, and 6 north-south rail lines." James Schnabel, *Policy and Direction: The First Year* (Washington, DC: United States Army, 1972), p. 11.

10. The saga of the stillborn trusteeship is described in James Matray, *The Reluctant Crusade: American Foreign Policy in Korea, 1941–1950* (Honolulu: University of Hawaii Press, 1985), pp. 52–124.

11. Edward Olsen, "South Korea Under Military Rule: Friendly Tyrant?" in *Friendly Tyrants: An American Dilemma,* eds. Daniel Pipes and Adam Garfinkle, p. 332. (New York: St. Martin's Press, 1991).

12.   Hahm, "Korean Perception of the United States," p. 42.

13.   For more information on the development of both Koreas, see Ralph Clough, *Embattled Korea: The Rivalry for International Support* (Boulder, CO: Westview Press, 1987); and Young Whan Kihl, *Politics and Policies in Divided Korea: Regimes in Contrast* (Boulder, CO: Westview Press, 1984).

14.   Callum MacDonald, *The War Before Vietnam* (New York: Free Press, 1986), p. 15. See also Okonogi Masao, "The Domestic Roots of the Korean War," in *The Origins of the Cold War in Asia,* eds. Yonosuke Nagai and Akira Iriye, pp. 299–320, (New York: Columbia University Press, 1977).

15.   For a discussion of America's departure, see Kim Chull Baum, "U.S. Policy on the Eve of the Korean War: Abandonment or Safeguard?" in *Korea and the Cold War: Division, Destruction, and Disarmament,* eds. Kim Chull Baum and James Matray, pp. 63–94 (Claremont, CA: Regina Books, 1993).

16.   Memorandum, Joint Chiefs of Staff, June 23, 1949, JCS 1483/74, RG 218, Box, Modern Military Records, National Archives, Washington, DC.

17.   For exculpations of Acheson, see John Merrill, "The Origins of the Korean War: Unanswered Questions," in *Korea and the Cold Wars,* eds. Baum and Matray, pp. 106–7; and Philip Geyelin, "Don't Blame Acheson," *Washington Post,* August 8, 1995, p. A19.

18.   Symptomatic of such overconfidence was a book published in 1950 and written before the North's invasion in June of that year, which declared that "in a military sense the North Korea regime was undoubtedly the stronger at the outset, but it was rapidly being overtaken by the South Korean government." George McCune and Arthur Grey, *Korea Today* (Cambridge, MA: Harvard University Press, 1950), p. 266.

19.   Matray, *The Reluctant Crusade,* p. 233.

20.   Although the Rhee regime is not without some blame for raising tensions on the peninsula before the war, there is no serious doubt that Kim Il-sung was the aggressor. See, e.g., Merrill, "The Origins of the Korean War," pp. 95–100, 107–8. Why Kim chose June 25 to strike is still not clear. Speculation includes the failure of DPRK guerrillas to topple Rhee, domestic political pressure on Kim, and an impending visit to South Korea by John Foster Dulles. MacDonald, *The War Before Vietnam,* pp. 27–28. One of the most detailed looks at the start of the conflict is provided by John Merrill, *Korea: The Peninsular Origins of the War* (Newark: University of Delaware Press, 1989).

21.   Glenn Paige, *The Korean Decision: June 24–30, 1950* (New York: Free Press, 1968), p. 132. Paige's book provides a detailed study of the decision to intervene. See also Matray, *The Reluctant Crusade,* pp. 236–37; and Rosemary Foot, *The Wrong War: American Policy and the Dimensions of the Korean Conflict, 1950–1953* (Ithaca, NY: Cornell University Press, 1985), pp. 58–62.

22.   Clay Blair, *The Forgotten War: America in Korea, 1950–1953* (New York: Times Books, 1987), p. 973.

23.   The conflict between the ROK and United States is explored in Ohn Chang-il, "South Korea, the United States, and the Korean Armistice Negotiations," in *Korea and the Cold War,* eds. Baum and Matray, pp. 209–29; and William Stueck, *The Korean War: An International History* (Princeton, NJ: Princeton University Press, 1995), pp. 210–15, 320–25, 330–39.

24.   Youngnok Koo, "The First Hundred Years and Beyond," in *Korea and the United States,* eds. Koo and Suh, p. 359.

25.   Ibid., p. 360. The torturous negotiations are covered in Baum and Matray, *Korea and the Cold War,* pp. 223–29.

26. Quoted in Stephen Goose, "The Military Situation on the Korean Peninsula," in *Two Ko-reas—One Future?*, eds. John Sullivan and Roberta Foss, p. 82. (Lanham, MD: University Press of America, 1987).

27. John Spanier, *American Foreign Policy Since World War II* (New York: Praeger Publishers, 1977, 7th ed.), p. 212.

28. Astri Suhrke and Charles Morrison, "Carter and Korea: The Difficulties of Disengage-ment," *The World Today* (October 1977): 371.

29. Manwoo Lee et al., *Alliance Under Tension: The Evolution of South Korean–U.S. Relations* (Boulder, CO: Westview Press, 1988), pp. 35–36.

30. Quoted in Ralph Clough, *Deterrence and Defense in Korea: The Role of U.S. Forces* (Wash-ington, DC: The Brookings Institution, 1976), p. 3.

31. "Weinberger Assures South Koreans 40,000 U.S. Troops Will Not Pull Out," *Washington Times,* April 3, 1986, p. A6.

32. See, e.g., A. James Gregor and Maria Hsia Chang, *The Iron Triangle: A U.S. Security Pol-icy for Northeast Asia* (Stanford, CA: Hoover Institute Press, 1984), pp. 69–70.

33. Quoted in Chae-Jin Lee, "U.S. Policy Toward South Korea," in *Korea Briefing, 1993: Fes-tival of Korea,* ed. Donald Clark, p. 59. (Boulder, CO: Westview Press, 1993).

34. Richard Solomon, "The Last Glacier: The Korean Peninsula and the Post–Cold War Era," *U.S. Department of State Dispatch,* February 11, 1991, p. 106.

35. Quoted in Harry Summers, "Pursuit of Peace in the Pacific," *Washington Times,* August 31, 1995, p. A15.

36. Department of Defense, *United States Security Strategy for the East Asia-Pacific Region* (Washington, DC: Department of Defense, February 1995), p. 10.

37. Robert Burns, "U.S. Sees Smaller, More Mobile Korea Force," Associated Press, October 18, 2003, http://aolsvc.news.aol.com; and Christopher Cooper, "U.S. Plan Puts Korea on Edge," *Wall Street Journal,* October 21, 2003, p. A4. Ironically, the North fears that the move might be the prelude to an attack on its nuclear facilities or even preventive war by the United States, since it moves forces out of easy retaliatory range.

38. Thom Shanker, "Rumsfeld Reassures Seoul on Regrouping G.I.'s," *New York Times,* No-vember 18, 2003, p. A11.

39. "Korea–U.S. Defense Posture," *Korea Now,* June 28, 2003, p. 4.

40. Colin L. Powell, remarks at Asia Society Annual Dinner, June 10, 2002, U.S. Department of State, www.state.gov/secretary/rm/2002/10983pf.htm.

41. "USFK Upgrade Aims Beyond Korea," Stratfor, June 2, 2003, www.stratfor.info/Story. neo? storyId=218261&countryId=113; and Robert Burns, "Air Forces Eyed to Fill Com-bat Power Gap," Associated Press, January 18, 2003, http://aolsvc.news.aol.com.

42. Choe Yong-shik, "U.S. Base Relocation Plan to Be Revised," *Korea Now,* September 20, 2003, p. 8.

43. David Briscoe, "U.S., South Korea Agree to Pull Troops Out of Seoul," Associated Press, January 17, 2003, http://aolsvc.news.aol.com.

44. Rumsfeld quoted in Robert Burns, "Rumsfeld Says S. Korea Should Defend Self," Asso-ciated Press, November 18, 2003. On the possible withdrawal of one-third of the U.S. troops stationed in South Korea, see Will Dunham, "Korea Move is Part of U.S. Global Force Realignment," Reuters, June 7, 2004.

45. William Stueck, *The Korean War: An International History* (Princeton, NJ: Princeton Uni-versity Press, 1995), p. 11.

46. For various analyses as to why the ROK succeeded, see Vittorio Corbo and Sang-Mok Suh, eds., *Structural Adjustment in a Newly Industrialized Country: The Korean Experience* (Baltimore, MD: Johns Hopkins University Press, 1992); Jene Kwon, ed., *Korean Eco-*

nomic Development (Westport, CT: Greenwood Press, 1990); Silvio de Franco et al., *Korea's Experience with the Development of Trade and Industry* (Washington, DC: World Bank, 1988); and Norman Jacobs, *The Korean Road to Modernization and Development* (Urbana, IL: University of Illinois Press, 1985). For a broad look at U.S.–ROK economic relations, see Dong Sung Cho, "From Unilateral Asymmetry to Bilateral Symmetry" and Eul Young Park, "From Bilateralism to Multilateralism: Korea's Economic Relations with the United States, 1945–1980," both in *Korea and the United States,* eds. Koo and Suh, pp. 219–60.

47.   Kyu-Ryoon Kim, "Economic Cooperation in Northeast Asia: The Role of Korea," *Korean Journal of National Unification,* Special Edition (1993): 167–77.

48.   James M. Lister, "Outlook for Korea's Economy," *Korea Insight* 6, no. 1 (January 2004): 1; Song Jung-a, "South Korea Sees 6% Growth Powered by Strong Exports," *Financial Times,* January 3–4, 2004, p. 2; and Andrew Ward, "S Korea's Central Bank Predicts 5.2% Growth Next Year," *Financial Times,* December 12, 2003, p. 8.

49.   See, e.g., Bob Davis, "South Korea Played the Reluctant Patient to IMF's Rescue Team," *Wall Street Journal,* March 2, 1998, pp. A1, A12; and Louis Kraar, "Wanted," *Fortune,* February 3, 2003, pp. 102–8.

50.   See, e.g., Kim Jung Min, "Backtracking," *Far Eastern Economic Review,* January 15, 2004, p. 49. It comes as no surprise that economic policy was a hotly contested election issue. Don Kirk, "After the Election, Reassuring Korean Business," *New York Times,* January 10, 2003, pp. C11, C17.

51.   Boon Ihlwan and Brian Bremner, "The Other Korean Crisis," *Business Week Online,* January 20, 2003, www.businessweek.com.

52.   Paolo Pasicolan, ed., *U.S. and Asia Statistical Handbook: 2003 Edition* (Washington, DC: Heritage Foundation, 2003), p. 83.

53.   See, e.g., Brian Bremner and Moon Ihlwan, "North Korea: How Dire a Threat?" *Business Week Online,* January 13, 2003, www.businessweek.com; Martin Sieff, "Pyongyang Is Unable to Turn On the Lights," *Washington Times,* January 8, 2003, p. A20; and Marc Lerner, "Kim Blamed for N. Korea Famine," *Washington Times,* January 6, 2003, pp. A1, A12.

54.   See, e.g., Bremner and Moon, "North Korea"; James Brooke, "Food Emergency in North Korea Worsens as Donations Dwindle," *New York Times,* December 5, 2002, p. A16.

55.   *The CIA World Factbook: 2003* (Washington, DC: Central Intelligence Agency, 2003), www.cia.gov/cia/publications/factbook/print/sn.html; www.cia.gov/cia/publications/factbook/print/kn.html.

56.   "North Korea's GDP Grows Four Years in a Row," *Korea Now,* November 29, 2003, http://kn.koreaherald.co.kr/SITE/data/html_dir/2003/06/14/200306140013.asp; and "Warning Over N. Korea Collapse," CNN.com, November 3, 2003, www.cnn.com/2003/BUSINESS/11/03/korea.rating.

57.   Ministry of National Defense, *Defense White Paper: 1990* (Seoul: Republic of Korea, 1991), p. 105.

58.   U.S. Department of Defense, "Report to Congress on the Military Situation on the Korean Peninsula," February 1987, p. 1.

59.   Hwang Dong Joon, "South Korea's Defense Industry: An Asset for the U.S.," Heritage Foundation Backgrounder, no. 38, December 10, 1985; and Stephen Goose, "The Comparative Military Capabilities of North and South Korean Forces," in *The U.S.–South Korean Alliance: Time for a Change,* eds. Doug Bandow and Ted Galen Carpenter, pp. 46–47. (New Brunswick, NJ: Transaction, 1992). For a discussion of the development of the ROK's military-industrial complex, see Chung-in Moon, "U.S. Third Country Arms

Sales Regulation and the South Korean Defense Industry: Supplier Control and Recipient Dilemma," in *Alliance Under Tension: The Evolution of South Korean-U.S. Relations,* in Manwoo Lee et al., pp. 81–90. (Boulder, Co.: Westview Press, 1988).

60. Ministry of National Defense, *Defense White Paper: 1991–1992* (Seoul: Republic of Korea, 1992), p. 119.

61. "Seoul's Space Program, Rising Nationalism Could Be Thorn in U.S. Ties," November 19, 2002, Stratfor, www.stratfor.biz; "We Have Liftoff," *Korea Now,* December 14, 2002, p. 16. This development has not been without some controversy given Washington's commitment to nonproliferation. See, e.g., "Unintended Consequences: Proliferation in South Korea," March 6, 2001, Stratfor, www.stratfor.bix; and "U.S. and South Korea Dispute Missile Development," November 12, 1998, Stratfor, www.stratfor.biz.

62. See, e.g., "South Korea: Joining Asia's Naval Arms Race," March 28, 2001, Stratfor, www.stratfor.info./Story.neo?storyID=10575.

63. Lim Jong-nam and Paul Eckert, "S. Korea May Deploy Nuclear-Powered Subs—Newspaper," Reuters, January 26, 2004.

64. Carl E. Haselden Jr., "The Effects of Korean Unification on the U.S. Military Presence in Northeast Asia," *Parameters* (Winter 2002–03): 122.

65. Langton, ed., *The Military Balance,* pp. 160–61.

66. Quoted in "CIA: War in Korea Unlikely Soon," *Washington Times,* December 5, 1997, p. A11.

67. Bruce Bechtol, "Who Is Stronger? A Comparative Analysis of the Readiness and Capabilities of the North and South Korean Militaries," *International Journal of Korean Unification Studies* 10, no. 2 (2001): 21.

68. Robert Hall and Ian Kemp, eds., "North Korea: The Final Act," *Jane's Intelligence Review,* Special Report, no. 2 (1994): p. 24.

69. International Institute for Strategic Studies, *The Military Balance: 1985–86* (London: International Institute for Strategic Studies, 1985), p. 118.

70. See, e.g., David Lague and Murray Hiebert, "Leaving Asia Exposed," *Far Eastern Economic Review,* February 6, 2003, p. 14.

71. Huessy, "A Final Word on Korea."

72. Compare, e.g., Langton, ed., *The Military Balance,* pp. 160–61, with International Institute for Strategic Studies, *The Military Balance: 1994–1995* (London: Brassey's, 1994), pp. 178–81.

73. U.S. Arms Control and Disarmament Agency, *World Military Expenditures and Arms Transfers: 1993–1994,* (Washington, DC: U.S. Government Printing Office, 1995) p. 70; and U.S. Arms Control and Disarmament, *World Military Expenditures and Arms Transfers: 1987* (Washington, DC: U.S. Government Printing Office, 1988), p. 64. All of these numbers are approximate. The estimates not only vary between organizations, such as the IISS and the Stockholm International Peace Research Institute, but also have been adjusted over time by the same organization, such as ACDA. Nevertheless, the figures are generally consistent. For instance, the Stockholm Institute figures the ROK's effort to have peaked at 6 percent of the gross domestic product (rather than the similar gross national product) in 1980 and 1981. Stockholm Research International Peace Research Institute, *SIPRI Yearbook 1988: World Armaments and Disarmament* (New York: Oxford University Press, 1988), p. 170.

74. Don Oberdorfer, *The Two Koreas: A Contemporary History* (Reading, MA: Addison–Wesley, 1997), p. 106.

75. "US Troops Pull-out to Cost $30 Billion," *Korea Times,* October 1, 2002, www.koreatimes.com.

76. Doug Bandow, *Tripwire: Korea and U.S. Foreign Policy in a Changed World* (Washington, DC: Cato Institute, 1996), p. 67.

77. See, e.g., James Schnabel, *Policy and Direction: The First Year* (Washington, DC: United States Army, 1972), p. 37.

78. Shipments included antiaircraft missiles, antitank missiles, tanks, and armored vehicles. "Moscow Pays Debt to Seoul with Arms," *Washington Times,* September 27, 1995, p. A10; and Anton Zhigulsky, "Russians Court S. Korea with Technology Transfer, Arms," *Defense News,* October 9–15, 1995, p. 12.

79. Quoted in Patrick Goodenough, "US–South Korean Alliance 'Precious,' President-Elect Says," Cybercast News Service, January 15, 2003, www.cnsnews.com.

80. Claude Buss, *The United States and the Republic of Korea: Background for Policy* (Stanford, CA: Hoover Institution, 1982), p. 142.

81. Quoted in ibid., p. 144.

82. Ministry of National Defense, *Defense White Paper: 1989* (Seoul: Republic of Korea, 1990), p. 118.

83. *Participatory Government Defense Policy 2003* (Seoul: Ministry of National Defense, 2003), pp. 72–74.

84. See, e.g., Hamm Taik-young, "Self-Reliance or an Arms Build-up? The 2004 Defense Budget Request of the ROK," Institute for Far Eastern Studies (September 2003), http://ifes.kyungnam.ac.kr.

85. "Korea–U.S. Defense Posture." The writers even dismiss the idea of adding one division to the ROK military to replace soldiers from America's Second Division as they move south.

86. *Participatory Government Defense Policy 2003,* p. 138.

87. Quoted in Hwang Jang-jin, "Roh Backs Increased Military Spending," *Korea Now,* June 28, 2003, p. 5.

88. *Participatory Government Defense Policy 2003,* p. 82; see also p. 84.

89. Jin-Young Chung, "Cost Sharing for USFK in Transition: Whither the US–ROK Alliance?" in *Recalibrating the U.S.–Republic of Korea Alliance,* eds. Donald W. Boose Jr. et al., p. 40, (Carlisle, PA: Strategic Studies Institute, 2003).

90. Ibid., pp. 43–44.

91. Quoted in Thom Shanker, "Rumsfeld, on Asia Tour, Hints of Shifts in U.S. Forces There," *New York Times,* November 14, 2003, p. A8.

92. See, e.g., Doug Bandow, "Mutually Assured Frustration," *American Spectator* (January 2004), www.spectator.org.

93. "US Troop Presence Depends on Role in Unification: Report," *Han Kook Ilbo,* January 24, 2003, www.korealink.com.

94. Kim Sung-han, "Anti-American Sentiment and the ROK–US Alliance," *Korean Journal of Defense Analysis* 15, no. 2 (Fall 2003): 119.

95. Bandow, *Tripwire,* pp. 7, 34–41.

96. Quoted in Doug Bandow, "Leaving Korea," *Foreign Policy,* no. 77 (Winter 1989–90): 90.

97. From private conversations during a visit to Seoul in July 1995.

98. Ralph Clough, *Embattled Korea: The Rivalry for International Support* (Boulder, CO: Westview Press, 1987), p. 99.

99. Ministry of National Defense, *Defense White Paper: 1991–1992,* p. 31.

100. Clough, *Embattled Korea,* p. 98.

101. Lee, "U.S. Policy Toward South Korea," p. 97.

102. See Ted Galen Carpenter, *A Search for Enemies: America's Alliances After the Cold War* (Washington, DC: Cato Institute, 1992), p. 86.

103. Quoted in Melvyn Krauss, *How NATO Weakens the West* (New York: Simon and Schuster, 1986), p. 188.

104. Ministry of National Defense, *Defense White Paper: 1992–1993* (Seoul: Republic of Korea, 1993), pp. 142–43. See also the discussion of a "shrinking" American role and a "Koreanization of Korean defense." Ministry of National Defense, *Defense White Paper: 1994–1995* (Seoul: Republic of Korea, 1995), p. 123.

105. Ministry of National Defense, *Defense White Paper: 1994–1995*, p. 221; see also p. 235. This has been a theme for a number of years. See, e.g., *Defense White Paper: 1991–1992*, p. 169.

106. Quoted in Franklin Weinstein and Fuji Kamiya, eds., *The Security of Korea: U.S. and Japanese Perspectives on the 1980s* (Boulder, CO: Westview Press, 1980), p. 84.

107. See Doug Bandow, "Korea: The Case for Disengagement," Cato Institute Policy Analysis, no. 96, December 8, 1987, pp. 6–9, 12–13.

108. See, e.g., Doug Struck and Glenn Kessler, "Clashing Agendas Threaten Start of North Korean Talks," *Washington Post*, April 20, 2003, p. A13; Paul Wiseman, "Steep Price Tag Expected for Victory in N. Korea," *USA Today*, February 28, 2003, p. 13A; Seymour Hersh, "The Cold Test," *New Yorker*, January 27, 2003, pp. 45–46; and Vernon Loeb and Peter Slevin, "Overcoming North Korea's 'Tyranny of Proximity,'" *Washington Post*, January 20, 2003, p. A16.

109. This is similar to the problem of Taiwan pressing its independence claims and relying on U.S. military support. See, e.g., Kenneth Lieberthal, "Dire Strait: The Risks on Taiwan," *Washington Post*, January 8, 2004, p. A23. Another case is the Philippines' attempt to rely on the United States in asserting claims over the Spratly Islands despite the lack of a functioning military. See, e.g., Doug Bandow, "Instability in the Philippines: A Case Study for U.S. Disengagement," Cato Institute Foreign Policy Briefing, no. 64, March 21, 2001.

110. Ministry of National Defense, *Defense White Paper: 1990*, p. 141.

CHAPTER 5

1. See, e.g., Patrick Carkin, "Hidden Casualties & Secret Diplomacy: The History of US Relations with North Korea," *CounterPunch*, January 3, 2003, www.counterpunch.org/01032003.html; "North Korea: Incidents and Infiltrations: Targeting South Korea," June 1993, 1Up Info, www.1upinfo.com/country-guide-study/north-korea/north-korea157.html; Donna Miles, "Drama Along the DMZ," *Soldier* magazine 50, no. 2 (February 1995): 4, www.army.mil. There have also been two recent sea battles between South and North Korean ships. Mark Valencia and Jon Van Dyke, "Drawing a Line in the Water," *Washington Times*, January 10, 2003, p. A14.

2. Korea Defense Veterans of America, KDVA home page, January 2003, www.kdvamerica.org.

3. Bong Youngshik, "Anti-Americanism and the U.S.-Korea Military Alliance," in *Confrontation and Innovation on the Korean Peninsula*, ed. James M. Lister et al., p. 21 (Washington, DC: Korea Economic Institute, 2003).

4. Quoted in Doug Bandow, "Seoul Long," *American Spectator*, November 1990, p. 35.

5. Robert Manning, "Toward What New Ends?" *Washington Times*, July 2, 2000, p. B3.

6. Quoted in Robert Burns, "U.S. Intends to Remain in S. Korea," Associated Press, June 15, 2000.

7. Ibid.

8.   Quoted in John Lancaster, "U.S. Presence Fixed on Korean Peninsula," *Washington Post,* June 24, 2000, p. A20.

9.   Quoted in ibid.

10. Richard Weitz, "One Reader's Perspective: Confronting a Nuclear Hermit," *In the National Interest,* January 15, 2003, www.inthenationalinterest.com.

11. Peter Brookes, "It Ain't Over," Cybercast News Service, August 1, 2003, http://www.cnsnews.com.

12. Peter Huessy, "A Final Word on Korea," *In the National Interest,* September 3, 2003, www.inthenationalinterest.com/Articles/Vol2Issues34/Vol2Issues34HuessyPFV.html.

13. "Strengthening the U.S.-ROK Alliance: A Blueprint for the 21st Century," CSIS and Seoul Forum, 2003, p. 17.

14. William J. Perry et al., "A Scary Thought: Loose Nukes in North Korea," *Wall Street Journal,* February 6, 2003, P. A18.

15. Patrick Goodenough, "Analyst Foresees US-South Korea Tensions Easing," Cybercast News Service, January 16, 2003, http://www.cnsnews.com. So does former secretary of state James Baker. James A. Baker III, "U.S. Needs to Put a Stop to N. Korea's Blackmail," *Los Angeles Times,* January 12, 2003, p. M5.

16. Balbina Y. Hwang et al., "North Korea and the End of the Agreed Framework," The Heritage Foundation, Backgrounder no. 1605, October 18, 2002, p. 3.

17. William Kristol and Gary Schmitt, "Lessons of a Nuclear North Korea," *Weekly Standard,* October 28, 2002, p. 8.

18. Greg Jaffe et al., "Pyongyang in Mind, U.S. Will Boost Forces in Asia," *Wall Street Journal,* February 3, 2003, p. A12; David Sanger and Eric Schmitt, "Admiral Seeks Deterrent Force in Korea Crisis," *New York Times,* February 1, 2003, pp. A1, A11.

19. See, e.g., Richard V. Allen, "Seoul's Choice: The U.S. or the North," *New York Times,* January 16, 2003, p. A31; Donald Lambro, "Shultz Weighs Impact of the Deployment," *Washington Times,* January 16, 2003, p. A17; Murray Hiebert, "Yankee Go Home," *Far Eastern Economic Review,* January 23, 2003, p. 17; Robert Novak, "Perhaps It's Time South Korea Tried Its Wings," *Washington Post,* January 6, 2003, p. A15; William Safire, "N. Korea: China's Child," *New York Times,* December 26, 2002, p. A21; "South Korea's Schroeder," *Wall Street Journal,* December 20, 2002, p. A14; National Review Editors, "Limited Options," *National Review Online,* January 10, 2003, www.nationalreview.com; Jack Kelly, "Crisis Management," *Washington Times,* January 12, 2003, p. B1; and Victor Davis Hanson, "Korea Is Not Quite Iraq," *National Review Online,* January 10, 2003, www.nationalreview.com.

20. Quoted in Howard French, "Shifting Loyalties: Seoul Looks to New Alliances," *New York Times,* January 26, 2003, p. 15.

21. Quoted in James Brooke, "North Korean Issues Warning, And Seoul Seeks Compromise," *New York Times,* January 5, 2003, p. 12.

22. Nicholas Kristof, "Cookies and Kimchi," *New York Times,* January 17, 2003, p. A25.

23. Adam Garfinkle, "Checking Kim: The Awful Question of What to Do," *National Review Online,* January 27, 2003, http://www.nationalreview.com/27jan03/garfinkle012703.asp.

24. William Berry, *North Korea's Nuclear Program: The Clinton Administration's Response* (Colorado Springs, CO: Institute for National Security Studies, 1995), p. 22.

25. Quoted in Clay Blair, *The Forgotten War: America in Korea, 1950–1953* (New York: Times Books, 1987), p. 44. Rhee unsuccessfully attempted to wring a similar declaration out of the Truman administration. James Irving Matray, *The Reluctant Crusade: American Foreign Policy in Korea, 1941–1950* (Honolulu: University of Hawaii Press, 1985), p. 191.

26. "Korea-US Relationship Growing Broader, Closer," *Bridging the Pacific,* no. 33 (January 2004): 1.

27. Marcus Noland and Taeho Bark, *The Strategic Importance of U.S.–South Korean Economic Relations* (Seattle: National Bureau of Asian Research, October 2003), pp. 7–8.

28. William Taylor Jr., *The Future of Conflict into the 21st Century* (Seoul: Korea Institute for Defense Analyses, 1987), p. 20.

29. Department of Defense, *United States Security Strategy for the East Asia-Pacific Region* (Washington, DC: Department of Defense, 1995), p. 10.

30. Some U.S. officials are complaining that the United States does not have enough troops to fight two overseas wars at once. But why should it be expected to fight in Korea when the South possesses ample manpower and economic resources? See, e.g., Rowan Scarborough, "U.S. Ability to Fight Two Wars Doubted," *Washington Times,* December 25, 2002, pp. A1, A9.

31. Working Group Report of the CSIS International Security Program, *Conventional Arms Control on the Korean Peninsula* (Washington, DC: CSIS, August 2002), p. 14.

32. "South Korea: Roh's Independence Push Speaks to Military Necessities," Stratfor, January 13, 2003. www.Stratfor.biz.

33. For one criticism of President Roh's proposal to push military outlays back above 3 percent of gross domestic product, see Hamm Taik-young, "Self-Reliance or an Arms Building-Up? The 2004 Defense Budget Request of the ROK," September 2003, http://ifes.kyungnam.ac.kr.

34. See, e.g., Nicholas Eberstadt, "Our Other Korea Problem," *National Interest* no. 69 (Fall 2002): 117–18.

35. Ministry of National Defense, *Defense White Paper: 1989* (Seoul: Republic of Korea, 1990), p. 27.

36. William S. Cohen, "Huffing and Puffing Won't Do," *Washington Post,* January 7, 2003, p. A17.

37. Lambro, "Shultz Weighs Impact of the Deployment." See also James Dao, "Why Keep U.S. Troops?" *New York Times,* January 5, 2003, p. WK–5.

38. Richard Halloran, "Should We Withdraw Troops from South Korea?" *Honolulu Advertiser,* January 5, 2003, www.nexis.com.

39. Robyn Lim, "Korea in the Vortex," *China Brief,* January 14, 2003, p. 6.

40. Allen, "Seoul's Choice."

41. Quoted in Robert Burns, "Pentagon to Keep Troops in Korea," Associated Press, June 16, 2000.

42. Department of Defense, *United States Security Strategy for the East Asia-Pacific Region, 1995,* p. 10.

43. Carl E. Haselden Jr., "The Effects of Korean Unification on the U.S. Military Presence in Northeast Asia, *Parameters* (Winter 2002–03): 120. See also those alliance advocates cited by Edward A. Olsen, "U.S.-ROK Security Treaty: Another Half Century?" *Korean Journal of International Studies* 29, no. 1 (Spring/Summer 2002): 29, 38–40.

44. Larry M. Wortzel, "Why the USA Is OK in the ROK," Heritage Foundation Press Room Commentary, January 30, 2003, www.heritage.org.

45. French, "Shifting Loyalties."

46. Kim Sung-han, "Challenges and Visions of ROK-U.S. Alliance: A Korean Perspective," paper presented to Korean Association of International Studies conference, Seoul, September 25, 2003, p. 27.

47. Avery Goldstein, "Fallout from the Summit: The Challenging Consequences of Korean Detente," Foreign Policy Research Institute, July 1, 2000, e-notes, www.FPRI.org.

48. Ivan Eland, "Is Chinese Military Modernization a Threat to the United States?" Cato Institute Policy Analysis, No. 465, January 23, 2003.

49. Wortzel, "Why the USA Is OK in the ROK."

50. See, e.g., David Pilling, "Japan's Defense Force Tries to Carve Out a New Image," *Financial Times,* February 3, 2004, p. 16; David Pilling, "Japan's Diet to Consider Bill to Change Constitution," *Financial Times,* January 24–25, 2004, p. 3; Yuki Tatsumi, "Where Do We Go From Here? Revising Japanese Defense Posture," *CSIS Japan Watch,* January 21, 2003; Norimitsu Onishi, "Mission to Iraq Eases Japan Toward a True Military," *New York Times,* January 16, 2004, p. A3; and "Japan's Military Mindset: Iraq and Beyond," Stratfor, January 9, 2004, www.stratfor.info/Story.neo?storyId=226807. Although there have long been forces in Japan seeking a more assertive policy, Tokyo's latest moves in that direction largely reflect fear over the DPRK's brinkmanship policies, which is perhaps one reason why Japan's shift has been greeted with such seeming equanimity. See, e.g., Tim Shorrock, "Japanese Hawks Soar on Korea Fears," Asia Times Online, November 26, 2003, www.atimes.com.

51. See, e.g., *Participatory Government Defense Policy 2003* (Seoul: Ministry of National Defense, 2003), pp. 87–88.

52. Bill Emmott, "Japan's English Lessons," *Foreign Policy,* no. 140 (January/February 2004): 56.

53. Cohen, "Huffing and Puffing Won't Do," p. A17.

54. Haselden, "Effects of Korean Unification," p. 121.

55. Quoted in David Pitt, "Seoul, U.S. Forces and the North: The Balance Is as Delicate as Ever," *New York Times,* April 8, 1987, p. A10.

56. William Gleysteen and Alan Romberg, "Korea: Asian Paradox," *Foreign Affairs* 65, no. 3 (Spring 1987): 1052.

57. Edwin Feulner Jr., "The U.S.-Republic of China Partnership in the Year 2000," Heritage Foundation Lecture, no. 85, 1987, p. 5.

58. Quoted in Marcus Corbin et al., "Mission Accomplished in Korea: Bringing U.S. Troops Home," Center for Defense Information, *Defense Monitor* 9, no. 2 (1990): 5.

59. Department of Defense, *United States Security Strategy for the East Asia-Pacific Region,* February 1995, p. 10.

60. Michael Klare, "East Asia's Militaries Muscle Up," *Bulletin of the Atomic Scientists* (January/February 1997), www.thebulletin.org/issues/1997/jf97/jf97klare.html.

61. Kim Sung-han, "Challenges and Visions," p. 29.

62. Wortzel, "Why the USA Is OK in the ROK."

63. Cohen, "Huffing and Puffing Won't Do."

64. New Delhi's current activities in Southeast Asia are quite extensive and help match what otherwise would be serious Chinese encroachments. See, e.g., Satu P. Limaye, "The Weakest Link, but Not Goodbye," *Comparative Connections* (4th quarter 2002), www.csis.org.

65. See, e.g., Victor Gobarev, "India as a World Power: Changing Washington's Myopic Policy," Cato Institute Policy Analysis, no. 381, September 11, 2000; and Larry Pressler, "India, A Natural Ally," *Washington Times,* January 27, 2003, p. A21.

66. See, e.g., Doug Bandow, "Needless Entanglements: Washington's Expanding Security Ties in Southeast Asia," Cato Institute Policy Analysis, no. 401, May 24, 2001.

67. Haselden, "Effects of Korean Unification," p. 121.

68. Lim, "Korea in the Vortex," p. 6.

69. Halloran, "Should We Withdraw Troops."

70. Quoted in George Gedda, "U.S. Troops to Remain in S. Korea," Associated Press, June 15, 2000.

71. Quoted in Patrick Goodenough, "US-South Korean Alliance 'Precious,' President-Elect Says," Cybercast News Service, January 15, 2003, http://www.cnsnews.com. See also Howard R. French, "Aides Declare U.S. 'Willing to Talk' in Korea Dispute," *New York Times,* January 14, 2003, p. A12. South Korean envoy Yoo Jay-kun made much the same pitch when visiting the United States in late January. Christian Bourge, "Seoul Envoy Sees Ties to U.S. Vital in Nuclear Crisis," *Washington Times,* January 24, 2003, p. A17.

72. See, e.g., John Lancaster, "U.S. Presence Fixed on Korean Peninsula," *Washington Post,* June 24, 2000, p. A20.

73. Ministry of National Defense, *Defense White Paper: 1994–1995* (Seoul: Republic of Korea, 1995), pp. 11–12.

74. Quoted in Valerie Reitman, "The U.S.'s Ongoing Battle in South Korea," *Los Angeles Times,* June 29, 2000, p. A4.

75. "Defending the Troops," *Washington Times,* June 28, 2000, p. A13.

76. "US Troop Presence Depends on Role in Unification," *Han Kook Ilbo,* January 24, 2003, www.Korealink.com.

77. Norman D. Levin and Young-Sup Han, *The Shape of Korea's Future: South Korean Attitudes Toward Unification and Long-term Security Issues* (Santa Monica, CA: RAND Corporation, 1999), pp. 16–18, 33–39.

78. "South Korea: Roh's Independence Push Speaks to Military Necessities," Stratfor, January 13, 2003, www.Stratfor.biz.

79. See, e.g., Doug Bandow, "Wrong War, Wrong Place, Wrong Time," Cato Institute Foreign Policy Briefing, no. 76, May 12, 2003.

80. Quoted in Carolyn Skorneck, "Lugar Won't Rule Out Use of Force to Eliminate North Korea's Nuclear Threat," *CQ Today,* January 21, 2004.

81. John McCain, "Rogue State Rollback," *Weekly Standard,* January 20, 2003, pp. 12–13. Columnist Fred Hiatt makes a similar argument, complaining that "South Korea's proximity to North Korea's army, in fact, may cloud its vision of the danger of a nuclear arsenal." Fred Hiatt, "Seoul May Not Know Best," *Washington Post,* January 6, 2003, p. A15.

82. Frank Gaffney, "North Korea Scorecard," *Washington Times,* January 14, 2003, p. A15.

83. See, e.g., Jason Dean, "'Status Quo' Has Different Meaning to China, Taiwan," *Wall Street Journal,* December 12, 2003, pp. A10, A11; Philip Pan, "Taiwan's President Unfazed by U.S. Warning," *Washington Post,* December 11, 2003, p. A47; Tim Culpan and John Pomfret, "Taiwan Reaffirms Plan to Hold Referendum," *Washington Post,* December 10, 2003, p. A27; Joseph Kahn, "Taiwan's Strategic Miscalculation," *New York Times,* December 10, 2003, p. A6; Dana Milbank and Glenn Kessler, "President Warns Taiwan on Independence Efforts," *Washington Post,* December 10, 2003, pp. A1, A27; and David E. Sanger, "U.S. Asks Taiwan to Avoid a Vote Provoking China," *New York Times,* December 9, 2003, pp. A1, A11.

84. Kim Sung-han, "Anti-American Sentiment and the ROK-US Alliance," *Korean Journal of Defense Analysis* 15, no. 2 (Fall 2003): 124.

85. Ministry of National Defense, *Defense White Paper: 1992–1993* (Seoul: Republic of Korea, 1993), p. 168.

86. Claude Buss, *The United States and the Republic of Korea: Background for Policy* (Stanford, CA: Hoover Institution Press, 1982), p. 143.

87. Ibid., p. 139.

88. Kim Chull Baum, "U.S. Policy on the Eve of the Korean War: Abandonment or Safeguard?" in *Korea and the Cold War: Division, Destruction, and Disarmament,* eds. Kim Chull Baum and James Matray, pp. 82–83, 89 (Claremont, CA: Regina Books, 1993). At least one Korean observer argues that the Pentagon belief that the peninsula was too

rough for tanks was more important than Rhee's bellicosity. Lee, p. 28. However, Rhee's threats are widely cited by historians. William Stueck, *The Korean War: An International History* (Princeton, NJ: Princeton University Press, 1995), p. 30; Blair, *The Forgotten War,* p. 44; Max Hastings, *The Korean War* (New York: Simon and Schuster, 1987), p. 43; Callum MacDonald, *Korea: The War Before Vietnam* (New York: Free Press, 1986), pp. 15–16; and Matray, *The Reluctant Crusade,* pp. 173, 183, 230, 233.

89. Having configured its forces based on America's presence, Seoul deserves time to build up its own military as necessary. But some frustrated commentators are less forgiving. Writes Pat Buchanan: "as the new South Korean regime has undercut U.S. policy and is pandering to anti-Americanism, we should tell Seoul all U.S. troops will be out of Korea within two years." Patrick Buchanan, "The Coming U.S. Retreat from Asia," January 8, 2003. www.townhall.com/columnists/patbuchanan/pb20030108.shtml.

90. Ralph Clough, *Embattled Korea: The Rivalry for International Support* (Boulder, CO: Westview Press, 1987), p. 96; Buss, *The United States and the Republic of Korea,* pp. 89–91.

91. Richard Nixon, *U.S. Foreign Policy for the 1970s; Shaping a Durable Peace* (Washington, DC: U.S. Government Printing Office, 1973), p. 110.

92. Earl Ravenal, "The Way Out of Korea," *Inquiry,* December 5, 1977, p. 15.

93. Ibid., p. 15.

94. Among those who noted the convenient timing of the new assessments was New York University's Melvyn Krauss. *How NATO Weakens the West* (New York: Simon and Schuster, 1987), p. 186.

95. So pitiful was the result that Carter does not even mention his efforts in his biography! *Jimmy Carter, Keeping Faith: Memoirs of a President* (New York: Bantam Books, 1982). Nor did his national security advisor, Zbigniew Brzezinski. *Power and Principle: Memoirs of the National Security Adviser, 1977–1981* (New York: Farrar Straus Giroux, 1985, rev.'d).

96. The plan is reviewed in the Ministry of National Defense, *Defense White Paper: 1994– 1995,* pp. 122–23, and Ahn Byung-joon, "The United States, Korea, and Arms Control: A Strategic Review," in *Korea and the Cold War,* eds. Baum and Matray, pp. 255–56.

97. See, e.g., Andrew Ward, "US to Pull Troops Out of Seoul in Rejig of S Korean Force," *Financial Times,* January 20, 2004, p. 6; David Briscoe, "Korea-U.S. Defense Posture," *Korea Now,* June 28, 2003, p. 4.

98. Franklin Weinstein and Fuji Kamiya, eds., *The Security of Korea: U.S. and Japanese Perspectives on the 1980s* (Boulder, CO: Westview Press, 1980), p. 70.

99. William Gleysteen Jr. and Alan Romberg, "Korea: Asian Paradox," *Foreign Affairs* 65, no. 3 (Spring 1987): 1048.

100. Peter Huessy, "Realism on the Korean Peninsula: Real Threats, Real Dangers," *In the National Interest,* August 13, 2003, www.inthenationalinterest.com/Articles/Vol2Issues32/Vol2Issue32HuessyPFV.html.

101. Rhee's views in this regard appear to have differed little from those of Kim Il-sung, since Rhee asserted that the matter of reunification was purely a domestic concern. See, e.g., Okonogi Masao, "The Domestic Roots of the Korean War," in *The Origins of the Cold War in Asia,* eds. Yonosuke Nagai and Akira Iriye, p. 313 (New York: Columbia University Press, 1977); Weinstein and Kamiya, *The Security of Korea,* p. 73.

102. It was not just military occupation, of course. It was also "Japan's attempt in the last decade of its rule to eliminate Korean identity altogether—by enforced Shintoism and taking of Japanese names, plus a language ban." *South Korea, North Korea: 1994–1995* (London: Economist Intelligence Unit, 1994), p. 4.

103. For a discussion of the tension in this relationship, see Clough, *Embattled Korea*, pp. 221–37.

104. Jason U. Manosevitz, "Japan and South Korea: Security Relations Reach Adolescence," *Asian Survey* 43, no. 5 (September/October 2003): 824.

105. John Miller, "The Glacier Moves: Japan's Response to U.S. Security Policies," in *Asia-Pacific Responses to U.S. Security Policies,* ed. Satu P. Limaye, p. 53 (Asia-Pacific Center for Security Studies, March 2003).

106. Sebastian Moffett and Martin Fackler, "Cautiously, Japan Returns to Combat, in Southern Iraq," *Wall Street Journal,* January 2, 2004, pp. A1, A4.

107. Ministry of National Defense, *Defense White Paper: 1994–1995,* p. 21.

108. See Alexandre Y. Mansourov, "Giving Lip Service with an Attitude: North Korea's China Debate," Asia-Pacific Center for Security Studies, December 2003, http://www.brook.edu/ dybdcroot/fp/cnaps/mansourov20031201.pdf.

109. Ministry of National Defense, *Defense White Paper: 1992–1993,* p. 23.

CHAPTER 6

1. A graphic example of that tendency can be found in the comments of Secretary of State Madeleine K. Albright, "1997 Forrestal Lecture: American Principle and Purpose in East Asia," United States Naval Academy, Annapolis, MD, April 15, 1997.

2. Paolo Pasicolan, comp. and ed., *U.S. and Asia Statistical Handbook, 2003* (Washington, D.C.: Heritage Foundation Asia Studies Center, 2003).

3. A similar situation occurred in Europe. The removal of Germany as a political and military player and the drastically weakened positions of Britain and France after World War II meant that there was no European strategic counterweight to the Soviet Union. By default, the United States moved in to fill that power vacuum, in effect playing the balancer role and becoming the leading "European" military power. For a discussion of that process, see John J. Mearsheimer, *The Tragedy of Great Power Politics* (New York: W. W. Norton, 2001).

4. Department of Defense, Office of International Security Affairs, *United States Security Strategy for the East Asia-Pacific Region,* February 1995, p. 23.

5. Ibid., p. 9.

6. For an extended discussion, see Ted Galen Carpenter, "Smoke and Mirrors: The Clinton-Hashimoto Summit," Cato Institute Foreign Policy Briefing, no. 41, May 16, 1996.

7. Following the summit, U.S. officials stated that although they hoped for greater Japanese logistical support for U.S. military missions in East Asia, Japan was "far from ready to send troops into battle alongside U.S. forces," adding that was "not something the United States wanted anyway." Quoted in Kevin Sullivan and John F. Harris, "Clinton Hails Partnership with Japan," *Washington Post,* April 18, 1996, p. A1.

   When asked what help the United States could expect from Japan, in light of the Clinton-Hashimoto summit, if a conflict were to break out in East Asia, former assistant secretary of defense Joseph Nye had extremely limited expectations. "If there were a war in Korea, I'm confident that we would have Japanese support, the use of Japanese bases, and help with supplies and so forth." Nye added that if the conflict were instead in the Taiwan Strait or the South China Sea, Washington would expect—and, in his judgment, would need—"considerably less" support from Tokyo. "Treaty Ratification Reassures Region," interview with Joseph Nye, *Washington Times,* April 19, 1996, p. A17.

8. U.S.-Japan Security Consultative Committee, Completion of the Review of the Guidelines for U.S.-Japan Defense Cooperation, New York, NY, September 23, 1997, http://www.jda.go.jp/e/policy/f_work/sisin4_.htm.

9. Ibid., pp. 2–3.

10. The United States has pursued—and continues to pursue—a similar policy in Europe. See Benjamin Schwarz, "Permanent Interests, Endless Threats: Cold War Continuities and NATO Enlargement," *World Policy Journal* 14, no. 3 (Fall 1997): 24–30; and Christopher Layne, "U.S. Hegemony and the Perpetuation of NATO," in Ted Galen Carpenter, ed., *NATO Enters the 21st Century* (London: Frank Cass, 2001), pp. 59–91.

11. "Excerpts from Pentagon's Plan: Prevent the Emergence of a New Rival," *New York Times,* March 8, 1992, p. A14.

12. White House, Office of the Press Secretary, "The National Security Strategy of the United States of America," September 2002, p. 29.

13. Philip Shenon, "Baker Asks Asians to Move Warily on New Pacts," *New York Times,* July 25, 1991, p. A14.

14. Quoted in Jim Mannion, "No Reduction in U.S. Forces in Asia Even if Korea Unites: Cohen," Agence France-Presse, April 6, 1997.

15. Department of Defense, Press Conference with Secretary of Defense William Cohen and Assistant Secretary of Defense for International Security Affairs Frank D. Kramer, November 23, 1998, transcript, p. 1.

16. For a discussion, see Doug Bandow, "Needless Entanglements: Washington's Expanding Security Ties in Southeast Asia," Cato Institute Policy Analysis, no. 401, May 24, 2001. Washington even tried to pressure Manila into agreeing to a sizable U.S. combat troop presence as part of the war on terrorism. Greg Miller, "U.S. Forces to Fight in the Philippines," *Los Angeles Times,* February 21, 2003, p. A1. The government of President Gloria Macapagal Arroyo, responding to intense domestic opposition, eventually turned down the U.S. request. Jim Gomez, "Philippines Ruling Out U.S. Combat Role," Associated Press, March 5, 2003.

17. Announcement by the chief cabinet secretary on Japan's Immediate Response to North Korea's Missile Launch, September 1, 1998, http://www.mofa.go.jp/announce/announce/1998/9/901–2.html.

18. For a discussion of that issue from diverse perspectives, see Selig S. Harrison, ed., *Japan's Nuclear Future: The Plutonium Debate and East Asian Security* (Washington, DC: Carnegie Endowment for International Peace, 1996). On recent developments, see Selig S. Harrison, *Korean Endgame: A Strategy for Reunification and U.S. Disengagement* (Princeton, NJ: Princeton University Press, 2002), chap. 19, "Japan and Nuclear Weapons," pp. 231–34; and Matake Kamiya, "Nuclear Japan: Oxymoron or Coming Soon?" *Washington Quarterly* 26 (Winter 2002–03): 63–75.

19. Hideshi Takeshida, a professor at Japan's Institute for Defense Studies, noted that his country "is always nervous when a problem arises with China." An important root of that nervousness, he contended, is the fear that China will retaliate against Japanese investors on the mainland. Quoted in Willis Witter, "U.S. Gets No Help from East Asians in Backing Taiwan," *Washington Times,* March 14, 1997, p. A15.

20. For discussions of these themes from a number of different perspectives, see Ted Galen Carpenter and James A. Dorn, *China's Future: Constructive Partner or Emerging Threat?* (Washington, DC: Cato Institute, 2000).

21. Examples of the argument that China's objectives are defensive rather than offensive include Charles W. Freeman Jr., "China, Taiwan, and the United States," in *Asia after the "Miracle": Redefining U.S. Economic and Security Priorities,* eds. Selig S. Harrison and

Clyde V. Prestowitz Jr., pp. 169–84, (Washington, DC: Economic Strategy Institute, 1998); Andrew J. Nathan and Robert S. Ross, *The Great Wall and the Empty Fortress: China's Search for Security* (New York: W. W. Norton, 1997); and Patrick Tyler, *A Great Wall: Six Presidents and China* (New York: Public Affairs, 1999).

22. For a discussion of the importance of China's growing economic power, see Daniel Burstein and Arne de Keijzer, *Big Dragon: China's Future: What It Means for Business, the Economy, and the Global Order* (New York: Simon and Schuster, 1998).

23. There are scholars who argue that China will not succeed in becoming a great power and that the internal stresses and strains within the republic's rigid political system will cause either a pronounced decline or an implosion. See Ross Terrill, *The New Chinese Empire: And What It Means for the United States* (New York: Basic Books, 2003); and Gordon Chang, *The Coming Collapse of China* (New York: Random House, 2001).

24. For an argument that such a rivalry between China and the United States is highly probable, see Richard Bernstein and Ross H. Munro, *The Coming Conflict with China* (New York: Alfred A. Knopf, 1997). For extreme versions of the "China threat" thesis, see Edward Timperlake and William C. Triplett II, *Red Dragon Rising: Communist China's Military Threat to America* (Washington, DC: Regnery, 1999); and Steven W. Mosher, *Hegemon: China's Plan to Dominate Asia and the World* (San Francisco: Encounter Books, 2000).

25. For two studies that reached similar conclusions on that score, see Ivan Eland, "Is Chinese Military Modernization a Threat to the United States?" Cato Institute Policy Analysis, no. 465, January 23, 2003; and Harold Brown, chair, Joseph W. Prueher, vice chair, and Adam Segal, project director, *Chinese Military Power: Report of an Independent Task Force* (New York: Council on Foreign Relations, 2003).

26. Office of the U.S. Trade Representative, *2003 National Trade Estimate Report on Foreign Trade Barriers,* April 2003, pp. 2, 6.

27. Chalmers Johnson and E. B. Keehn make a solid case that the notion of America's military presence in East Asia giving the U.S leverage on trade issues is an illusion. Chalmers Johnson and E. B. Keehn, "The Pentagon's Ossified Strategy," *Foreign Affairs* 74 (July-August 1995): 103–14.

28. For a detailed discussion of the Taiwan Relations Act, see Lester L. Wolff and David L. Simon, eds., *Legislative History of the Taiwan Relations Act: An Analytic Compilation with Documents on Subsequent Developments* (Jamaica, NY: American Association for Chinese Studies, 1982). The text of the act is on pp. 288–95. For a comparison of the U.S. defense "obligations" contained in the act and the very real defense obligations in the mutual defense treaty that it replaced, see Ted Galen Carpenter, "Let Taiwan Defend Itself," Cato Institute Policy Analysis, no. 313, August 24, 1998, pp. 11–12.

29. Quoted in David E. Sanger, "U.S. Would Defend Taiwan, Bush Says," *New York Times,* April 26, 2001, p. A1. For an analysis of the dangers inherent in such a pledge, see Ted Galen Carpenter, "Going Too Far: Bush's Pledge to Defend Taiwan," Cato Institute Foreign Policy Briefing, no. 66, May 30, 2001.

30. Steve Glain, "U.S. Probably Shouldn't Count on Help from Japan in Resolving Taiwan Flap," *Wall Street Journal,* March 11, 1996, p. A1; "Downer Urges Restraint in China-Taiwan Tension," Melbourne Radio Australia, in *Foreign Broadcast Information Service (FBIS) Daily Report—East Asia,* March 13, 1996, electronic version, document Odo8cfk040v69n; "Alatas on Tense China-Taiwan Relations," Jakarta Radio Republik Indonesia, in *FBIS–East Asia,* 96–050, March 13, 1996, p. 50; "Further Comment on Assistance to U.S.," *Business World* (Manila), in *FBIS–East Asia,* March 13, 1996, electronic version, document Odoag3j03m9trn; and statement by Tan Sri Ahmad Kamil Jaa-

far, secretary general of the Foreign Ministry of Malaysia, March 1996, text provided by Malaysian embassy, November 18, 1996.

31. See Ted Galen Carpenter, "With Friends Like These," *Washington Post,* April 18, 2001, p. A11.

32. Philip P. Pan, "China's Improving Image Challenges U.S. in Asia," *Washington Post,* November 15, 2003, p. A1.

33. Christopher Layne, "Less Is More: Minimal Realism in East Asia," *National Interest* 43 (Spring 1996): 64–77.

34. For a discussion of the discontent in Okinawa, where most of the U.S. troops stationed in Japan are deployed, see Doug Bandow, "Okinawa: Liberating America's Last East Asian Military Colony," Cato Institute Policy Analysis, no. 314, September 1, 1998. On the growing discontent in South Korea, see Doug Bandow, "Bring the Troops Home: Ending the Obsolete Korean Commitment," Cato Institute Policy Analysis, no. 474, May 7, 2003, pp. 8–10. See also James Brooke, "U.S. Soldiers in South Korea Feel Growing Anti-Americanism," *International Herald Tribune,* January 8, 2003, p. 1; and Hae Won Choi, "Long a U.S. Ally, South Koreans Sour on America," *Wall Street Journal,* December 24, 2002, p. A8.

35. For an extended discussion of the undesirable side effects of the U.S.-Japanese alliance, see Ted Galen Carpenter, "Paternalism and Dependence: The U.S.-Japanese Security Relationship," Cato Institute Policy Analysis, no. 244, November 1, 1995.

36. "Leaving South Korea," editorial, *Wall Street Journal,* May 14, 2003, p.A14.

37. For a discussion, see Leon T. Hadar, "Averting a 'New Kosovo" in Indonesia: Opportunities and Pitfalls for the United States," Cato Institute Policy Analysis, no. 367, March 9, 2000.

38. Patrick Goodenough, "Australia Takes New, More Assertive Role in Region," Cybercast News Service, June 27, 2003, http://www.cnsnews.com.

39. David Fickling, "Australia Double Defence Spending in Desire to Become Top Military Player," *Guardian,* February 5, 2004, p. 4.

40. See, e.g., Yoichi Funabashi, *Alliance Adrift* (New York: Council on Foreign Relations Press, 1999); Michael J. Green and Patrick M. Cronin, eds., *The U.S.-Japan Alliance: Past, Present and Future* (New York: Council on Foreign Relations Press, 1999); Mike Mochizuki, ed., *Toward a True Alliance: Restructuring U.S.-Japan Security Relations* (Washington, DC: Brookings Institution Press, 1997); and Stuart Harris and Richard N. Cooper, "The U.S.-Japan Alliance," in *America's Asian Alliances,* eds. Robert D. Blackwill and Paul Dibb (Cambridge, MA: MIT Press, 2000), pp. 67–79.

41. Beijing reacted badly even to the meager changes in the U.S.-Japan defense guidelines. See Willis Witter, "Japan's Hints of Defense of Taiwan Enrage China," *Washington Times,* August 25, 1997; Chalmers Johnson, "Who Is U.S.-Japan Pact Aimed At?" *Los Angeles Times,* September 8, 1997; and Reuters, "China Warns U.S., Japan on Security Pact," *Washington Post,* September 1997.

42. Esther Schrader, "U.S. to Realign Troops in Asia," *Los Angeles Times,* May 29, 2003, p. A1.

43. Eric Talmadge, "Koizumi Urges Missile Defense," *Washington Times,* May 30, 2003, p. A13.

44. Quoted in Stephen Lunn, "Japan Vows to Get in First Shot at North Korea," *Weekend Australian,* February 15, 2003, p. 16.

45. See "Remarks by Mr. Yauo Fukuda, Chief Cabinet Secretary, Regarding the Dispatch of Destroyers and Another Vessel," November 8, 2001, press release in possession of the author. http://www.kantei.go.jp/foreign/policy/2001/anti-terrorism/1108anpo_e.html.

46. Teruaki Ueno, "Japan Passes Landmark Iraq Troop Deployment Bill," Reuters, July 4, 2003.

47. That growing assertiveness has attracted the attention of a number of experts on East Asia. See, e.g., Eugene A. Matthews, "Japan's New Nationalism," *Foreign Affairs* 82, no. 6 (November-December 2003): 74–90.

48. Nao Shimoyachi and Reiji Yoshida, "Diet Enacts Legislation for War Contingencies," *Japan Times,* June 7, 2003, online edition.

49. Howard W. French, "Japan Adopts Laws Strengthening Military Powers," *New York Times,* June 7, 2003, p. A6.

50. Richard Halloran, "Warships Suggest Discarded Pacifism," *Washington Times,* July 13, 2003, p. A5.

51. Statement by H. E. Dr. Kuniko Inoguchi, Ambassador, Permanent Representative of Japan, to the Conference on Disarmament, the Second Session of the Preparatory Committee for the 2005 Review Conference of the Parties to the Treaty on the Non-Proliferation of Nuclear Weapons, April 29, 2003, Geneva, http://www.disarm.emb-japan.go.jp/Statement/NP030429.

INDEX